Kentucky

Johnny Green joins here
Bowling Green
OCTOBER 7, 1861

Nashville

Tennessee

CUMBERLAND GAP

Murfreesboro DEC. 1862

Lewis executed here

Johnny dances Weavely Wheat
Manchester

Knoxville

Chattanooga NOV. 1863
Smallpox here

CHICKAMAUGA SEPT. 1863

Dalton WINTER 1863-64

N. Carolina

Lightning bug trouble

S. Carolina

Gen'l Polk killed

KENNESAW MOUNTAIN

Decatur

ATLANTA SUMMER 1864
Jonesboro

Johnny rescues wounded

"The blackest day of our Lives"
APRIL 22, 1865 Camden

Columbia Big fire here

Johnny captured here
AUG. 28-31, 1864

Georgia

Johnny tries to stop Sherman

Charleston

Savannah DEC. 1864

Fort Sumter

CW00822477

Johnny Green
of the Orphan Brigade

Johnny Green
of the Orphan Brigade

THE JOURNAL OF A CONFEDERATE SOLDIER

Edited by A. D. Kirwan

With a new foreword
by Kent Masterson Brown

THE UNIVERSITY PRESS OF KENTUCKY

Publication of this volume was made possible in part
by a grant from the National Endowment for the Humanities.

Scholarly publisher for the Commonwealth,
serving Bellarmine University, Berea College, Centre
College of Kentucky, Eastern Kentucky University,
The Filson Historical Society, Georgetown College,
Kentucky Historical Society, Kentucky State University,
Morehead State University, Murray State University,
Northern Kentucky University, Transylvania University,
University of Kentucky, University of Louisville,
and Western Kentucky University.

Editorial and Sales Offices: The University Press of Kentucky
663 South Limestone Street, Lexington, Kentucky 40508-4008

06 05 04 03 02   5 4 3 2 1

Frontispiece: John Williams Green, Company B, 9th Kentucky Infantry.

Catalog record available from the Library of Congress.
ISBN 0-8131-2221-X

CONTENTS

Illustration inserts follow pages 76 and 180.

BATTLE MAPS

FOREWORD

The exploits and losses of the Orphan Brigade of Kentucky, without a doubt the most remarkable military organization in any Civil War theater, rival and indeed surpass those of other famous commands, including the Stonewall Brigade, the Texas Brigade, and Cleburne's Arkansas Brigade. The Orphans campaigned over more territory (eight states), suffered higher casualties, and lost more brigade commanders than any other comparable unit in the war. And as if those trials were not enough, the brigade was never able to return to fight for its native state of Kentucky after February 1862.

The Orphan Brigade was composed of the Second, Fourth, Sixth, and Ninth Kentucky Infantry regiments, the artillery batteries of Capts. Robert Cobb, Edward P. Byrne, and Rice E. Graves, and, at times, the Third and the Fifth Kentucky Infantry. At Shiloh the Orphans brigaded with the Fourth Alabama Battalion, Thirty-first Alabama Infantry, and Crews's Tennessee Battalion. From Shiloh to Chattanooga they fought alongside the Forty-first Alabama Infantry.

The story of the Orphan Brigade is written in the blood of its officers and men; Fort Donelson, Shiloh, Vicksburg (1862), Baton Rouge, Stone's River, the relief of Vicksburg (1863), Chickamauga, Chattanooga, Rocky Face Ridge, Resaca, Dallas, Kennesaw Mountain, Peachtree Creek, Intrenchment Creek, Utoy Creek, and

Jonesboro are among the battles and operations in which the brigade was engaged. Its losses were horrific: at Shiloh it was decimated; at Stone's River the Orphan Brigade lost 431 men in forty-two minutes, over one-third of its total strength; at Chickamauga it lost nearly one-third of its men; and in 120 days from Dalton, Georgia, to Atlanta and Jonesboro, the Orphan Brigade lost 1,860 men, 23 percent more than were present on the muster rolls of its five Kentucky regiments. Men who were wounded returned to the brigade, only to be wounded again (and again) or killed.

When the war finally came to an end, the veterans of the Orphan Brigade became idols to their fellow Kentuckians, who accorded them "a kind of title of nobility."[1] Naturally, those old Orphan Brigade veterans were determined to remind the citizenry of Kentucky of their role in the war. They gathered in ever-diminishing numbers at annual reunions held in towns across the Commonwealth from 1882 to 1896, erecting monuments in cemeteries and courthouse grounds to remember fallen comrades.

Fortunately, some of those old veterans wrote down what they remembered of the war. No unit that fought in the Civil War, north or south, was the subject of a grander, more complete written history than the Orphan Brigade. Ed Porter Thompson, a lieutenant in Company E, Sixth Kentucky Infantry, from Metcalf County (Kentuckians have always identified themselves with their counties), published *History of the First Kentucky Brigade* in 1868. His book was expanded and reissued in 1898 as *History of the Orphan Brigade*, a massive 1104–page volume of memoirs, biographies, and detailed rosters of the officers and men of all of the regiments and artillery batteries that composed the command; it was reprinted by Morningside Bookshop in 1973. Lt. Ed Porter Thompson was every inch a soldier, returning to the army despite being severely wounded and captured by the enemy at Stone's River. His incomparable history stands today as the definitive record of the Orphan Brigade.

Former Company I, Sixth Kentucky Infantry member Gervis D. Grainger of Simpson County published the forty-five-page *Four Years With the Boys in Gray* (1902), a memoir of his years in the Orphan Brigade. Like Thompson, Grainger saw heavy action. He was captured at Jonesboro but escaped. While he was in custody, orders from Gen. Stephen Burbridge, the hated commander of the military district of Kentucky, twice subjected him to casting lots for execution by shooting in retaliation for guerrilla outrages. At war's end, Grainger attempted to assassinate General Burbridge in Cincinnati, Ohio. Happily, he was stopped by friends and hurried away. Grainger's memoir was reprinted by Morningside Bookshop in 1972.

Lot D. Young, a first lieutenant in Company H, Fourth Kentucky Infantry, published *Reminiscences of a Soldier in the Orphan Brigade* (1918), a ninety-nine-page memoir. Young, who hailed from Nicholas County, was severely wounded and disabled at Jonesboro. His delightful reminiscences cover not only the war, but also his visits to battlefields after the war. Young recalls the fighting at Stone's River with great feeling. He remembers Capt. William P. Bramblett[2] of Bourbon County, who "glanced" at Young just seconds before he fell with a wound from a shell burst that soon proved fatal. That glance Young never forgot, nor have his readers. Years later, at a commemorative service at Murfreesboro, Young recalled the battle and the deaths of so many comrades there, including Captain Bramblett. Overcome, he clung to a nearby tree and wept while a children's chorus sang "My Old Kentucky Home."

No other diary or memoir from the Orphan Brigade was published after Young's until the late Albert D. "Ab" Kirwan, who served the University of Kentucky as a distinguished professor of history, president, and one-time football coach, annotated and published *Johnny Green of the Orphan Brigade: The Journal of a Confederate Soldier* (University of Kentucky Press, 1956). Green's "journal" is, in reality, a memoir, the writer's retrospective view of the events through which he had served, embellished with newspaper and other published accounts that Green had collected after the war. It is nevertheless a gem. Green saw heavy action, taking part in all of the battles that the Orphans fought, save Baton Rouge when he was severely ill. His long, uninterrupted service makes him one of the very best narrators of the Orphan Brigade's story.

It was not until 1980 that the Orphan Brigade became the subject of another book; historian William C. Davis, author of the award-winning biography of Gen. John C. Breckinridge, published *The Orphan Brigade: The Kentucky Confederates Who Couldn't Go Home* (Doubleday), a most readable history of the brigade. Davis later edited and annotated the wartime diary of Nelson County soldier John S. Jackman in *Diary of a Confederate Soldier: John S. Jackman of the Orphan Brigade* (University of South Carolina Press, 1990). His diary is truly that, an unembellished day-by-day account of the war from Shiloh to Pine Mountain, where Jackman received a head wound, to his train ride home at war's end. Interestingly, Johnny Green speaks of John Jackman, a member of the same company, in his journal, and Jackman records many episodes with Green in his diary. The two soldiers knew each other well, and their accounts make wonderful companion pieces.

Recently, another publication on the Orphan Brigade emerged. Ben L. Bassham edited and annotated Conrad Wise Chapman's Civil War memoir *Ten Months in the "Orphan Brigade"* (Kent State University Press, 1999). Chapman, a struggling artist in Rome, Italy, found his way to Bowling Green, Kentucky, and joined Col. Lloyd Tilghman's Third Kentucky Infantry. Although Chapman's regiment was a part of the Orphan Brigade only through the summer of 1862, his memoir is a fascinating read. Ultimately, Chapman became the great wartime artist of the Confederacy.

Through it all Johnny Green's journal has stood the test of time. Because it is a wartime journal embellished with post-war reflections and additions, Green's narrative makes for wonderful reading. It is also good history. Few commands saw such heavy action as the Orphan Brigade and none suffered the losses it did. The story of the Orphan Brigade is not only the story of the fabled Army of Tennessee, but, to a great degree, of the war outside of the Virginia theater. No one tells that story better than Johnny Green.

This edition of *Johnny Green of the Orphan Brigade* is issued with new illustrations in an effort to "bring to life" some of the personalities and events Johnny Green records. Thanks are due to the Library of Congress, the National Archives, and Bill Straus of Lexington for their assistance, as well as Rebecca Rose and all my dear friends at the Museum of the Confederacy, who, along with I. Beverly Lake of Wake Forest, North Carolina, kindly photographed and granted permission for me to publish the photographs of the magnificent battleflags of Johnny Green's regiment.

I know Johnny Green and "Ab" Kirwan would be proud.

Kent Masterson Brown

NOTES

1. Ed Porter Thompson, *History of the Orphan Brigade* (1898), p. 21.

2. Young uses the spelling "Bramblett," which also appears in an 1895 Confederate Veteran Association membership book and on a more recently erected headstone marking the captain's grave in the Confederate lot of Paris Cemetery, Paris, Kentucky. However, the name also appears as "Bramblette" and "Bramlett" in various newspaper clippings at the public library in Paris. An extensive family genealogy posted on the Internet spells the name "Bramblette" (see www.rootsweb.com/~orphanhm/bramblette.htm).

INTRODUCTION

This is the story of the Civil War in the West told by a soldier in the ranks who experienced as much of it, perhaps, as any man in either army. Johnny Green, a Kentucky boy not yet twenty years of age, enlisted in the Confederate Army at Bowling Green, Kentucky, in the autumn of 1861. From then until the surrender in April, 1865, he was in continuous service, drilling, marching, or fighting.

Green was a sensitive observer who had a flair for descriptive writing. He saw the things he should have seen and recorded them in delightful fashion. His journal has real literary merit, and in addition, it is a complete and unified narrative. In a sense, it is a biography of Green as he moved through a series of great events, with his emotions and experiences recorded in a way that shows the development of his character and personality.

Almost miraculously Green seemed to escape serious injury. At Shiloh he was shot just over the heart. The impact knocked him down, but he remained conscious. "I felt sure it had gone clear through me," Johnny wrote, "& it flashed through my mind that I would live until the arterial blood started back to my heart, when I would drop dead, as I had once seen a deer do which my father shot through the heart." After taking what he thought was one last shot at the enemy he was surprised to find himself still alive. The bullet had passed through the stock of his gun before splitting on the iron ramrod, and the fragment that had struck him in the chest had buried itself in a little pocket Testament which he carried there. At Chickamauga he was hit in the groin with a grape shot which whirled him around and threw him on his back. He thought his leg was torn off, but examination found the grape in his pants pocket, its force spent when it struck the metal clasp of his pocketbook. The clasp was doubled around the ball. On another occasion he had to scale a high fence while charging the enemy. As he climbed over, his canteen caught on the top rail and suspended him in the face of a galling enemy fire, his feet unable to reach the ground. Minié balls and grape were showering around him as he was held there a target for the enemy. But as he was making desperate efforts to free himself, a Yankee bullet which grazed his shoulder cut the strap and set him free.

Such hairbreadth escapes come to seem almost commonplace in the war experiences of this Kentucky boy. Nor does it seem that the drama grew in the telling. For Johnny Green throughout his long life enjoyed the reputation of being a scrupulously honest man. Moreover, the whole tone of Green's narration is one of simple statement of fact as he saw it, without embellishment and without heroics. And finally, an even more dramatic escape, which reflected great heroism on the part of Johnny Green, is related by the official historian of Green's brigade. Green mentions this act of heroism only casually in this journal, however.

The journal abounds in accounts of military operations and of fighting, yet Green shows flashes of humor, some pleasant and some grim. There is the anecdote of the Irish soldier at Stone's River who had borne his wounded comrade, shot in the leg, a great distance over rough ground only to find, when he had reached safety, that his comrade had received en route a bullet in the head and was dead. "I thought," the Irishman expostulated to his dead companion, "you said it was your leg you were shot in."

Then, too, there are picaresque incidents galore in these pages: pranks played by soldiers seeking fun at the expense of regulations, and sometimes at the expense of more fundamental morality. Some soldiers bored a hole from underneath through the bed of a wagon and through the bottom of a whisky keg placed thereon and drained off whisky undetected by the officer in charge. Another thirsty private took a position outside camp and, impersonating a guard, confiscated all whisky of those who passed. Secreting his liquid prize inside a pumpkin shell, he carried it safely into camp, where he and his buddies proceeded to enjoy it. A couple of Kentucky boys enlisted the aid of an Alabama "Yellowhammer" to help themselves to gift packages not their own. But perhaps we should reserve that tale for Johnny Green himself to tell.

There is poignancy in the journal, and despite the callousness and brutality of war, some individuals, Green among them, have been able to retain humane and sensitive instincts. The account of the execution of young Lewis is stark tragedy, and one can well understand after reading it that "gloom settled over the command" when the young lad lay in his grave.

A scene which he beheld after the battle of Shiloh stirred Green almost to poetic depths. A Northern and a Southern soldier lay in a death embrace. Although they had killed each other, the face of neither showed any trace of pain or anger. "Had the Angel of peace come to each of them?" mused the young man. "I dont know but what we should have put them both to sleep in the same grave, but we did not. The warrior will be rewarded for a patriotic death where they have gone but I know peace reigns there supreme."

There is pathos in the lingering agony of young Will Pope at Corinth, who was reconciled to death when assured that "if a boy dies for his country the glory is his for ever." There is the tender and generous act of mercy when Gus Moore, who had been on picket duty all day, swam the Chattahoochee at dusk to barter some coffee from the Yankee pickets so that he could brew a cup of the stimulating beverage for the fever-racked Johnny Green. There is the heroism of Lieutenant McLean, his leg torn off by an enemy shell, calmly cautioning his men to "Be steady!" lest the enemy, seeing their confusion, "make it worse for us." There was nobility as well as brutality in this war.

XV

II

If Johnny Green participated in an extraordinary number of campaigns, it was because of the unit to which he belonged, the First Kentucky or Orphan Brigade. The origin of the name Orphan Brigade is uncertain. One veteran, writing many years after, stated that the name was given the Brigade by its division commander, John C. Breckinridge, at the battle of Stone's River in January, 1863. According to this account Breckinridge, contemplating the broken state of the unit as it reformed after its bloody repulse on the afternoon of January 2, exclaimed, "My poor Orphans! My poor Orphans!"[1]

But the official historian of the Brigade offers a more plausible explanation. "Its attitude towards its native state," he said, "—expatriated by reason of identification with a cause which Kentucky had not formally approved; its complete isolation from its people; its having been time and again deprived of its commander by transfer to other service or death in battle—these . . . may have suggested the name."[2] Whether this adequately explains the origin of the name or not, certain it is that during almost its entire existence the Brigade was "orphaned" from home. After its retreat from Bowling Green in February, 1862, its members never set foot on their native soil again until after their surrender and parole in April, 1865. During the intervening years they had marched, fought, and bled from one end of Tennessee to the other, through "the burning hot sands" of Mississippi and Louisiana, over the rough foothills and mountains of north Alabama and Georgia to the sea, and in the dying months of the war through the swamps of the Carolinas. It is doubtful if any other brigade saw such continuous and far-flung service.

The Kentucky Brigade was organized on October 28, 1861, at Bowling Green, Kentucky, from the various independent regiments of Kentucky volunteers which had been raised during the summer of 1861 by individuals in southern Kentucky and across the border in Tennessee. Originally it consisted of the Second,

1 Lieutenant L. D. Young, *Reminiscences of a Soldier of the Orphan Brigade* (n.p., n.d.), 51.
2 Ed Porter Thompson, *A History of the Orphan Brigade* (Louisville, 1898), 29.

Third, Fourth, Fifth (later the Ninth), and Sixth regiments of infantry, Graves' and Cobb's batteries of artillery, and the First Kentucky Cavalry together with John Hunt Morgan's cavalry squadron. John C. Breckinridge assumed command on November 16.

There were various minor skirmishes in the fall and early winter of 1861-1862. Early in February, 1862, the Second Regiment and Graves' Battery were detached and sent to Fort Donelson in time to be surrendered with the rest of the garrison there on February 17. Meanwhile, the remainder of the Brigade retreated through Nashville and Murfreesboro to Burnsville in the vicinity of Corinth, Mississippi.

At Shiloh, where the Brigade fought as a unit for the first time, it was part of the reserve corps of which Breckinridge had been appointed temporary commander, the Brigade itself being directed by Colonel R. P. Trabue of the Fourth, who was the senior regimental commander. In the retreat to Corinth after the battle the Brigade was given the important assignment of rear guard.

Shortly after Shiloh, Breckinridge was promoted to major general and given command of a division. At the same time the Kentucky Brigade was, for a few months, broken up into two separate brigades, each augmented by Alabama and Mississippi troops. One of these brigades was under the command of Ben Hardin Helm, a Kentuckian of distinguished family and a brother-in-law of Abraham Lincoln. The Ninth Kentucky, Johnny Green's regiment, was part of Helm's brigade. This organization was continued until September, 1862, when the Alabama and Mississippi regiments, together with the Third Kentucky, were detached from the two brigades, and the Fourth, Sixth, Ninth, and Second (returned from its northern prison) were united into the First Kentucky Brigade. Colonel Roger W. Hanson of the Second Regiment, who outranked Trabue, was given temporary command, Ben Hardin Helm having been wounded at Baton Rouge two months before.

Meanwhile, the Confederate Army evacuated Corinth on May 29 and Breckinridge's division was again assigned to cover the retreat; the Ninth Kentucky was part of the special rear guard of infantry under command of Colonel Thomas H. Hunt.

xvii

The rear guard rejoined the army at Tupelo, Mississippi, on June 7 and 8.

While at Tupelo the army was inspected by a personal aide of President Jefferson Davis, and his report to the President gives a picture of camp life during a relatively inactive period. In general, he wrote, the discipline of the army was excellent and respect for private property prevailed. "In the vicinity of the camps . . . , the fences are unharmed and the fields unwasted." Five hours daily were devoted to drill, and the veteran units he found very proficient in that important detail. Hospitals were inadequate and poorly managed, and the sick and wounded had to be dispersed and cared for among the neighboring plantations. Surgeons had not been regularly appointed, their position was undefined, and they apparently did not receive "the respect and consideration [from commanders] necessary to the performance of their duties." The quality of rations and the irregularity of their issue was a source of some complaint. A large quantity of salt beef had been received which was "spoiled and unwholesome" as the result of improper packing. The supply of flour was short, but there was an abundance of corn from which to make meal. Bush huts were occasionally used for shelter, and sometimes tents, but the almost universal protection was the canvas fly suspended on poles and beneath which ten men could sleep. The men messed together in small squads and were said to "cook badly." Most of the brigades had brick bake ovens where bread for the entire brigade was prepared. The bread varied from excellent to bad in accordance with the ability of the many bakers. Wells had been dug, and there was an ample supply of cool and clear water. The camps were clean, the sinks properly arranged and attended to, and the kitchens equipped with pits for refuse. "In a word," he concluded, "the police of the camp is admirable, and indicative of a high state of discipline."[3]

But the Kentuckians were not to enjoy these relatively comfortable conditions for long. On June 25 Breckinridge's division left for Vicksburg, where Union Admiral David Farragut had

[3] *War of the Rebellion: A Compilation of the Official Records of the Union and Confederate Armies,* 128 vols. (Washington, 1880-1901), Series 1, X, pt. 1, pp. 780-83. Hereafter this work is cited as *O.R.*

concentrated a fleet of gunboats and was planning to land troops to seize the city. Here the Kentuckians suffered from the intense heat, and many, including Johnny Green, were stricken with malaria from the mosquito-infested swamps around the city. After six weeks there the Brigade surgeon reported that the health of the troops had been "almost ruined" by the malarial atmosphere. During that period the number of men fit for duty had been reduced from 1,822 to 548.[4]

On July 27 the Union fleet steamed away and Breckinridge's division was sent to Baton Rouge to reduce the Federal garrison there. Breckinridge's attack, initially successful, was repulsed by the fire from the Union gunboats stationed there. Later, however, the Union garrison abandoned Baton Rouge. This was the only engagement his regiment participated in which Johnny Green missed. Ill with fever at Vicksburg, he dragged himself from his sickbed when he learned of the mission but was peremptorily ordered back to the hospital.

After the battle of Baton Rouge the Fourth, Sixth, and Ninth regiments traveled to Knoxville, Tennessee, there to be formed with the Second into the First Kentucky Brigade, Breckinridge's division, as previously related. The Brigade started from Knoxville to march to join General Braxton Bragg in his Kentucky campaign, but at Cumberland Gap word came that Bragg was retreating from Perryville. Sorely disappointed at being denied at the last moment a chance to return to Kentucky the Brigade retired, first to Chattanooga and then to Murfreesboro, which it reached on October 28. Here, in December, Hanson was promoted to brigadier general and given permanent command of the Brigade, with Breckinridge still in command of the division of which it was a part. There were numerous skirmishes and raids in this locale, the most noted of which was the attack on the Union garrison at Hartsville, where Morgan with his cavalry and the Second and Ninth regiments isolated and captured a force larger than his own.

In late December, Major General William Rosecrans, who had succeeded Don Carlos Buell as commander of the Army of the Ohio, moved out from Nashville to attack Bragg, who had regrouped his army at Murfreesboro. The engagement started

4 *O.R.,* XV, 1125.

on December 31 on the banks of Stone's River and was to prove the bloodiest battle in the West. On January 2 came the ill-fated charge of Breckinridge's division in which the Orphan Brigade lost more than one fourth of its number. Among the killed was the Brigade's commander, General Hanson; and Ben Hardin Helm, recovered from his injury at Baton Rouge, succeeded him. Helm soon became the idol of his men, and although Green speaks well of all his officers, it is apparent that Helm had a special place in his affections.

From Murfreesboro the army retreated to the vicinity of Tullahoma, Tennessee, again under the rear guard protection of the Kentucky Brigade. Here several months were spent in maneuvering and in skirmishing, and here also probably occurred the contest in which the Kentucky Brigade was judged the best drilled in the Army of Tennessee.

On May 24, 1863, Breckinridge took his division back to Mississippi to join General Joseph E. Johnston in his attempt to relieve the garrison at Vicksburg. Arriving in Jackson, Mississippi, in early June they spent the rest of the month there while Johnston tried vainly to raise sufficient force to attack General Ulysses S. Grant's besieging army. On July 1 Breckinridge was ordered to move to attack Grant. This march to the Big Black River was, wrote the Brigade historian, "The most trying ever made by the command. The day was hot, almost to suffocation . . . , the roads were dry, and the sand rose in clouds to envelop the heated, panting column. Water was so scarce that even a reasonable supply could not be procured, and extreme thirst contributed to the fatigue. . . . Many fell out exhausted by the way, and some died of sunstroke."[5] But the Vicksburg garrison surrendered on July 4, and Johnston hurried his army back to Jackson. For a week Johnston defended himself from Union attack here, but evacuated the city on July 16 when Union reinforcements threatened to encircle him.

The Confederate force settled down at Morton, Mississippi, forty miles east of Jackson, for a month of rest and inaction. From there in late August, Breckinridge left with his division to reinforce Bragg in Chattanooga. On September 19 and 20 the Brigade took part in the great battle at Chickamauga Creek

[5] Thompson, *Orphan Brigade*, 207.

XX

where the Union Army was broken and part of it driven pell-mell back into Chattanooga. Here the greatly loved Ben Hardin Helm was killed, and Colonel Joseph H. Lewis, of the Sixth Kentucky, succeeded to the command of the Brigade. Lewis was to retain this command until the end of the war.

At Tyner's Station on November 5 the Fifth Kentucky Regiment of Infantry was transferred to the Brigade, replacing the Forty-First Alabama, which had been temporarily assigned to it. The Brigade was now composed of the Second, Fourth, Fifth, Sixth, and Ninth Kentucky regiments. No organic changes were made henceforth, and these five regiments surrendered together at the end of the war.

Now began the siege of Chattanooga by the Confederates. Grant replaced Rosecrans, organized a shorter line of supply, brought up reinforcements, and on November 24-25 launched an attack which drove the Army of Tennessee off Missionary Ridge. The Kentucky Brigade took what had by now become its customary place in the rear guard as the army retreated through Ringgold to Dalton in north Georgia, where it went into winter quarters.

At Dalton, General Joseph E. Johnston replaced Bragg as army commander. Here, too, General Breckinridge's connection with the Orphan Brigade was severed. He had been its leader either as brigade or division commander from the time of its organization. Now he was given an assignment in southwestern Virginia, and Major General William B. Bate of Tennessee succeeded to the command of his division. Here, too, at Dalton occurred the great religious revival that swept the Army of Tennessee in the winter of 1863-1864 and about which Johnny Green made some interesting observations.

The long spring of calm was broken in early May, 1864, when Sherman launched his campaign for Atlanta. The next eight weeks were arduous ones for the Army of Tennessee and the Kentucky Brigade as Sherman slowly forced them back. Rocky Face Ridge, Resaca, Calhoun, Allatoona, Kennesaw, Pine Mountain, Marietta—all were landmarks as Johnny Green and his comrades marched and countermarched, stood picket, or fought in the trenches against Sherman's powerful army. But Johnny and, according to him, the Brigade were not discouraged.

They believed that "Gen'l Joe," as they affectionately referred to Johnston, knew what he was doing and would turn on Sherman at the proper time and do him in.

But unfortunately Richmond authorities did not share Johnny Green's confidence in "Gen'l Joe," and when he retreated across the Chattahoochee into Atlanta, he was removed and replaced by General John B. Hood. Then began the series of battles for Atlanta: at Peachtree Creek, at Decatur, at Ezra Church, and finally at Jonesboro, in all of which Johnny and the Kentucky Brigade played a central part. But at the end of August the gray lines were broken and Hood had to evacuate Atlanta. Hoping then to lure Sherman back into Tennesee by operating on his line of communications, Hood moved past Sherman to the north. Sherman sent General George H. Thomas after him, but remained himself in Atlanta, where he prepared for his march to Savannah.

When Hood moved north, the long association between the Kentucky Brigade and the Army of Tennessee was broken. Johnny Green had been captured at Jonesboro, but he was exchanged after a few weeks and rejoined his comrades at Forsythe, Georgia, where the Brigade was in the process of being mounted as cavalry. Still under the command of General Lewis, the Brigade became part of the cavalry forces of Major General Joseph Wheeler and for the next six months remained on the flank of Sherman's army as it marched, first to Savannah and then to Raleigh, North Carolina, where the end came. The Brigade, now down to company size, could do little to impede Sherman's march. It and Wheeler's other forces annoyed Sherman, but they were too feeble to impede him seriously.

This closing chapter of the War in the West is a story of blind, unreasoning, almost superhuman courage and fortitude on the part of the men who fought on for what had for some time been a hopeless cause. Yet they seemed until the very end unable to grasp the meaning of defeat. It is pathetic to witness the surprise, and even shock, with which Johnny Green received news of the surrender. He was sure, even on the last day, that right was on his side and that, somehow, in some way, right would triumph. There can be little doubt that this last day of the war was, as he recorded, "the darkest day of our lives."

III

The saga of the Orphan Brigade reveals that it was no ordinary body of men, even in such a worthy company as the Army of Tennessee. One might well surmise from the number of important special missions which were assigned it, especially from the fact that it invariably was given the vitally important and dangerous task of guarding the rear on retreat, that it was universally regarded as a superior fighting force. Testimony of qualified and unbiased witnesses supports that assumption.

It should be borne in mind that the men of the Orphan Brigade were volunteers in the purest meaning of that term. In the beginning all Confederate, as also Union, soldiers were volunteers. But as the early romantic impressions of war and early enthusiasm of patriotism waned, conscription became necessary. The Confederacy began conscripting early in 1862, and from that time on as attrition depleted the ranks of the old volunteer units, they were refilled with the fruits of the conscription act. Some of these conscriptees were in the army against their wishes, and some even against their principles. Frequently morale problems, grumbling, straggling on the march, deserting when the opportunity presented itself, they must have considerably diminished the fighting enthusiasm of the units to which they belonged.

But the Orphans had all joined up in the first year of the war, when recruits from Kentucky were "clamorous to be received."[6] Kentucky at the time had declared her neutrality, and sentiment in the state was pro-Union, soon to become overwhelmingly so. There was, therefore, little pressure on them, even of sentiment, impelling them to enlist. Indeed, they went in many cases in opposition to the wishes of their families and friends and the opinion of their community. Whether they went from constitutional conviction or from emotional attachment to a cause matters little; they were determined and devoted men, the circumstances of whose enlistment were quite different from those whose states had seceded. Furthermore, the Confederacy was without power to enforce the draft in Kentucky, from which

[6] William T. Withers to Secretary of War L. P. Walker, July 12, 1861, in *O.R.*, Series 1, IV, 367.

its troops were expelled early in 1862. Consequently, as battle and disease took their toll in the Brigade, the vacant places were not filled with unwilling draftees; they were simply left vacant, and the survivors closed ranks and carried on. The regiments and batteries comprising the Brigade at their organization had counted approximately 5,000 men. When they marched out of Dalton in May, 1864, this number had dwindled to 1,420. After the Brigade was mounted in the fall of 1864, it numbered about 900, but two hundred or more of these were never mounted.[7]

Despite this heavy attrition which in three years reduced the Orphans by four-fifths their enthusiasm and discipline never waned. General Wheeler in his report of the Savannah campaign wrote, "No men in the Confederate States have marched more, fought more, suffered more, or had so little opportunities for discipline; yet they are today as orderly and as well disciplined as any cavalry in the Confederate service. . . . I must particularly commend my . . . Kentucky troops, who . . . I brought from the Coosa River to Savannah without a single desertion."[8]

But Wheeler was only one of the Confederate high command who testified to the caliber of the Orphans as a fighting unit. On the outskirts of Nashville a week before the battle which was to destroy his army General Hood, who had left the Brigade in Georgia with Wheeler, wired General P. G. T. Beauregard, pleading for it to be sent him, "As soon as the interests of the public service will allow."[9] In view of the fact that the Brigade numbered at the time fewer than a thousand and would have added little numerically to Hood's army, this special plea for their aid is indeed remarkable.

Braxton Bragg was never popular with the Orphans and saw little of them before the winter of 1862-1863. They had fought, of course, at Shiloh, but not in his corps. Shortly thereafter they had been sent to Mississippi and were there during his Kentucky campaign, and he did not see them again until he reached Murfreesboro, Tennessee, in November, 1862. Yet two months later at Stone's River he carefully selected them as "our best troops" for the climactic charge on the Union left on Jan-

---

[7] Thompson, *Orphan Brigade*, 280-81.
[8] *O.R.*, Series 1, XLIV, 412.
[9] *Ibid.*, XLV, pt. 2, p. 669.

uary 2. And Bragg's chief of staff thought of the Brigade as the "elite of the Confederate Army."[10]

General D. H. Hill saw the Orphans in battle only once, at Chickamauga where he commanded a corps made up of Breckinridge's and Pat Cleburne's divisions. Hill had commanded a famed division of his own the year before in Lee's Army of Northern Virginia, and there he had been closely associated with such noted units as Jackson's "Stonewall" Brigade, Hampton's Legion, and Hood's "Fighting Texans." But after watching Ben Hardin Helm's and Cleburne's troops repulsed as they threw themselves again and again on Thomas' barricaded position his admiration was unbounded and he thought he had never seen their equal. Years later he recalled their "unsurpassed and unsurpassable valor," and credited them, not without reason, with setting the stage for Longstreet's great victory on the other flank. It was their incessant pressure on Thomas, he said, which convinced Rosecrans that the bulk of the Confederate Army was concentrated there and caused him to weaken his own right to meet it, thus opening the gate for Longstreet's sweep. "Never," he said, had he seen "nobler troops led on a more desperate 'forlorn-hope'—against odds in numbers and superiority in position and equipment," than Helm's and Cleburne's that day.[11]

If Hill's and Bragg's high regard for the Orphans was made on short acquaintance and was a "first impression," there is little reason to believe that longer association would have altered their opinions. General Thomas C. Hindman's brigade had fought beside the Kentuckians at Shiloh and at Corinth. The two brigades had become seasoned companions-in-arms at Stone's River, at Chickamauga, and at Missionary Ridge. Promoted to division command, Hindman was temporarily in command of Hardee's Corps in January, 1864, at Dalton. Only two months had elapsed since the army had collapsed disgracefully under Bragg at Missionary Ridge, and the time had been spent profitably by Johnston in rebuilding its morale. Johnston ordered a review, and the conduct of his corps so pleased Hindman that he issued a congratulatory order. While complimenting the corps in general he

[10] Colonel David Urquhart, in Robert Underwood Johnson and Clarence Clough Buell (eds.), *Battles and Leaders of the Civil War*, 4 vols. (New York, 1887), III, 607. Hereafter this work is cited as *Battles and Leaders*.
[11] *Battles and Leaders*, III, 656, 657.

singled out the Kentuckians for special praise. "Without distracting from the praise due all," he said, "the Major-General deems it but just to mention the Kentucky Brigade as especially entitled to commendation for soldierly appearance, steadiness of marching, and an almost perfect accuracy in every detail."[12]

Joseph E. Johnston was another who had seen the Orphans tested over a long period. They had been with him in Mississippi in the summer of 1863, when he was vainly trying to save the garrison in Vicksburg. They had spent the next winter with him at Dalton and were to be daily with him in the eight weeks of almost constant battle from that place to Atlanta. When Breckinridge was transferred to Virginia early in 1864, he asked Johnston to let him take the Kentuckians with him on the understanding that President Davis would replace them with an "equivalent" brigade. "The President has no equivalent for it," Johnston is said to have replied. "It is the best brigade in the Confederate Army."[13] Years after the war Judge Emory Speer of Georgia wrote that Johnston had told him that "The Orphan Brigade was the finest body of men and soldiers he ever saw in any army anywhere."[14]

It is possible that the statements he made to Breckinridge and to Judge Speer were not Johnston's considered opinion, although, indeed, the circumstances under which they were made would indicate that they were. If there can be such a doubt, there is documentary evidence which should dispel it. Early in January, 1864, Secretary of War J. A. Seddon was toying with the idea of converting the Kentucky Brigade into cavalry and sending it on a mission back to Kentucky where it might recruit additional cavalry. It had been represented to Seddon that seven or eight thousand men might be added to the Confederate forces by this means, and he wrote Johnston for his opinion of the move. Johnston's reply was an unequivocal negative. Terming the Brigade "an excellent one," he wrote that he would not exchange it for the "7,000 or 8,000 mounted men it is proposed to raise by abolishing it." At the time the Brigade numbered only 1,065 effectives.[15]

[12] Thompson, *Orphan Brigade,* 23.   [13] Thompson, 23-24.
[14] Thompson, 24.
[15] *O.R.,* Series 1, XXXI, pt. 3, pp. 826, 877; XXXII, pt. 2, pp. 520-21.

Not only did friends pay tribute to the Orphans, but the enemy did also. Colonel George P. Este, commanding the Third Brigade, Third Division, of Sherman's Fourteenth Army Corps, who repulsed an attack by the Orphans at Jonesboro on August 31, 1864, admitted that the Kentucky troops "fought with the greatest determination." They were, he said, "Confessedly among the best of the rebel army."[16]

Finally, we have the word of a distinguished scientist about the caliber of the Orphans. Nathaniel Southgate Shaler, the noted Harvard geologist and anthropologist, was a native Kentuckian whose sympathies were with the Union during the war. Years later he was making a study which called for the observation of some group of about 5,000 soldiers who were of homogeneous ethnic background and whose ancestors had been for several generations on this continent. After considerable research the only group he could find which met these qualifications was the Kentucky Brigade, and he made an intensive study of its history. "From the beginning," he said, "it proved as trustworthy a body of infantry as ever marched or stood in the line of battle." He pointed out that in the hundred days of the Atlanta campaign it was almost continuously in action or on the march. More than eleven hundred strong at the beginning of that campaign, the Brigade suffered 1,860 fatal or hospital wounds. "At the end of this time there were less than fifty men who had not been wounded during the hundred days." Yet 240 men were present for duty and fewer than ten had deserted.

"A search into the history of warlike exploits," Shaler wrote, "has failed to show me any endurance to the worst trials of war surpassing this. . . . The men of this campaign were at each stage of their retreat going further from their firesides. It is easy for men to bear great trials under circumstances of victory. Soldiers of ordinary goodness will stand several defeats; but to endure the despair which such adverse conditions bring for a hundred days demands a moral and physical patience which, so far as I have learned has never been excelled in any other army."[17]

[16] *Ibid.*, XXXVIII, pt. 1, p. 811.
[17] Nathaniel Southgate Shaler, *Nature and Man in America* (New York, 1897), 277.

IV

John W. Green was born on his grandfather's plantation in Henderson County, Kentucky, on October 8, 1841. His father, Hector Green, had been born in Fauquier County, Virginia, descendant of a family which had settled there in 1710.[18] Hector Green had married Louisa Eleanor (known as Ellen) Ruggles of Roxbury, Massachusetts, whose father, Nathaniel Ruggles, was the representative of the Suffolk (Massachusetts) District in the United States Congress at the time of his death. According to the family records the first Ruggles, Thomas, settled in Roxbury in 1637.[19]

Hector and Ellen had three sons: Charles Catlett, the eldest, David Simmons, and John Williams, the youngest. After the grandfather lost his property, Hector and his young family moved to Louisville, where Ellen died and where the family supported themselves with some difficulty. John was graduated from Louisville Male High School and then secured employment with the firm of Hunt and Badger, Louisville merchants. When the secession depression caused the firm to cease business operations, John went to Florence, Alabama, where he was employed by the firm of McAllister and Company. Here he was when the war broke out. He made his way to Bowling Green, Kentucky, where on October 7, 1861, the day before his twentieth birthday, he enrolled in Company B of a regiment being formed there by John H. Hunt.[20] Meanwhile, Charles Catlett had moved to Virginia, where he had married, and David had gone to Memphis, where he was learning to become a Mississippi River pilot under the tutelage of Mark Twain. Neither of John's brothers was to take active part in the Civil War.

During the war John rose to the rank of regimental sergeant major, but he nursed some disappointment because of his failure to become a commissioned officer. He gave vent to his feelings

18 Mrs. John W. Green to "My dear Lillian" [Mrs. David Simpson], March 7, 1926. Letter in possession of John S. Green, Louisville.
19 Same to same, December 23, 1924.
20 John Green's obituary in the Louisville *Courier-Journal,* June 14, 1920, recounted much of his life. I have supplemented this by interviews with John S. Green, January 27, 1954, and Marion Green, April 14, 1953.

at the conclusion of hostilities by throwing away the sword of his rank, a deed he was later to regret. In the journal John makes several references to his shortness of stature. He was five feet, six inches tall, of slight build, and had dark hair, gray eyes, and dark complexion.

This intrepid Kentucky soldier who survived the perils of battle as well as privation and disease lived a full life as a successful businessman and respected citizen. After the war he settled in Louisville, where he entered the banking firm of Quigley and Martin. Several years later he joined the firm of Morton, Galt, and Company, and then formed a brokerage firm with Lucian Galt. This firm was dissolved in 1879 when John formed a brokerage partnership with his brother David. This partnership continued until John's death in 1920. At the time of his death he was a director of the Louisville Title Company and of the Columbia and Fidelity Trust Company, two of the largest financial houses of Louisville. He was a communicant of St. Paul's Episcopal Church and a member of the board of the Church Home. He was active in many civic enterprises and "ignored no public or private duty, no matter how onerous."

Meanwhile, John's father, Hector, had remarried after the death of Ellen and had become the father of seven additional children. Hector, who tried his hand in the professions of medicine and surveying as well as in several business ventures, seemed never able to support his family. The care of his younger half brothers and sisters thus became a charge of John's, whose growing prosperity enabled him cheerfully to provide for them.

John married Annie Amis of Louisville, and they had three children, Elizabeth, Marion, and a twin brother of Marion who lived only a few days. Elizabeth died before her twenty-eighth birthday, so that only Marion, who still resides in Louisville, survived her father. A nephew, John S. Green, son of John's brother Charles Catlett, and the two sons of John S. Green, Jack Green and C. Hunter Green, also reside in Louisville. A daughter of John S. Green, Mrs. Racey Biven, lives in San Pedro, California.

The sanguine and courageous disposition which he gave evidence of in his journal remained with Johnny Green until the day of his death. In the spring of 1920 he was stricken with arthritis. Although suffering intensely he gave no indication of depression to his wife and daughter who were in constant attendance. It was a great shock, therefore, when on the morning of June 13 he died of a self-inflicted wound.

V

This journal is in the handwriting of John W. Green and is in a leatherbound, pocketsize notebook of 290 pages. Green stated on the first page that he was writing it "from notes and from memory" for the benefit of his daughters, and as near as can be ascertained he wrote it in its present form sometime about 1890. His daughter says that he worked on it over a considerable period of time and that during its preparation he made constant reference to a large box containing papers. Doubtless these were diary notes which he made at the time of the event recorded, for details are too numerous, too circumstantial, and too authentic to be the product of mere memory. The original notes and papers, however, have disappeared.

Much of the book was written in the present tense, and frequently Green made reference to what was at the time an uncertain future, but which by 1890 was a well-known past. There was, for example, the occasion at Missionary Ridge when he stumbled upon the cottage in which lay the soldier stricken with smallpox. Green wrote: "During the battle of the next few days, there was one consoling thought. I knew if I should be killed on the field I would not have to suffer the pain of small-pox. *But as I was not killed I may have small-pox yet"* (my italics). This might indicate that at the time he made the entry the incubation period of the disease had not yet elapsed and he still feared he might contract the dread malady. It is most unlikely that this was a ruse of Green's to give the account a contemporaneous ring. It would be out of character for Green to stoop to such acts of deception. By all accounts he was a plain, unaffected, thoroughly honest man of no pretense. Moreover, he was not writing for publication but only for the education and entertainment of his young daughters, and it could not matter to them whether the account was contemporaneous or not.

And finally, the suggestion is completely discredited because if Green was cunning enough to deceive here, he would have done so throughout the journal, and there are many instances where he frankly made statements which arose from facts obviously learned after the war.

There is, for instance, the reference Green made to a Confederate deserter at Chattanooga revealing to Grant the fact that Buckner's corps had been sent to Knoxville. It is not likely that Green had means of knowing this at the time. But Grant recorded this, in substance, in his official report, and this was published some years before Green wrote his journal in its present form. Then, too, writing in October, 1863, Green noted that Captains Buchanan and Hewett "served to the day of surrender on Genl Lewis' staff," a thing he could not possibly have known before April, 1865. Had Green been so careful to deceive in the smallpox incident, he could not have been so careless here. It is clear that the former account was contemporaneous and the latter was not.

Abundant examples could be cited illustrating both contemporaneous and edited accounts, but they would be merely repetitious. It can be concluded that the book was largely written, as Green stated on the first page of the manuscript, from notes contemporaneously recorded, but which were in many cases edited later by the author.

Green was quite literate and wrote in an unstilted and attractive style. He knew how to spell almost every word he used (*Breckinridge, Beauregard,* and *cavalry,* I think, were beyond him), but like most of us he grew careless at times, and some words are spelled in several different ways. *Cavalry* bothered him most, and although he used it dozens of times, only seldom did he ever get it right. He tried *Cavelry, cavelry, cavlery,* and finally sensing that the fourth letter was the source of his trouble, he left it out and wrote *Cav'lry.* Other words which gave him trouble were: *pickets (picketts), bayonets (bayonetts), Baton Rouge (Batton), enemy (ennemy), brigade (briggade), bullet (bullitt), buried (burried), firing (fireing), pursued (persued),* and *Yankee,* for which he had an infinite variation. I have corrected in the text the spelling of *Breckinridge, Beauregard, Baton Rouge,* and other proper nouns without explanation. All other spelling has been left unchanged except where it might lead to the reader's confusion.

Green paid little attention to paragraphing or to rules of punctuation. I have for readability made paragraph divisions and have done considerable punctuating. I have also divided the journal into chapters and given them titles. I have placed capital letters at the beginning of all sentences, but I have left his lower-case letters at the beginning of some proper nouns. In all other respects the published work corresponds with the manuscript.

VI

This journal was first brought to my attention by W. K. Stewart of Louisville, who had previously examined it and through whose influence it was made available to me. The publication itself has been made possible through the kindness of the daughter of John W. Green, Miss Marion Green, who is the owner of the journal. John S. Green and his wife Maude gave me valuable biographical information. I also wish to thank Bruce F. Denbo and Kenneth W. Elliott of the University of Kentucky Press; their careful editing and wise suggestions have smoothed many rough spots left both by the author and by the editor. I am grateful to the University of Kentucky Research Fund for a grant used in preparation for publication. William K. Hubbell has drawn the battle maps and the end maps. Mrs. Monroe Billington, Mrs. Lloyd Keeton, and my wife, Betty Kirwan, have typed and retyped the manuscript. To all of them I am grateful.

1 CALL TO COLORS

At the outbreak of hostilities Kentucky placed herself in the anomalous position of refusing to furnish troops to suppress the rebellion, and even of arming herself to repel efforts of the Federal government to suppress it, and yet refusing to join the Confederacy. By this action the government of the state had virtually abandoned control over its citizens, who began to ally themselves with either party as they chose.

Some of the Southern party early organized themselves into units and left the state for Virginia, where they joined the army of Joseph E. Johnston and fought at Bull Run. Meanwhile, honoring for a time the letter if not the spirit of the state's technical neutrality, the Unionist party opened a recruiting station at Camp Joe Holt, near Jeffersonville, Indiana, across the river from Louisville. At about the same time Camp Boone was opened in Montgomery County, Tennessee, just across the border from Kentucky, as a recruiting center for Kentuckians of Confederate sympathies. Here gathered members of the State Guard and local militia from all sections of Kentucky, fleeing before the Unionist sentiment rising in the state.

Soon both sides were violating Kentucky's neutrality furtively, but early in September, Confederate General Leonidas Polk seized Columbus in the extreme western part of the state. Thereupon General Ulysses S. Grant seized Paducah, and General Robert Anderson moved a Union force into Louisville.

The formal truce in Kentucky was now at an end. General Albert Sidney Johnston, commander of all Confederate forces west of the Appalachian Mountains, with headquarters at Nashville, ordered General Simon Bolivar Buckner, a Kentuckian, to Bowling Green, which soon became the stronghold of the Confederate center in Kentucky. Recruits, among them Johnny Green, poured into the city, and it was at this time that Colonel Thomas H. Hunt organized the Ninth Kentucky Regiment.

$\mathcal{F}$EELING THAT when I have been called to Heaven to join a long line of God loving ancestors, especially my dear Sainted mother who taught me to love my Creator & Heavenly Father with all my heart & to love my neighbor as myself; my daughters would have great interest in knowing many things about my life which they had not heard before; I jot down these lines.

I was born Oct 8th 1841 on a large farm in Henderson Co Ky about 8 miles from Henderson on the Madisonville road.

My Grand father John Green came from Fa[u]quier Co Va & settled this tract of about one thousand acres & improved it until he had one of the finest farms in the state. I think he was born in Culpepeper [Culpeper] & married Miss Winnifred Catlet[t] of Fauquier. His slaves were of the best & most intelligent sort, whose lives were made happy by the comforts provided for them, freedom from all responsibility & the knowledge of the fact that their master was one of the best & most important men in the county.

My childhood was one of supreme happiness. When uncle Norv our negro miller would set me on the mill sweep beside him as he was riding around & around driving the horse to grind the corn, I was as happy as the bird who seemed to be trying to whistle louder than this jolly miller. To watch our negro blacksmith as he hammered the red hot iron, gave me a pleasure which made my eyes sparkle in rivalry with the sparks which I watched with such interest fly from the red hot iron.

Everything used on the place was made by my Grandfathers slaves. His carpenter made my two wheeled cart in which it gave me such pleasure to haul my older brother; for the small boy always takes his fun in laboring for the big one (if the big one is smart).

When uncle Shoewax made my first pair of red top boots, I strutted up & down with more vanity than a peacock, then rushed to the rope walk to show them to Uncle Mack who was rope maker & then to show them to aunt Jinney who made all the cloth to make the clothes for the slaves.

But my dear old Grand father was made High Sheriff of the county & because of too much kind heart & leniency on his part, at the close of his term of office he found he was almost bankrupt. It was somewhat in this manner. He had an execution for instance which it was his duty to levy upon the property of an acquaintance, he levied upon some lumber, some corn & some hogs. The man pleaded most faithfully that he intended to sell those things & pay the debt & induced my grandfather after levying upon the things to make him (the debtor) bailiff to take charge of & guard the property under promise that within a certain time he would bring to my Grand father a purchasor who would take the things & pay the debt. The time passed & nothing was heard from the man. Grand father went to see him to require a settlement. Every thing was gone; when asked what had become of the corn, he had fed that to the hogs, "Well where are the hogs?" Oh he had killed them & eaten them.

"Well you did not eat the lumber. Where is it?"

"Oh you have that."

"What do you mean?" said Grand father.

The man replied, "Why Williams sold you that lumber

4

to build that house you built & gave the widow Howe."

"Well I paid Williams," said Grand father, "so give me that money."

"Why," replied the man, "I cant. I owed Williams more than that & he just took that in part pay."

This & many other cases about as bad forced the dear old Grand father to sell his farm & some of his slaves.

My maturnal Grandmother Mrs Sallie Ruggles, widow of Hon Nathaniel Ruggles U.S. congressman representing Suffolk district of Mass. bought one hundred acres of my Grand father Green's farm & had the same deeded to my mother & her children.

The slaves which had to be sold were permitted to seek for new masters to suit themselves; several purchasors who were willing to pay the price were rejected because the slave did not wish to be sold to that person. In no instance was husband & wife or mother & child separated except where the mother was willing to have my Grand father retain the children. Aunt Sophie rejected three proposed masters because they never came from Virginia & might be poor white trash for all she *knowed*.

My father & mother together with my grandfather, my uncle Rob't who was a cripple my two brothers & myself moved to a little farm which my father rented near Cairo, Henderson Co Ky, until the house on my mothers one hundred acres was ready for us, when we moved there. At this time I was about five years old. We still had five slaves left & life to my two brothers & myself was as happy as to a prosperous hive of bees & my parents christened our home "The Hive."

My father having graduated as a physician began the practice of medicine. He would never send a bill to a friend & his enemies if he had any did not employ him; therefore his profession afforded but little profit. I remember once my mother reminded him of a bill he could collect but his reply was, "My dear you know that child died & you dont suppose

I would send a bill for medical services when the patient died."

The custom then was for the doctor to furnish the medicine when he gave the prescription & as my father was such a poor collector it soon became evident that he could not support a family by the practice of medicine, so mother convinced him that the more practice he got the poorer he would become. He then became county surveyor of Henderson County but the spirit of change set him to longing to emigrate & after discussing Oregon & Texas he decided to emigrate to Texas.

My mothers little farm was sold, his debts paid, & with the remainder father went to Texas to locate while my mother, my two brothers & I visited my mothers first cousin John S. Williams & his family in Louisville Ky.

Father bought land near Gonzalies Texas, made first payment & came back for his family, but upon weighing the importance of schools for us boys he abandoned the Texas plan as well as the land & my dear mother taught school in Louisville & father sought some employment, but mother had to provide the greater part of the support for the family.

She had a little ready money inherited from her mother; some of this she lent to start my fathers brother Robert in business. His partner swindled him out of most of it but he got a mortgage on a poor farm in Mead[e] Co Ky to secure the debt to a small extent.

My mother after much suffering died of a cancer of the face. The family lived together in Louisville for a few years, each of us boys having gone to work; but the hire of two slaves still owned by father & the wages of my brother David & myself supported the family. David after a time got a situation on the Genl Pike, a steam boat running from Memphis to New Orleans & other southern waters, & I was clerking in the banking house of A. D. Hunt & Co; father & my brother Charley went to Memphis & embarked in business. This left me in Louisville with my helpless uncle

6

Robert to support which with the greatest economy I did on $275 per annum & the hire of one Slave Andrew about $100 per annum, but the patience with which my poor uncle endured the discomfort of having me learn to shave him (for every week I had to shave & bathe him he being almost as helpless as a baby) & the affection with which he looked up to me was full compensation to me. I was happy in the performance of my duty; I was looking forward to fitting myself by close study & long patience to becoming a physician; to this end I employed my evenings in studying & attended the dissecting class at the University one winter, my good friend Dr A. B. Cook having given me the ticket.

But the war of secession was rapidly approaching. It first paralyzed business & my situation was lost because my employers determined to discontinue business. I had to send Uncle Robert to his brother Peter who lived in Union County & I accepted a clerkship with McAlester Simpson & Co Florence Ala.

My mother was a Boston woman her father having been a member of the United States congress from that district at the time of his death. I had learned to love the Union & earnestly hoped that dissolution might be averted, but looked upon coercion as fratricidal and unconstitutional & when Abraham Lincoln issued his proclimation calling for men & money as he said to enforce the laws I knew it was for unconstitutional coercion & sad as it made me to take up arms against the country that I loved I recognized that my first duty was to the cause of Constitutional government & I made arrangements as soon as possible to give up my situation & enlist in the Confederate army to fight for the right of a state to govern itself; as there was no right given or implied in the constitution to coerce a state to remain in the Union, as much as I loved our country I could not reconcile the coercion of a sister state with Self Government. The South claimed only the right for each state that so desired peaceably to withdraw. The other states had full power to continue as they were.

(The distinguished Jerre Black—(Atty Genl of the United States) gave to Pres Buchannan a written opinion that no state could under the constitution be forced to remain in the union.) [1]

When I resigned my clerkship to go into the army of the Confederate States I was less than 20 years old, I had not seen my father for about two years & realizing that going into the army when war was upon us meant large chances of getting killed I determined to first go & tell him good bye. He lived then at Corrydon Henderson Co Ky—my journey was interrupted at Nashville Tenn; as Genl Albert Sidney Johns[t]on[2] had siezed all the railroads & was sending Genl Buckner[3] & the troops at his disposal to Bowling Green.

With a Mr Carter Harrison of Russellville Ky I hired a horse & buggy & drove to that town, & from Russellville by stage coach to Hopkinsville & from there to my father's by farm wagon.

After telling father good bye & buying myself some blankets & suitable underclothes I rode back to State Line

[1] Attorney General Jeremiah S. Black further pointed out in this opinion, however, that the President had no power to recognize the independence of or absolve from her federal obligations any state attempting secession. He added that the "General Government may lawfully repel a direct aggression on its property" but could not fight offensive war "to punish the people [of a state] for the political misdeeds [secession] of their State government." Opinion of November 20, 1860, in *Digest of the Official Opinions of the Attorney-General of United States* (Washington, 1885), 131-32. Black was an advocate of a firm policy by the federal government in the secession crisis.

[2] In September, 1861, Albert Sidney Johnston, a native Kentuckian, was appointed commander of all the Confederate forces west of the Appalachian Mountains. He established his headquarters at Nashville and was commander in chief of the army of which the Orphan Brigade was a part. He was killed at Shiloh April 6, 1862.

[3] Brigadier General Simon Bolivar Buckner, also a native Kentuckian, was in command of the Confederate forces at Bowling Green, Kentucky, where the Kentucky or Orphan Brigade was recruited and organized. He went with the Second Kentucky Regiment of Infantry, a unit of the Orphan Brigade, to Fort Donelson in February, 1862, and became a Federal prisoner, along with the rest of the garrison, when Grant captured the fort. He was exchanged and rejoined the army some months later, and although he commanded a division and later a corps in the Army of Tennessee, to which the Orphan Brigade was attached, he was never again closely associated with it.

(now Guthrie). I got aboard a freight train, spread my blanket on the floor, threw myself down on it & woke up the next morning in Bowling Green. I had determined to join the Citizen Guards[4] of Louisville Ky which I had learned had gone to Bowling Green to join the Confederate army. A portion of this company had come south; by this time the Home guards were in controll of every thing in Louisville & no one was permitted to come south if it was thought he was a southern sympathizer. In order to get through the lines these boys [the Citizen Guards] loaded their equipments into a farm wagon, threw some straw over them, & then on top of that threw stable manure, & a member of their company dressed as a countryman hauled the equipments through the Federal lines while the other boys Scattered & made their way as best they could to Muldraugh's hill where they found the wagon & their equipments waiting for them.

After buying something to eat I set out in quest of the Citizen Guards. I went to Genl Buckners head Quarters, he directed me so that I soon found their camp. Col Thos H. Hunt[5] of Louisville was in command, he was organizing a regiment which at this time was called the 5th Ky Inftry. Later because of some conflict in the dates of commission's the number was changed to the 9th.

---

4 A military organization recruited by Buckner, ostensibly for the defense of Kentucky against an aggressor, the Citizen Guards were soon identified as sympathetic to the Confederacy. They were also known as State Guards. The Home Guards were the Union counterpart of the Citizen Guards.

5 Thomas Hart Hunt (1815-1884) was born and grew to manhood in Lexington, Kentucky. In 1848 he moved to Louisville, where he engaged successfully in merchandising and in manufacture of rope and bagging. When the secession crisis arose, he joined the State Guards and was appointed colonel of the Second Regiment. In October, 1861, he resigned this commission and made his way to Bowling Green, where he proceeded to recruit the Fifth (later the Ninth) Regiment of Kentucky Infantry, of which he was appointed colonel. He distinguished himself at Shiloh, Vicksburg (1862), Baton Rouge (where he commanded the brigade after the injury to General Ben Hardin Helm), and Stone's River. In April, 1863, he resigned from the army in order to care for his family. After the war he settled in New Orleans, where he died in 1884. At the time of his death he was secretary of the World's Exposition, then being held in New Orleans. Thompson, *Orphan Brigade*, 429-33.

9

About this time Mr John C. Breckinridge[6] Vice Pres of the United States under Buchannan & afterwards United States Senator for Ky resigned & came south & was made a Brigadeer General & ordered to report to Genl Simon Bolivar Buckner who organized the Orphan Brigade then known as 1st Ky Brigade & placed genl Breckinridge in command & Col Hunt's regiment was in this brigade. I was sworn in, Oct 7th 1861, given one of the grey uniforms, a gun & equipments which the Citizen Guard boys had brought south with them as above related. I was placed in a mess with David W. Caruth,[7] Len S. Miller,[8] Billy Pope,[9] H. P. (Gos) Elston,[10] Bob Tyler[11] & John B. Pirtle.[12] We had good wall tents with

[6] Breckinridge assumed command of the Kentucky Brigade in November, 1861, at the time of its organization. A few months later he was promoted to major general and given command of a division, of which the Brigade was part. He was intimately associated with the unit, as division commander, until the spring of 1864, when he was transferred to southwestern Virginia (Thompson, 361-62). Breckinridge was a colorful figure, much loved by the Brigade. General Thomas Jordan, Albert Sidney Johnston's adjutant general, has left his impression of Breckinridge. Encountering him on the field at Shiloh at the height of the battle, he says, "His dark eyes seemed to illuminate his swarthy, regular features, and as he sat in his saddle he seemed to me altogether the most impressive-looking man I ever had seen." *Battles and Leaders,* I, 601. Jordan was not unaccustomed to impressive-looking men.

[7] David W. Caruth, a native of Louisville, served in every engagement in which the Brigade took part. He was wounded at Missionary Ridge November 25, 1863, but returned to active duty in time for the Atlanta campaign. He was made second sergeant of Company B in January, 1864. He was a successful businessman in Louisville after the war. Thompson, *Orphan Brigade,* 818.

[8] Len S. Miller of Louisville fought with the Brigade until the fall of Atlanta. He was then attached to the Army of Tennessee and fought in the battle of Nashville December 15, 1864. Thompson, 821.

[9] William Pope of Louisville was wounded at Shiloh, suffered an arm amputation, and died shortly afterward. Thompson, 822.

[10] Sergeant H. P. Ellston of Louisville was killed at Shiloh. Thompson, 818.

[11] Robert S. Tyler fought with the Brigade at Shiloh but was transferred to Morgan's Cavalry shortly thereafter. Thompson, 823.

[12] John B. Pirtle was born in Louisville in 1842. He enlisted in Company B, Ninth Kentucky, but was commissioned for distinguished service at the battle of Shiloh, though not yet twenty years of age. He rose to the rank of captain and served successively on the staffs of Colonel R. P. Trabue, General Ben Hardin Helm, and General William B. Bate. He took part in all major engagements of the Brigade and was wounded at Resaca and Jonesboro. After the war he became a successful businessman and civic leader in Louisville. Thompson, 505-506.

10

wooden floors in them but to new recruits seven men in a tent on the floor with only a blanket between us & the boards at first seemed pretty hard sleeping but it was not long before we looked back upon these comforts as princely luxuries.

Routine Camp life consisting of Drill & Guard duty occupied the time until rather late in Nov when a party of Federals was reported to be threatening the R. R. running to Memphis. We made a hurried march out towards Mud river to intercept them but learning that they had withdrawn we returned after a terrible march through mud & rain. But this, severe as the experience seemed then, was nothing to what we underwent later. We soon went down to Russellville to Join Capt John W. Caldwell's[13] Co & Capt Mitchell's.[14] They were incorporated into our regiment, the first as Co A & the other as Co C. It was here that the Citizens Guards combined with other companies, some of the men, myself among them, going into Co B in consideration of their making one of our officers Joe Benedict[15] Second Lieutanant. And some of the other men went into Company C to secure a Lieutenancy for Price Newman[16] an other officer

[13] John William Caldwell was born in Russellville, Kentucky, January 15, 1836. At the outbreak of hostilities he was practicing law in his native town. He raised a company in Logan County and entered the Confederate service in September, 1861, with the rank of captain. His company was designated Company A, Ninth Kentucky Infantry. He was wounded at Shiloh and shortly thereafter was promoted to major and then to lieutenant colonel. Upon Colonel Hunt's resignation in April, 1863, he was promoted to colonel. He was wounded again at Chickamauga, but returned to duty. Being the senior colonel in the Brigade, he commanded it on several occasions when General Lewis acted as division commander. He served with the Brigade throughout the war and at its end resumed the practice of law in Russellville. He was repeatedly the Third District congressman. Thompson, 434-38.

[14] William Mitchell of Hartford, Kentucky, was killed at Shiloh April 6, 1862. Thompson, 825.

[15] Joe Benedict of Louisville was elected second lieutenant October 2, 1861, and was promoted to first lieutenant March 6, 1863. He fought at Shiloh, Vicksburg, Hartsville, Stone's River, and Jackson. Ill health forced him to resign in March, 1863. He died in New Orleans in 1895. Thompson, 815.

[16] Price Newman of Louisville was elected second lieutenant of Company C, Ninth Regiment, in November, 1861, and was chosen captain at the reorganization of the unit in May, 1862. He fought with distinction in all major engagements of the Brigade. He died in Louisville in 1894. Thompson, 825.

11

of the old Citizens Guards. This was done because our Co
was not full & the ranks were not filling up.

We came back from Russellville to Bowling Green by
R. R., the rain pouring down all day. Reaching Bowling
Green at dusk we marched through mud & rain to a point
on the right ha[n]d side of the turn pike looking north &
called the place Camp Price for Genl Sterling Price who had
just done such gallant fighting in Mo.

I was drenched to the skin, tired, muddy & sick, every
bone in my body aching, but I said to my messmates I would
bring straw to spread in our tents to sleep on. (We were
fortunate enough at this time to have tents.) I took my
blanket, filled it with all the straw I could pack into it,
brought [it] to our tent & being almost dead on my feet
threw myself down on it & tossed until morning.

When day came my messmates found I had broken out
with measles & Col Hunt sent me to the hospital. He rode
down to the hospital in Bowling Green & got the matron to
give me the best accommodation & attention; my bed was a
bunk filled with straw with one blanket to lie on & one to
cover with. I knew nothing for a few days & when my fever
began to abate I could not speak above a whisper. The only
treatment I remember receiving was that about every hour
the good kind hearted matron would bring me a tin cup full
of hot sage tea.

My brother David came to see me just at this time &
burst out crying because I was sick abed & could not speak
above a whisper. I convalesced rapidly & went to Memphis
on a ten days sick leave & met my brother David when his
steam boat the Kennawah [Kanawha?] Valley on which he
was second clerk came into port.

I took the round trip from Memphis up White River
with him. The Capt was glad to give that much to a confederate soldier & especially to a Soldier who was the brother
of his clerk. It was a great pleasure to us brothers to be together on this trip. I never saw so much wild game in my

life as the boat brought back to Memphis: wild ducks, geese, turkeys, deer & bear & a wounded swan.

I returned to Bowling Green just in time to set out on the march from Oakland to Dripping Springs.[17] The rain was coming down in a bleak steady down pour as we took up the line of march with our faces towards Louisville. The boys raised a yell to cheer their spirits. The road was very muddy & crossed by frequent little streams flooded to their fullest. As we would wade into the ice cold water, so deep as to come much above our k[n]ees, we would sing, "Cheer boys Cheer we march away to battle."

Not a complaining voice was heard, not one heart that did not beat with pride to brave discomfort for the cause we had espoused. I had a fine grey army over coat which I bought when I enlisted. It was quite long & as I waded the streams the coat tail would float out behind & the boys would call out, "I want to be ferried across on duck leg's coat tail." Capt Clint McClarty rode a horse & as I was about to wade across the fourth & deepest stream the capt rode up to me & said, "Here you duck legged little rebel you jump up behind me & let me ferry you over." Capt McClarty & I were fast friends from that hour until the time of his death.

On Dec 20th late in the day, learning that the federal forces were moving towards Dripping Springs we marched hurriedly to that point to intercept the enemy. The weather was terrible, rain & sleet all day & when halted we were drenched to the skin. It turned verry cold & soon our clothes were frozen stiff on us. We were in time to head off the yankee column & they came no nearer, but fell back towards Glasgow.

Strict orders had been issued against burning rails, but we were actually freezing & had no axes to cut fire wood. We were compelled to have fires & Col Hunt realized our necessity, he therefore said to the regiment when he gave

17 Oakland was a settlement about thirteen miles northeast of Bowling Green. Dripping Springs was six miles farther.

orders to break ranks, "Boys you must not burn any whole rails." We soon found some of the boys who had matches & made roaring fires from pieces of rails. The truth is, it was but little time before every rail in that fence had been converted into pieces. We thawed out, found some whole rails, laid them side by side, spread our blankets upon them to keep off the frozen ground & with our feet to the fire went to sleep despite the sleet which fortunately had now almost ceased. But it was growing colder every minute.

Dec 22nd 1861. This day we took another chase after the Yankees & marched to Merry Oaks about 10 miles from Dripping Springs but saw nothing of the enemy, the weather still very bleak & rough.

Dec 23d marched back to Oakland. It seems we have scared the yanks off & are to make ourselves as comfortable as we can here. This place belongs to Mr Wilder of Louisville. He has lots of wheat in the granary & a steam mill to grind it. Hiram Garr[18] of Capt Bousche's[19] Co was detailed to act as miller & grind some of this wheat to give us flour to make biscuit. Garr was a steam boat engineer but in some unaccountable way the boiler blew up just when he had gotten well started to grinding & for the one mess of biscuit he provided for us he paid his life, for he was killed by the explosion. There were several others in the mill at the time but he was the only one hurt.

We had tents at this time but the weather was very cold with snow on the ground. We had not learned to build chimneys to our tents & we spent a very cold Christmas here. We were however fortunate enough to buy a turkey. Dave Caruth cooked the turkey & I made & cooked the biscuit. We thought we had a sumptuous dinner for soldiers but

---

[18] Garr was a Louisvillian. Thompson, 852.

[19] Christian Bosche was a German immigrant who had settled in Louisville. He was a lieutenant at the time of this incident but was elected captain April 25, 1862. He served with the Brigade throughout the war and died in Louisville in 1890. Thompson, 852.

14

hoped soon to march victoriously into Louisville & recount our interesting experience.

About Jan 4th 1862 we left Oakland, marched a few miles & went into winter quarters at Camp Clear Water, there was not sufficient drinking water for us at Oakland. Camp Clear Water is in an open field near a large woods & near a bold [cold?] spring of delicious clear water. We now set to work to make ourselves comfortable; we had to stay through a very cold winter in tents & the question was how to heat them. We had neither brick nor stone so we determined to build chimneys to our tents out of the sod which was close by & plentiful. All set to work, some cutting sod, some bringing it to the tent & some building; very soon a fire place & chimney was built to each tent. We would turn up one half of the front & place the fire place & chimney there leaving the other half for the door.

It is wonderful how comfortable we made ourselves. Stakes were driven in the ground about two feet in front of the fire, a plank was nailed on top of these stakes for a seat, an other plank was placed on edge against the stakes to make a foot board to our bed & the floor of the tent was filled with straw for the bed, which we found much more comfortable than to have board floors.

I had taken as my part of the messwork, the cooking of the bread, we were at this time drawing rations of flour & other good food. My first attempt at bread making came near causing the rest of my mess to mob me but I pleaded for one more chance before being condemned. I had good Kentucky money in my pocketts & so concluded to let it do my bread baking for me & I set out for a farm house in the neighborhood to bargain for the baking of our buscuits but my offer of money was declined. The dear good woman, a widow Ford, said, "No indeed young man I'll take no pay; but you bring your flour up here every day & I'll have your biscuits baked for you." May the Lord bless her & give her a choice seat in the choir of Heavenly Hosts. All that winter my bread baking was done for me simply by my walking to & from that dear good Mrs Ford's home.

We left camp Clear Water at 7 AM Feb 12th altogether in doubts as to our movements but strong in our faith that Albert Sidney Johnston would do the right thing.[20] We marched but 4 miles this day; on Feb 13th crossed Barren River & marched 15 miles to Franklin, quite cold. Gathered broom Sedge to make our bed as we could get no straw. Feb 14th marched to camp Trousdale; very cold the ponds & creeks frozen hard—attempted to sleep in frame sheds, dirt floors, no chimneys—made fires on the floor but little chance for the smoke to get out & it nearly suffocated us. We tore some of the roof off but still we were like smoked rats. The next morning had to break the ice in the creek for water. I was soon at the creek for a souse to revive me from the effects of the smoke.

Feb 15th marched 14 miles to Goodletsville,[21] bivouacked with six inches of snow on the ground. We were fortunate enough to get a lot of wheat straw for our beds. We were completely covered with snow when reveille sounded in the morning. This day they double-quicked us for several miles because of an alarm that the Yankies were trying to cut us off from Nashville & we thought we were to have a chance for a fight but it was a false alarm.

Feb 16th 1862 Crossed the bridge at Nashville just after night. It had been sleeting all the afternoon, our march was very muddy cold & wet. So great had been our hurry that we had no chance to fill our canteens. Every thing in Nashville was in such a rush that semi-panic Seemed to prevail. After marching through the city the column halted for a few minutes on the turn pike; we heard the trickling of water in the

20 The capture on February 6 of Fort Henry on the Tennessee River by Grant with the aid of Foote's gunboats convinced General Johnston that Fort Donelson could not be held and that the army at Bowling Green must retreat to Nashville and beyond. Accordingly orders were issued to that effect. *O.R.,* Series 1, VII, 863, 864.

21 Goodletsville is a hamlet about ten miles north of Nashville.

16

gully besides the pike & such was our thirst that some of us kneeled down by the side of the running water & drank. You can imagine our disgust when we went into Nashville the next day to find that the street gutters emptied right into the stream we drank from.

We halted 4 miles south of Nashville to camp for the night. Our wagons with tents & camp outfit had been sent ahead so we had cold comfort in prospect for the night as it was still sleeting & the mud seeped over shoe tops everywhere you would step; but we cut cedar boughs & piled under bushy cedar trees & tried to think we were as comfortable as snow birds. Two of us would bunk to-gether, one would spread his blanket on the cedar boughs & the two would cover with the other blanket & soon we slept the sleep of the just.

We heard conflicting rumors about the battle at fort Donaldson [Donelson], One that we had whipped the Yanks four days in succession & one that our boys were all captured. Strange as it may seem both rumors were true. When our boys were out of provisions & amunition the yanks took them in, our boys had to surrender.

Feb 17th 1862 Our tents were brought to us & we rested; it was however the muddiest, most dismal place in the world. We cut poles & laid in our tent for a floor & put the cedar boughs over them.

Feb 18th 1862 Marched 5 miles.

Feb 19th rested in our tents; rained all day.

Feb 20th marched 9 miles, camped in Cedar forest left hand side of the road.

Feb 21st marched 13 miles to Murfreesboro. We pitched our tents but did not ditch them. The rainy season is continuous & during the night the deluge came; it filled the floor of our tent with water fully three inches deep. Indeed the whole face of the earth throughout our camp was under water (very flat country). I had a severe chill followed the

17

next day by fever, but Calomel & Quinine soon had me all right again.

Some of the boys who were set to guard the commisary stores got into trouble because a barrel of whiskey from the commisary wagon was stolen that night & all the messmates of the guards were too drunk next morning to answer roll call. They had gotten a gimlet & bored through the bottom of the wagon up through the barrel & as the whiskey ran out they caught it in bucketts. The boys on guard had to serve on extra duty notwithstanding their protestations that they saw no body do it. It is quite probable that they took good pains not to see any one while they were doing it. Our Commisary Capt Phil Vicaro[22] got so mad that after taking three or four stiff drinks himself he knocked in the head of the other barrel he had & poured the whiskey on the ground. After this he could never pass by the regiment without the whole crowd yelling out, "Pour it Out, Pour it Out."

Feb 28th left Murfreesboro & by slow marches went through Moorsville & Huntsville Ala to Decatur Ala. At Moorsville we had an equinoxial storm which blew down everyone of our tents & just deluged us; some of us squatted on the ground & covered ourselves with our tents & took the storm as best we could, of course, every thing was drenched. Some others took refuge in a gin house which withstood the fury of the storm.

At Huntsville the ladies of the City presented a silk flag to the sixth Ky Regmt. At this place is a big spring that supplies the whole city with water & has a spillway flowing in a stream three feet deep by about 8 feet wide.

At Decatur the whole country was flooded. The wagon train crossed the Tenn River on the Railroad track, planks were laid on the track to make a roadway for wagons & teams. I borrowed Col Hunt's horse to ride over to Decatur to buy myself a pair of shoes. As I was crossing on the R. R. fill with

[22] Phil Vacaro of Louisville served as captain and commissary throughout the war. Thompson, *Orphan Brigade*, 823.

18

20 feet of water on each side, a train met us & the tussel I had to keep that horse from jumping into the river or getting under the train was indeed strenious.

We took the train at Decatur & went to Burnsville Miss where we went into camp in an old Cotton field on March 22nd. Quite vigorous camp duty, drill & guard mounting until April 3d 1862, the weather is very warm. Night of April 3d ordered to cook three days rations & prepare to attack the enemy—the whole command greatly rejoiced at the prospect of battle.

Daylight April 4th marched by Farmington & Monterey to a point near Shiloh Church.[23] At Monterey was a black smith shop busy turning out old fashioned pikes to arm some of our troops who had no guns.

Night of the 4th of April bivouacked on the side of the road. Poured rain all night. April 5th moved slowly towards Shiloh, roads terribly heavy & we had to wait for the artillery to come up; occasional rains throughout the day; last nights deluge wet our rations but notwithstanding wet bread is not very appetizing we ate up the three days rations in half that time & consequently we are all very hungry. Halted about 5 Oclock April 5th near a turnip patch, helped ourselves to turnips. A rabit jumped out of a bunch of brush & ran until headed by some soldiers, then he turned in an other direction & was headed again, then he ran towards our command. He had left the last pursuer far behind when I took up the chase. He was tired & confused, I thought I had him but he suddenly darted towards a line of high weeds & disappeared. I followed in hot pursuit & tumbled headlong into a ditch filled with water up to my middle. But Brer Rabit was there too & was a poor swimmer. I pulled him in. We barbecued him & our mess lived high that night on turnips, Rabit & ash cake; for one of the boys got a negro woman in

---

[23] Shiloh Church is about three miles west of the Tennessee River at Pittsburg Landing and is twenty miles northeast of Corinth, Mississippi. Much of the battle of April 6-7, 1862, was fought near the church, which has given its name to the first major battle of the War in the West.

19

the neighborhood to make us some bread and as her skillet was already taxed to its greatest capacity, all she could give us was ash cake (Corn meal mixed with salt & water, put between two cabbage leaves & cooked in the red hot ashes) .

2 SHILOH

With the defeat of the Confederate forces at Mill Springs and with the fall of Forts Henry and Donelson the Confederate line of defense in Kentucky was broken and its forces at Bowling Green were in danger of encirclement, as also were Polk's at Columbus. The Tennessee and Cumberland rivers were now broad highways for Union invasion, and Nashville was uncovered. Johnston ordered a hasty retreat of Confederate forces from Kentucky through Tennessee and a concentration at Corinth, Mississippi, a few miles from the Tennessee border. Here by the first of April he had assembled a force of about 40,000 to check further Union advances.

After the Confederate evacuation Bowling Green and Nashville had been occupied by General Don Carlos Buell, commander of the Federal Department of the Ohio. Meanwhile, after the capture of Donelson, Grant had moved his army by transport up the Tennessee and had them stationed by April 1 at Pittsburg, a landing on the west bank of the river about twenty miles northeast of Corinth. Grant maintained his headquarters at Savannah, nine miles north on

*the east bank of the Tennessee, awaiting the arrival of Buell,
who had been ordered to concentrate his army with Grant's.
Buell and his lead division under General William Nelson
reached Savannah on the evening of the fifth, but for some
reason Grant and Buell did not communicate with each other
that night, and Grant left early the next morning for Pittsburg, leaving word for Buell to follow with his army.
Grant's army numbered slightly less than 40,000, and Buell's
was almost as large, so that if they should join, they would
outnumber Johnston almost two to one.*

*Knowing that Grant and Buell were concentrating on
his front, Johnston planned to attack Grant before Buell
should arrive. Johnston's army was divided into three corps
—under Braxton Bragg, who had recently arrived from Pen-
sacola, William J. Hardee, and Bishop–General Leonidas
Polk—and a reserve force under Breckinridge. The Orphan
Brigade was part of the reserve and, since Breckinridge's
elevation, was commanded temporarily by Colonel R. P.
Trabue of the Fourth Kentucky.*

*Johnston's orders contemplated a surprise dawn attack
on the Union army on April 5, but a confusion in marching
orders, together with heavy rains which impeded the march,
threw his army a full day behind schedule. Furthermore,
an unplanned skirmish between an advance unit and a Federal cavalry regiment on the evening of the fifth convinced
some of the Confederate high command that their movement
was disclosed, and they wanted to turn back, certain that
the Union army would be prepared for them. But Johnston
was determined to execute his plans and ordered the attack
for dawn on the sixth.*

*Grant's army occupied a strong natural position extend-
ing from the river at Pittsburg to Shiloh Church about three
miles to the west and with his front facing to the south and
southwest. His right flank was protected by Owl Creek, a
wooded and steep-banked stream which emptied into Snake
Creek before both joined the Tennessee three-fourths of a*

22

mile north of Pittsburg. His left flank was secured by Lick Creek, an equally wooded and ravined stream which covered his left front and emptied into the river two miles south of the landing. There was, therefore, no possible point to attack save on a relatively narrow front between the headwaters of the two creeks. As Grant himself later admitted, had this front been entrenched, the position would have been virtually impregnable. But entrenching had not been practiced in the West at this time, and besides, Grant was not expecting an attack. On the evening of the fifth, with a Confederate army of 40,000 only one and a half miles from his picket line, General William T. Sherman, who was in command in Grant's absence, had notified Grant that "The enemy has cavalry in our front, and I think there are two regiments of infantry and one battery of artillery about two miles out." And Grant was sending equally reassuring messages to his superior in St. Louis.[1]

At dawn of the sixth the attack was launched. Taken completely by surprise, the Federals fought gamely. But slowly they were forced back so that by evening the Confederates occupied the Union camp and the Union army was huddled in an ever-narrowing circle between the two creeks and the river. There was heavy fighting all along the line, but the deadliest action occurred near Shiloh Church, where Sherman commanded, and near the center at a wooded knoll which became known as the Hornet's Nest. This latter point was taken when a Union division commanded by General B. M. Prentiss was surrounded and captured in the late afternoon.

About 2:30 in the afternoon General Johnston was mortally wounded, and the command passed to General Pierre G. T. Beauregard. The Confederate success continued until late afternoon. Then Beauregard issued his controversial order to retire when, some said, more than an hour's day-

1 O.R., Series 1, X, pt. 2, pp. 93, 94.

23

light remained—time enough, they thought, to have driven the Union army into the river.

During the night Buell arrived, as also did General Lew Wallace with 5,000 men who had spent the preceding day only five miles away, marching and countermarching in an effort to reach the field. On the morning of the seventh, therefore, a revitalized Union army took the offensive. Slowly but steadily they forced the Confederate army back until afternoon, when Beauregard ordered retreat.

This was Johnny Green's baptism of fire. The Orphan Brigade, being part of the reserve, did not become engaged until 9:30 a.m. on the sixth, but thereafter it was in the thickest of the fighting, both in the vicinity of Shiloh Church and of the Hornet's Nest, and it participated in the movement which resulted in the capture of Prentiss at the latter place. The Confederate plan of attack at Shiloh by corps front—that is, each corps stretched along the entire front one behind the other—was most unusual and resulted in a hopeless confusion and intermingling of different units.[2] Colonel Trabue said that he rode until 11:00 p.m. that night to find a general officer to report for orders and then sent an aide who rode throughout the night for the same object, but that their efforts were without success.[3]

At the conclusion of the second day's fighting, the Orphan Brigade was part of the rear guard which protected the army's retreat to Corinth. The Brigade had entered the battle with almost 2,400 men and had suffered casualities of 844, a shockingly high 35 per cent. Of these 844 killed and wounded, Johnny Green's Ninth Regiment had provided 134.[4]

---

[2] Later, Beauregard and Johnston's son engaged in bitter controversy over the authorship of the plan, with Beauregard claiming it for his own (*Battles and Leaders*, I, 552-55, 579-82). Under the circumstances it is difficult to understand why either should want to claim authorship.

[3] *O.R.*, Series 1, X, pt. 1, p. 616.   [4] *Ibid.*, 621.

24

*A*PRIL 6TH 1862 Sunday, each orderly Sergt shook the men of his company to waken them without noise. We wanted to surprise the Yankies & attack them at day light. We began to make coffee but just as it was boiling Genl Breckinridge galloped along the line & said, "Boys fall in. You have better work before you than eating."

Just then the firing commenced & we hurried towards Genl Hardee's line who had begun the fight.⁵ As we drew near the battle we were halted & told to unsling knapsacks. We were ordered to pile them & detail a guard to watch them. Volunteers were called for but not a man wanted to miss the fight, the sergt had to make a detail for this service. One of the boys who was detailed to stay behind the knapsacks, finding that he was one of the few soldiers who had any biscuit in his haversack, offered to give three biscuit & then increased the offer to his entire supply, 4 biscuit, to any boy who would exchange with him; he almost made Tom Porter mad by telling him he was not able to go into a fight (Tom was really sick & in the surgeons care) but Tom would not swap,

⁵ The Orphan Brigade was ordered from the reserve to support Hardee in the vicinity of Shiloh Church, which was the Confederate left and the Union right. From then until the end of the battle in the afternoon of the next day it was in the hottest of the fighting. *O.R.*, Series 1, X, pt. 1, pp. 385-88, 392-94, 567-70, 613-21.

and the detail had to stand as it was. Poor Tom was killed before ten oclock that morning.

Genl John C. Breckinridge having been placed in command of a division placed Col R. P. Trabue[6] in command of our brigade.

We double quicked for nearly two miles to reach the point where our help was most needed; the fight grew fast & furious. The enemy opened on us with artillery. Cobbs[7] battery wheeled into line & returned their fire [while] we hurried past to take our position. Just then one of the enemy's shells killed two of Cobbs men & carried completely away both hands of an other who wrung the bleeding stumps & said, "My Lord that stops my fighting." The next shell from the enemies guns passed just 18 inches in front of me & killed three of the four men in that set of fours And took off the leg of the other man.

In a few minutes we were in the thickest of the fight. Four of our color corporals were killed. I was chosen to take the post of one of them & before the battle was over two of those chosen to take their places were killed & two others

6 Robert Paxton Trabue (1824-1863) was born in Adair County, Kentucky. His grandfather, Colonel Daniel Trabue, had accompanied George Rogers Clark on his expedition against Kaskaskia, Cahokia, and Vincennes, and had settled in Kentucky after the Revolution. Robert Paxton was educated in law and was practicing that profession at the time of the Mexican War. He enlisted as a volunteer and rose to the rank of captain. After the Mexican War he settled in Natchez, Mississippi, and practiced law there. When the Civil War broke out, he applied for authority to raise a regiment of Kentucky troops for the Confederate army. He was made colonel of the Fourth Kentucky Regiment of Volunteers in September, 1861. He and his regiment were at Corinth in March, 1862, and when General Breckinridge was given command of the Reserve Corps, Trabue was placed in command of the Kentucky Brigade and led it at Shiloh. At the reorganization of the Brigade after the battle of Shiloh, Trabue resumed command of his regiment. Illness prevented his participation at the battle of Baton Rouge, but he resumed command shortly thereafter and led his regiment at Stone's River. When General Roger Hanson fell during that battle, Trabue again commanded the Brigade. A month later, on a mission to Richmond, Virginia, he became violently ill and died on February 12. Thompson, *Orphan Brigade*, 403-407.

7 Robert L. Cobb helped organize and recruit the battery of artillery which bore his name. He was its captain until Chickamauga, when he was made chief of artillery on Breckinridge's staff with the rank of major. He served with the Army of Tennessee throughout the war. Thompson, 862.

26

were wounded,[8] I being one of them. The litter bearers seeing that I was apparently seriously wounded took hold of me to carry me to the rear & off the field to have my wound dressed. By this time I had regained consciousness & told them I would not go. I said, "There is too much work here for a man to go to the rear as long as he can shoot a gun." Fortunately the ball which struck me glanced off my hard head, stunning me for a moment & making me very bloody, but the blood soon ceased to flow.

We had lots more of fighting that day but I was spared further wounds save a hole in my jacket & a scalp wound. About 5 oclock we joined in the sharp fight which resulted in the capture of Genl Prentice's[9] corps. We swaped our very indifferent guns for their splendid Endfield [Enfield] rifles. We sent the prisoners to the rear & pressed on with little difficulty as we met with slight resistance; we came to the bluff bank of the river & saw the gun boats & thousands of disorganized yankies; the gun boats opened fire on us but killed more of their men than of ours. These were our prisoners whom we were sending to the rear. We were ordered to lie down while waiting for orders to advance. One of our batteries took position on the river bank & replied to the gun boats.

Colonel Hunt rode along our line & said to me, "John you are as bloody as a butcher & did not go off the field; that is the way for a soldier to do. If all the boys will do that way we will be sure to win." He had me appointed to the position of Color Corporal which position I was then temporarily filling.

[8] This statement is slightly at variance with Colonel Trabue's report, according to which the Ninth Regiment lost seven color corporals, only four of whom were killed. Green's statement is that six were killed and two wounded. Trabue also mentions the wounding of a color sergeant. *O.R.*, Series 1, X, pt. 1, p. 619.

[9] Brigadier General B. M. Prentiss commanded the Sixth Division (not a corps as stated by Green). It was his troops upon whom Hardee's attack first fell. He defended his position stoutly for almost twelve hours, but late in the afternoon he found himself surrounded as a result of the falling back of the troops on either side and surrendered at 5:30 P.M. *Ibid.*, 278-79.

We laid down in line of battle with the shells from the gun boats passing over our heads. We expected momentarily to be ordered forward when we thought we would capture Grants entire disorganized army; but just before dusk we were called to antention & marched by the flank to the rear about two miles & camped in a yankee camp from which we had driven the enemy that morning.

We were greatly disappointed that we were not pushed forward for we believed we had the enemy utterly routed. Our matchless Genl Albert Sydney Johnston had been slain & Genl [P.] G. T. Beauregard had succeeded to command. We had great confidence in him, but in many mouths was the remark, "If Genl Johns[t]on had lived he would have pushed forward & we would have captured them all. Now they will all be gone by morning."[10]

But so complete had been our victory that we had little doubts that all we would have to do next day would be to bury our dead & gather up the guns & supplies from the battle field. The commisary & quartermaster & Sutler Stores were abundant; our mess had that night all the tea, coffee, sugar, cheese, hard tack & bacon they could want; & some of them found wine & liquor in the surgeons supplies. Some of my mess made a fire to boil water while I got a bucket (for our

---

10 It was commonly believed both in the army and out that Grant's army was soundly whipped and required only one final Confederate assault to cause its capitulation. William Preston Johnston, son and biographer of Albert Sidney Johnston, said, "Complete victory was in his [Beauregard's] grasp, and he threw it away (*Battles and Leaders*, I, 568). General Bragg criticized the order in his official report of the battle and said that the fall of Johnston prevented a complete victory (*O.R.*, Series 1, X, pt. 1, pp. 469-70). General Polk, speaking of the situation at the time of the order, said, "We had one hour more of daylight still left, were within 150 to 400 yards of the enemy position, and nothing seemed wanting to complete the most brilliant victory of the war but to press forward and make a vigorous assault on the demoralized remnant of his forces" (*Ibid.*, 410). Beauregard justified the order on the grounds that the Confederate troops had been fighting constantly for eleven hours and were in no condition to face Buell's fresh troops, some of whom had arrived on the field, that the Confederate troops were disorganized and had to be regrouped, and that some of them were out of ammunition (*Battles and Leaders*, I, 590-91).

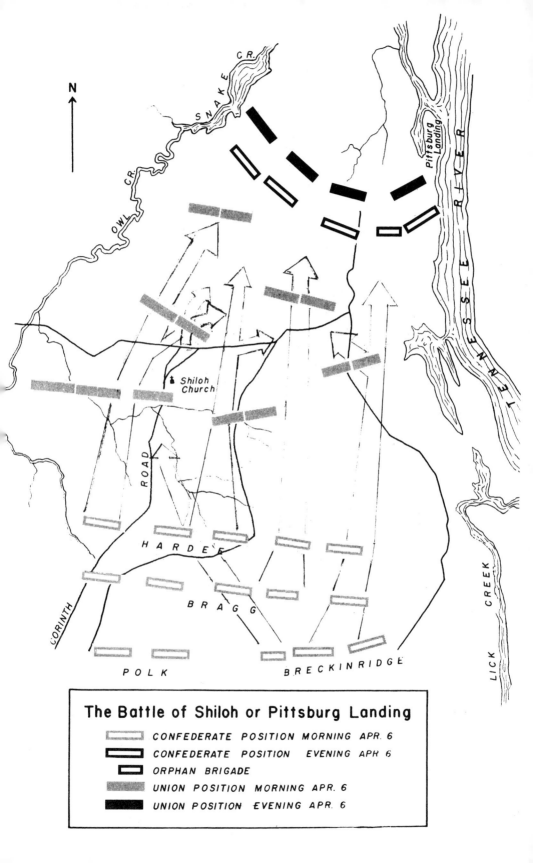

The Battle of Shiloh or Pittsburg Landing

☐	CONFEDERATE POSITION MORNING APR. 6
☐	CONFEDERATE POSITION EVENING APR. 6
☐	ORPHAN BRIGADE
▓	UNION POSITION MORNING APR. 6
■	UNION POSITION EVENING APR. 6

friends "the enemy" had abundant supplies of every thing) & went for water. I found it in Shiloh branch of Owl creek. The moon was under a cloud, but I thought I saw a log extending from the bank out into the creek. I stepped upon the supposed log but just then the moon emerged from under the cloud & I saw that my log was a dead man lying partly on the bank & partly in the water. I filled my bucket with water from the creek & we soon had both tea & coffee, for cooking utensils as well as every thing a Soldier could want were abundant.

We supposed the Yankies had all escaped across Tennessee River & as we were worn out we soon went to sleep. I remarked to Gos Elston (H. P. Elston) one of my messmates, "Gos! I thought the yanks had gotten you when we charged into Prentice's [Prentiss'] camp, for you were way ahead of all of us & I saw three different yanks pull at you. I cracked away at the last fellow & put a stop to his mad career just as he fired but I did not see you any more until they had all surrendered & I feared you had fallen just as he did."

Gos replied, "Greenie! you can bet your last dollar that Elston will come out safe, unless it be just a slight wound to give me a furlough; & wont you fellows envy me then when you come marching by & see me looking pale & interesting being tenderly cared for by some sweet & lovely girl."

That night it rained hard but we were comfortably stored away in yankee tents & slept soundly.

Monday April 7th 1862. Wakened by reveille—began in great glee to get breakfast—almost half through breakfast when ordered to fall hurriedly into line. At a short distance from us the small arms began firing a terrific volley. Col Hunt very sternly ordered us to throw away all bootie & get ready for battle. "Unk' Cowling"[11] Orderly Sergeant of Co C had a big round western reserve cheese on his bayonet which

---

[11] Henry G. Cowling of Louisville took part in the earlier battles of 1862, but was overage and was discharged in November. Later he served in the ordnance department at Augusta, Georgia. Thompson, *Orphan Brigade*, 827.

was fixed to his gun. Col Hunt almost took his head off &
made him throw the cheese away.

The artilery began to roar, we double quicked into position. Byrne's[12] battery galloped into line on our right,
limbered up & opened on the yankee line. We fired one
volley, but were then ordered to reserve our fire until the
enemy got close to us; we laid down & the fight settled down
into an artilery duel with our brigade in support of Byrne's
battery.

After this artillery fight had kept up for some time
Morgan's[13] squadron formed on our left & charged the enemies' guns & when within thirty yards of them found a fense
between them & the battery & therefore they could not capture it & were forced to wheel to the left & retreat. As they
came back to us many an empty saddle was seen. Some of
the men were seen to fall in the charge but the horses, when
not killed also, kept on in the charge as though spurred on
by the spirit of the gallant rider just slain. We charged
against this point & met with stubborn resistance but before
we reached them they withdrew their battery & hurried out
of our reach.

Finding that some of our forces just to our right were
hard pressed Col Hunt ordered us forward to their assistance,
when we soon drove the foe before us & they seemed to
abandon this part of the line. We then double quicked some
distance to the right of our line under orders to report to
Genl Beauregard. Colonel Hunt rode up to General Beauregard & Saluting said, "Genl I am instructed to report with
my command to you."

12 Edward P. Byrne was a native Kentuckian residing in Washington
County, Mississippi, in 1861. With the coming of secession he organized a
battery of artillery made up of both Mississippians and Kentuckians. The
battery did valiant service at Shiloh, but he and his fellow officers of the battery were aggrieved at failing to win promotion there and resigned. The battery was thereupon broken up among other units, but Byrne served thereafter as a cavalry and horse artillery officer. Thompson, 857-60.

13 John Hunt Morgan, the famed cavalry leader, frequently participated in
battles at the side of the Orphan Brigade and at this time was part of its
organization.

Genl Beauregard saluted, but saying not a word to Col Hunt turned to our command & said, "Forward."

Col Hunt said, "Steady men," & although the enemies bullets & shels were shrieking all around, the Col again saluted the Genl & said, "Give me your commands Genl & I will have them executed," whereupon Genl Beauregard said, "Put them in right here"; & at Col Hunt's order to "fix bayonets!" "Charge!" we rushed forward & cleared the enemy out of one of their camps which they had reoccupied during the night.

Poor Gos Elston was seen to fall mortally wounded here, but we were soon hurried to an other part of the field & saw no more of him & such was the case with many another gallant boy who here offered up his life for the right of Constitutional Government.

We arrived at a point where our line was hard pressed, we were ordered to charge & went in with a yell, we drove the yankees before us & followed them across an open field through one of their camps. One yankee who stood his ground firing from behind one of their tents had drawn a bead on Captain Price Newman who was in hot pursuit at the head of his company. I fired at Mr Yank as I advanced, but missed him; he fired at Capt Newman not fifteen feet distant, who fell headlong. I rushed for a clump of bushes to take shelter long enough to reload & just as I had loaded & was raising my gun to fire I fell from a bullit which struck me just over the heart. I felt sure it had gone clear through me & it flashed through my mind that I would live until the arterial blood started back to my heart, when I would drop dead, as I had once seen a deer do which my father shot through the heart. I rose to my knees, took a hurried aim & fired at a clump of the enemy. By this time I was surprised to find that I was still alive. I felt my breast to learn the extent of my wound when I found one piece of the bullit laying against my skin inside my clothes just over my heart. The ball had passed through the stock of my gun, split on the iron ramrod of my gun, and the other piece had passed through my jacket & burried itself in a little testament in my jacket pocket. The force of the blow knocked me down but nothing more serious had befallen me.

We advanced a few hundred yards further but found the enemy in great force, posted behind breast works made of logs. We were then ordered to fall back as we were in advance of the line on both our left & right, leaving our flanks exposed. A yankee battery began to shell us and as we were ordered to retreat across an open field in full view of that battery we ran at full speed. General Breckinridge, who had just come to this part of the line, saw us & thought we were routed. He galloped up to us & called to us to halt, which we did at once notwithstanding the fierce artillery fire we were exposed to. He said, "Can it be that Kentuckians are running off the field of battle!" But when told that we were simply obeying orders & falling back to form on a line with our other troops, he fell back with us & we reformed to conform to the rest of our line of battle.

Here I was surprised to see Capt Newman at the head of his Company. When asked about his resurrection, he explained that he stumbled over a guy rope to that yankee's tent just as the yank fired at him & the fall no doubt saved his life. When he rose from the ground his pistol was loaded & the yanks gun was empty, so he had his shot & his aim did not miscarry as did Mr Yanks.

We held our position about Shiloh Church until about sun down when firing had ceased, except an occasional shot from the skirmishers. We were greatly exhausted & suffering for water (biting off the end of your cartrage will get some powder in your mouth & this increases your thirst). The yankees seemed as much exhausted as we & after lying still for about half an hour our forces were withdrawn & fell back in a leisurely march about two miles where we bivouacked for two days on a portion of the battle field.

April 8th. Sent details to gather up from the battle field

arms, tents, & supplies which were sent back to Corrinth Miss where our wounded were all sent. The night of the 7th the heavens were opened & the rains decended as they did in Noah's day; but we were so exhausted that we laid down in the mud & got what sleep we could. I remember that I had dropped off to sleep when such a flood was running down the side of the hill I was attempting to sleep on that it got in my nose & almost strangled me before I woke. I managed to pose myself in such a position with my head resting on my arms placed on the ground, my back bowed in the air, & the rest of my weight resting on my knees, leaving an open channel under my middle for the floods to rush through, as to prevent my being washed away & I managed to catch a nap or two.

Details were busy all day burying the dead, (both our dead & those of the enemy). Many a mothers darling lay stark & cold. I shall never forget the face of a young Lieut from Louisiana with smoothe face & the bluest blue eyes, as he lay with his revolver in his right hand, a most peaceful smile on his face & a great big yankee laying across him cold in death with his musket still firmly grasped in his hand. The yankees gun was empty & the Lieutenants pistol had two empty chambers. The Lieutenant had a death wound made by a musket ball & the other man had two pistol ball holes clear through him; neither face had any expression of pain or anger. Had the Angel of peace come to each of them? I dont know but what we should have put them both to sleep in the same grave, but we did not. The warrior will be rewarded for a patriotic death where they are gone but I know peace reigns there supreme.

Our Brigade took 2,400 men into this fight & lost 844 in killed & wounded. Adjutant Billy Bell[14] (a brother of Mess[rs.] John Bell & Robert of Louisville) was mortally wounded by a minnie ball which passed clear through his

14 Lieutenant William Bell died of his wound in Memphis. Thompson, *Orphan Brigade*, 807.

breast in the first charge we made. Just as we put the enemy to flight the ball passed clear through him & he fell from his horse but he rose to his feet again when we were ordered forward. He was attempting to mount his horse when Col Hunt called to the infirmary corps to take Adjutant Bell back to the hospital. The adjutant said, "Col I shall follow you as long as there is breath in my body." Col Hunt again called in a peremptory tone, "Take Adjutant Bell to the hospital, he is unable to fight longer"; & on we rushed upon the enemy.

Thos Caldwell, a Russellville boy only sixteen years old, was killed here, & never did a more galant boy fall.

After the battle we remained upon a part of the battle field for three days. I remember the night of April the 9th the weather had gotten very chilly. We had gotten some yankee blankets in place of ours which we stacked with our knapsacks but in the confusion we never saw them again; but to lie down on, & cover with a blanket again was comfort indeed.

After three days we fell back to Corinth Miss. Our Brigade covered the retreat, having been chosen for that honerable post of danger; but we saw no more of the enemy for some time.

We had completely routed the enemy on the first day of this battle of Shiloh as we called it (Pittsburgh Landing as the yankees called it) but just at the moment of victory our Idolized General Albert Sidney Johnston was slain by a yankee minnie ball & it was some time before Genl Beauregard was notified[15] of the loss & before he had gotten the

15 Johnston's aide and brother-in-law, Colonel William Preston, was present when Johnston died at 2:30 P.M. He stated that he sent word through Governor Isham Harris to Beauregard at once. Beauregard recorded that Harris reported to him shortly after the death of Johnston, which event Beauregard also fixed as occurring at 2:30 P.M. (*O.R.*, Series 1, X, pt. 1, pp. 403, 387). Writing in 1887 Beauregard fixed the time of Harris's reporting to him as "shortly after 3:00 P.M.," which would have been approximately thirty minutes after Johnston's death (*Battles and Leaders*, I, 590). It was not until after 6:00 P.M. that the order to withdraw was issued, so that approximately three hours elapsed between Beauregard's assuming command and ordering the withdrawal.

situation well in hand night came on & we fell back about two miles as above stated & at the close of the second days battle although we were greatly disappointed at not capturing Grant's army, yet we felt greatly elated over having routed on the first day an army equal in size to our own & having on the second day met a fresh army of the same size brought by Genl Buel[16] to reinforce Grant & repulsed their every attack when they endeavored to retake from us the field of battle.

This our baptism of fire was a terrible ordeal; about 1/3 of our entire army was killed or wounded.[17] Many of the flower of the manhood of our country lay cold in death. Ben Weber[18] the nephew of Lie't Crouch[19] who was then in command of our company (Capt Wickliffe[20] & 1st Lieut Sch-

[16] By forced marches three of Buell's divisions—Nelson's, Crittenden's, and McCook's (about 25,000 men)—reached the field of battle on the late afternoon and night of April 6. These reinforcements gave Grant overwhelming numerical superiority on April 7 and were unquestionably the decisive factor in the Union victory on that day. Grant in his report gave little credit to Buell (*O.R.*, Series 1, X, pt. 1, pp. 109-10). Writing many years later he said, "Victory was assured when [General Lew] Wallace arrived even if there had been no other support." He added, "I was glad, however, to see the reenforcements of Buell and credit them with doing all there was for them to do" (*Battles and Leaders,* I, 476-77).

[17] The official returns show effectives present before and after the battle as 40,335 and 29,636 respectively, or a loss of 10,699 (*O.R.*, Series 1, X, pt. 1, 396). This is a loss of a little more than 26 per cent.

[18] Ben Weber was from Bardstown, Kentucky. Thompson, *Orphan Brigade,* 824.

[19] N. A. Crouch of Bardstown was promoted to the rank of captain June 10, 1862. He fought in all engagements until Resaca, where he was temporarily unfitted for duty. He later took part in the mounted engagements, however. Thompson, 815.

[20] John Cripps Wickliffe, son of a distinguished father, was born in Nelson County July 11, 1830, and began the practice of law there with his father in 1853. In September, 1861, he organized and was elected captain of Company B, Ninth Regiment. With the exception of Shiloh and Stone's River he took part in all campaigns of the Brigade. In May, 1862, he was chosen major of the Ninth and was promoted to lieutenant colonel in the next April upon the resignation of Colonel Hunt. At the close of the war he resumed the practice of law in Bardstown and in Louisville. He served as circuit judge from 1870 to 1880. From 1885 to 1889 he was United States district attorney. From 1893 to 1895 he was adjutant general of Kentucky, with the rank of brigadier general. Thompson, 447-50.

waub[21] having both been wounded) was shot through the heart while standing touching my left elbow; he fell & called out, "Uncle Nat good bye; give them all my love at home," turned over once in his agony & was dead. Henry Vickers[22] at my right was shot in the elbow & said, "Johnnie I am afraid I will bleed to death."

I said, "No I will take your handkerchief & tie it around your arm so as to stop the bleeding."

I fired at a man just ready to fire at one of us & then tied up his arm so as to staunch the flow of blood. He then said to me, "I cant shoot with my arm in this fix; do you suppose it would do for me to go to the rear?"

I said, "Of course! you cant do any good here; you ought to go to the rear," & he went. Just then Corporal Casey,[23] an other one of the color corporals, was shot through the head & drop[ped] dead never uttering a word & it was here that John Head[24] gave up his life for the cause we loved & a few minutes afterwards Daniel Jenkins[25] & Sylvester Smith[26] offered up the same sacrifice for our country & it was but a few mintes later that Will Pope received a severe wound in the arm shattering the elbow.

Poor Will! he was one of the loveliest boys in our Company. He was taken back to Corinth & his arm amputated but he was quite cheerful & said, "Poor Elston boasted that he was sure to come through the war with nothing worse than a slight wound & here it is that he is gone & I am left with the honorable wound." But soon gangreen appeared in his wound & his arm was again amputated higher up, but this

21 G. G. Schaub of Bardstown was second lieutenant at this time, not being promoted to first lieutenant until June 10, 1862. He was so severely wounded in the arm at Shiloh that he was unfit for further service and resigned in March, 1863. Thompson, 815.

22 Vickers was discharged soon after Shiloh as a result of this wound. He was from Hawesville. Thompson, 829.

23 A. Casey was from Logan County. Thompson, 808.

24 Head was from Bardstown. Thompson, 820.

25 Jenkins was from Bullitt County. Thompson, 821.

26 Smith did not die until May 23, at Corinth. He was from Bardstown. Thompson, 823.

36

did not arrest the gangreen. He steadily grew worse but met death with a patriot's spirit. I talked with him the day he died, when he knew death had marked him for his own, & he said to me, "Johnnie if a boy dies for his country the glory is his for ever isn't it?" He died that night & I was the corporal of the guard of honor that burried him with military honors in the soil of Mississippi, that far southern sister in whose defense many of our Kentucky boys gave up their lives.

3 BATON ROUGE

From Shiloh the Confederate army retreated to Corinth, where it was besieged by the Union army, now commanded in person by General Henry W. Halleck. After keeping the Federal commander guessing for six weeks as to his plans, Beauregard quietly slipped away to Tupelo on May 30, leaving the important rail junction in the hands of the enemy.

Meanwhile New Orleans had also fallen, and a combined army-navy force had been sent up river to attack Vicksburg. This was many months before Grant's notable campaign against that Confederate strong point, which, indeed, was not strongly garrisoned or fortified at this time. Breckinridge's division, including the Kentucky Brigade, was dispatched to relieve the garrison there. The attackers confined their efforts to intermittent bombardment from gunboats and experimentation with construction of a canal short cut so that Federal transports could bypass Vicksburg. When neither effort proved effective, the Union force steamed away.

With the relief of Vicksburg, Breckinridge marched south against Baton Rouge, which was occupied by a Union garrison. His attack was to be supported by the Arkansas, a powerful Confederate ironclad which had more than held its own with Union gunboats at Vicksburg. But the Arkansas' engines failed as she moved into battle, and she fell a victim of the Union boats at Baton Rouge. Meanwhile Breckinridge had driven the Union garrison to the protection of its gunboats, and further he dared not venture. The Union garrison was then evacuated, and Baton Rouge fell once more into Confederate hands.

In the meantime Beauregard's poor health forced his retirement from command of the Army of Tennessee, and he was succeeded by Braxton Bragg. Bragg and Kirby Smith, who commanded Confederate forces in East Tennessee, agreed on a joint movement into Kentucky, which was temporarily defenseless. Bragg had been led to believe that sentiment in Kentucky was overwhelmingly pro-Southern and only awaited the presence of a force such as his to induce the people to rise in support of the Confederacy. Events were to prove that he was poorly informed, but the prospects looked bright in the summer of 1862.

Bragg and Smith entered the state in September and after some slight success were checked by the pursuing Buell on October 8 at Perryville. Discouraged, Bragg retreated into Tennessee.

When the Kentucky campaign was launched, Breckinridge and the Kentucky Brigade were still in Mississippi. Naturally eager to return to Kentucky, they sought and obtained permission to join the expedition. They moved by circuitous route to Knoxville and thence to Cumberland Gap. Here word reached them that Perryville had been fought and that Bragg was in retreat. "With sad hearts," said Johnny Green, "we turned from our cherished hope."

*O*UR ARMY ARRIVED at Corinth Apr 11th, four days after the last days fight at Shiloh. Here we got tents & went into camp & cleaned up. Many of us brought from the battlefield clothes that we had captured from the quarters of yankee officers. I remember that I was delighted with some fine under clothes that I had captured until I discovered that I had captured some undesirable inhabitants along with the clothes which caused me to feel utterly disgraced until I found that nearly all the boys had received a visitation from the same uncomfortable visitors, & nothing short of boiling every stitch of clothing while we sat by in nature's garb would rid us of their company.

All was comparatively quiet except that we did some work fortifying our position until May 15th when skirmishing began. A battle order was issued & we formed ready to receive the enemy, but after light skirmishing the enemy retired. General Halleck[1] had succeeded to command of the yankee army & he was daily gaining reinforcements. Again on the 20th skirmishing & every preperation for battle & on

[1] Henry W. Halleck was at this time the Federal commander of the Department of the Mississippi with headquarters at St. Louis. After the battle of Shiloh he took active command of Grant's, Buell's, and John Pope's armies and laid siege to Corinth, Mississippi, where Beauregard's army had retreated after Shiloh. *O.R.*, Series 1, X, pt. 2, p. 105.

the 22nd it seemed a fight to the finish was at hand & from the preparation made by the surgeons for the care of the wounded we felt that ere the sun went down many a scene of carnage would be witnessed & on May 28th we formed line of battle & advanced a mile or two towards the enemy but nothing more serious than skirmishing & some artillery fire at long range occured. That night we evacuated Corinth[2] & fell back towards Baldwin. Our Brigade covered the retreat. We halted at the Tuscumbia river, camped in the edge of a Swamp & picketed the road until the enemy came up in force, when we destroyed the bridge & fell back after a skirmish between the pickets in which seve[r]al were wounded.

We slept in this post one night; when I wakend up in the morning as I opened my eys I saw a great big rattlesnake coiled up on top of my blanket. I rolled out in a hurry, at the same time calling out to my messmate who was sharing my blanket, "Rattle snake in bed with us!" He got out in a hurry too, but mr rattler after poking out his tongue once or twice crawled quietly away beside a log near by & coiled up again; Jim Burba,[3] one of our Co, cut a forked stick, crept up on the other side of the log & pinioned Mr Rattle snake with his head under the fork of the stick & captured him alive. With this pet in his hands he was running nearly every body out of camp until the Capt made him kill the creature.

June 1st we marched all day & night with a halt of only one hour for a nap. The enemy were trying to cut us off from the main army & we had to reach Black Land before they did, or fight; when within a half mile of that place we learned that a detachment of the enemy had already occupied the position. Col Hunt threw out skirmishers & an advance guard & prepared to attack the enemy but they, having become alarmed for fear they had cut off more than they could chaw, hurried to get out of our way notwithstanding they had made

2 Corinth was evacuated on May 30. *Ibid.*, pt. 1, p. 763.
3 James Burba was from Nelson County and fought with the Brigade in all its battles. Thompson, *Orphan Brigade*, 817.

41

such great effort to force their horses forward in order to
reach that point in time to intercept us, but finding that the
rear was covered by infantry instead of cavelry they were in
a great hurry to get out of our pathway.[4]

At Tupelo we rejoined the army on June 7th 1862.
Here we suffured much from scarcity of water. But we were
soon started off on a march to Tallahatchie bridge on the
Mississippi Centr'l R R. by way of Pontotoc to oppose a
federal column reported to be advancing from that direction.
Finding that the federals had sent part of that column to Ky
& part to Vicksburg, we took the cars on June 25 at Abbeville
Miss & started to Vicksburg taking our cooking utensils with
us but the wagons were sent over land along with the quartermaster who was to gather up such supplies as could be bought
in that country to carry down to supply the defenders of
Vicksburg.

Our brigade reached Vicksburg June 30th 1862. Grant[5]
was assembling a force to capture Vicksburg. On July 2nd[6]
the fleet of mortar boats opened their fire on the City & kept
it up steadily until the evening of July 25. Every few minutes
they would fire a shell (both night & day) & at four different
times they let loose all their guns at once & then it would be
a literal hail of shot & shell, the wonder was that the town

4 The Union force at Blackland on June 3 was a regiment of cavalry under
General Gordon Granger, who was on reconnaissance duty. He reported that
when he found the Confederates there in force he withdrew after a minor
engagement. *O.R.*, Series 1, X, pt. 1, p. 732.

5 Green is in error in stating that the Federal operations around Vicksburg
in the summer of 1862 were under the direction of General Grant. At this
time Grant was in north Mississippi under the command of General Henry
W. Halleck. The Union troops near Vicksburg were under the immediate
command of Brigadier General Thomas Williams and were sent there from
New Orleans by the direction of Major General Ben F. Butler. The troops
were accompanied by a naval flotilla under Flag Officer David G. Farragut.
Another flotilla under Flag Officer Charles H. Davis descended from Memphis
to join the force on July 1. *O.R.*, Series 1, XV, 22-35, 39.

6 Actually the firing of the gunboats on the city began May 26 and continued without cessation until June 14. On June 20 the mortar boats arrived in
front of the city and the attack was resumed, rising to a great fury on June
28 when part of the fleet ascended the river past the city. The firing continued until July 27, when the fleet steamed away. *Ibid.*, 8-10.

& all of us were not utterly annihilated but for nearly one month we watched day & night lying on the hills & in the streets of Vicksburg to guard against a surprise. We expected Grant [that is, Williams] to attempt to land from the fleet & carry the town by assault for his force was three times as great as ours.[7] But he tried to dig a ditch opposite Vicksburg which should carry the waters of the Mississippi through a short cut on the other side of the river & thus let him march against us on dry land, but his ditch did not work so he abandoned this first siege of Vicksburg.[8]

Considering the fact that we were for nearly a month under continuous fire we lost but few killed & wounded.[9] I think it was somewhat due to the fact that they were mostly mortar shells & as they go first way up in the air & are only destructive as they come down they have not as many chances to kill a person as when a cannon or rifle ball comes skimming along just above the ground so if it mises one it has a chance to hit another. But those mortar shells were almost as big as a flour barrel & that is what the boys would call them as they would hear them coming. When they would burst in air & come singing down hunting for you every fellow would want to dodge for it sounded just as though it was coming for him, or if it struck the ground before it exploded

[7] The Union force was approximately 4,500 effectives with ten field guns. The Confederates after the arrival of Breckinridge's division probably outnumbered them. The Confederate general M. L. Smith in his report admitted that after Breckinridge's arrival he had "equality in numbers" with his enemy. *Ibid.*, 9, 25.

[8] At this time the Mississippi River in its meanderings actually flowed by Vicksburg three times in an S-shaped curve. The ditch Green speaks of was an ill-advised attempt on the part of General Williams (and of Grant in the next year) to cut a canal through the bottom to the loop of the S, not for the purpose of changing the river course, but in order to float his transports north of Vicksburg by this new channel and attack from that direction. Grant the next year wanted to go in the opposite direction and reach high undefended ground south of Vicksburg. Neither attempt was successful. Grant later concluded that even if the canal had been successfully completed, it would have been useless tactically. *Ibid.*, 27-33; XXIV, pt. 1, pp. 44-45; *Personal Memoirs of U. S. Grant*, 2 vols. (New York, 1885), I, 445-47.

[9] Casualties were seven killed and fifteen wounded. At least one civilian, a woman, was killed. *O.R.*, Series 1, XV, 10, 12.

43

it would actually dig a hole that you could bury a horse in. But we got used to it & many diversions were invented to amuse us. One Third of the command was on look out all the time but the others would be either sleeping, cooking or romping.

One day the boys captured two hogs which had been left to hunt for their own living & while they would do for a soldier to eat they were as lean as race horses & the boys got up a race between them with a rider astride the back of each. Several men held each hog until the rider was firmly seated on the hogs back & holding fast to his ears, when the word was given to start. Off they started & cheers went up to applaud the riders. This set loose several of the yankee guns & one flour barrel shell came right down in our midst, fortunately striking no one but scattering dirt over hogs, riders & every body & scaring the hogs so that their pace was increased to frantic gate but one threw his rider & escaped. Charley Edwar[d]s'[10] steed headed direct towards a bluff fifty feet high & all our combined efforts could not stop him or change his course, & he & his gallant rider pitched head foremost over this bank, landing in a deep hole at the bottom. Poor Charley's back was broken & he died in a few minutes but the hog was unhurt until he was slaughterd & eaten by Charley's mess. This cast a gloom over all, but soon we learned that the yanks were preparing for a night attack upon the lower water battery which was three miles away & we fell into line & marched to its defense leaving the infirmary corps to burry poor Charley Edwards. The attack on the Water battery however resulted in nothing but a midnight bombardment which was beautiful to behold but a little bit scarey as they had our range perfectly.

July 26th 1862. We discover that the Yanks have withdrawn their fleet & their troops are leaving the other side of the river, sickness has been playing great havoc in their ranks

---

10 Edwards, a Kentuckian, had enlisted less than three months before. Thompson, *Orphan Brigade*, 850.

& they are needing men elsewhere so they have left us in complete controll. We are also greatly exhausted from loss of sleep & constant exposure to the torrid rays of the Mississippi sun, but worst of all is the dreadful water we have to drink. If we get it from the river it is half mud & if taken from wells it is almost milk white from the soapstone soil it seeps through, or some other kind of clay. I had a severe attack of break bone fever & was delirrious for days. I can now realize how deceptive is the mirage of the desert, for Dave Caruth who was convalescent & acting as my nurse twice found me 100 yards from my sick bed with a tin pan in my hand chasing a spring which I was sure I could see just a little distance ahead of me, but which constantly slipped away from me just as I stooped to dip up a drink; he could not convince me that the spring was not just in sight but being too weak to walk unaided he induced me to let him help me back to my blanket bed under promise that he would get me a drink out of that spring as soon as I should lay down. When he brought me a tin cup of the miserable water which was all we could get I cried from disappointment. But as adverse as the conditions were to my recovery I was soon convalescent & learned that our command was ordered to Baton Rouge to capture that place. I put on my shoes & pants, got my gun & went to the surgeon in charge of the hospital camp where I was, & told him I would not stay away from my regiment when they were ordered to battle. But he would not hear to it, & finally failing to convince me that I was not able to go he cut the discussion short by saying if I did not go back to my tent (or rather tent fly, for that is all we had) he would order me under arrest. I was mad enough then to cry but did not; but very unwillingly accepted the unavoidable & remain in the Doctors care while our command went down to Baton Rouge by rail & fought the battle of Baton Rouge Aug 5th 1862. It was here that our Brigadier Genl Helm[11] was wounded & his aid de

[11] Ben Hardin Helm was born in Hardin County, Kentucky, June 2, 1831.

45

camp Lieutenant Alex Todd[12] killed & Col Hunt commanding our brigade & Liet Col John Caldwell com[man]ding our Regiment were wounded & many officers & men were killed & wounded. In our regiment the loss of Killed & wounded was 46 out of 223[13] who went into the battle. This was a gallant fight planned & executed by Genl John C. Breckinridge & Genl Van Dorn,[14] Gen Danl Ruggles[15] a distant kinsman of mine being second in command. The infantry drove the enemy in until they had them all near the river seeking the protection of their gun boats. The plan was to have our ram the Arkansas[16] which was a terror to their gun boats to attack their fleet at day light simultaneously with our attack by the infantry; Breckinridge waited for

His father, John L. Helm, was twice governor of Kentucky, and his mother was the daughter of perhaps the foremost member of the bar, Ben Hardin of Bardstown. Helm was graduated from West Point in 1851, but resigned from the army within the year because of ill health. He then studied law and practiced in Elizabethtown and later in Louisville. In 1856 he married Emily Todd of Lexington, younger half sister of the wife of Abraham Lincoln. When the war came, he cast his lot with the South and was commissioned colonel of the First Regiment of Kentucky Cavalry. Shortly after the battle of Shiloh he was promoted to brigadier general and accompanied Breckinridge to Vicksburg, where he commanded the Second Brigade, which included the Ninth Kentucky. At Baton Rouge he was disabled by a fall from his horse. In January, 1863, he was appointed to command the Kentucky Brigade and remained with it until his death at Chickamauga, September 20, 1863. Thompson, *Orphan Brigade*, 380-87.

12 Alexander Todd was the brother of Emily Todd Helm and a brother-in-law to Lincoln.

13 Major John C. Wickliffe, who commanded Green's regiment at Baton Rouge, reported nine killed, twenty-four wounded, one missing—a total of thirty-four casualities out of 184 effectives. *O.R.*, Series 1, XV, 88.

14 Major General Earl Van Dorn, a native Mississippian, fought early in the war in the Trans-Mississippi Department and later mostly in his own state. He became a noted cavalry leader and was given much credit for his raid which destroyed Grant's base at Holly Springs, Mississippi, December 20, 1862. As a result of this raid Grant abandoned his plan of marching overland against Vicksburg. Van Dorn was killed at his desk by a personal enemy in May, 1863.

15 Brigadier General Dan Ruggles, a Mississippian, was commanding a small force at Camp Moore near Baton Rouge when he was placed under Breckinridge's command. Thompson, *Orphan Brigade*, 123.

16 The *Arkansas* was a powerful ironclad ram which had been built in the Yazoo River and which had already performed valiant service against the Union gunboats around Vicksburg. See *O.R.*, Series 1, XV, 15-17.

hours after he had driven the enemy in, thinking to renew the attack so soon as the Arkansas should come up but when she got within five miles of the enemy her machinery broke, & she became utterly unmanageable. The enemy's gun boats discovering her smoke moved out to attack her & her commander realizing her helpless condition loaded her guns, headed her direct towards the enemy's fleet, set her on fire & landed his men to watch the gallant but helpless vessel fight her own battle; when the fire reached the guns they fired their heavy charges & soon the magazine exploded & created consternation among the enemy's approaching fleet for she had a few days before created such havoc among their vessels that they viewed her with superstitious fear. Learning of the loss of the Arkansas we did not renew the attack, but the enemy brought up transports & took their forces from this place to New Orleans so with the exception of not capturing the garrison we accomplished our purpose for we cleared the river of them at this place so as to open up communication with the trans-Mississippi department.

We camped on Comite river near Baton Rouge until Aug 19th. Part of Genl Breckinridges forces were sent under command of Genl Ruggles to fortify & hold Port Hudson & Genl Breckinridge brought our brigade back to Jackson Miss foot sore, rag[g]ed & hungry, though we fared a little better after the fight than before. We went down to supprise the enemy, which we did, making such a hurried movement that we had no food except what we took in our havresacks. We left the commisary stores & cooking utensils to follow us. The day before the battle we had nothing to eat but roasting ears & these we ate green because we had not time to stop long enough to roast them. Our command, with the horses, consumed 40 acres of green corn one evening; for we stopped only long enough to gather the corn & feed the horses, we then moved forward to take position to make the attack at day light.

The torrid heat together with fatigue & the wretched

47

water we had to drink reduced our ranks from June 28th when we had 1800 down to 580 men on Aug 11th. Such were the ravages of sickness, exposure & battle to our brigade.

We remained in camp at Brandon Miss until Sep 10th when we went by rail to Cold Water Creek a little above Holly Springs. We here heard that Genl Bragg was moving up into Ky & that we had been ordered to join him but we were not permitted to start until the 19th of Sept. 1862. But when once started our hearts beat high with the hope of once again treading our mother soil. Our General Hardin Helm had been wounded at Baton Rouge by his horse being shot & falling on him, [so] we were commanded now by Col R. P. Trabue of the 4th Ky Regt of Inftry. We went by rail first back to Jackson, thence to Meridian, thence to York station which was as far as we could go by rail on our way to Demopolis. From York Station to Demopolis we marched & at Demopolis we took steam boat for Mobile; at Mobile we were loaded on freight cars, some box, some open; but we learned it would be some hours before our train could start. So every body was crazy to go up to the Battle House & get a square meal but strict orders had come from brigade head Quarters that not a man should be permitted to leave the regiment. We were puzzled how to get up town for that longed for supper; we wanted some Mobile oysters. Dave Caruth hit upon a plan. Lt Joe Benedict was in command of our Co & Dave said to him, "Lt Some of our men are missing from the Co. and all the boys are dying to get up town to get a good square meal, now we want you to go to the Col & tell him some of your men are missing & ask if you may make a detail to go after the missing members of the Co & when you get this order take the whole Co as the detail."

Lt Benedict consented to try it on & it worked to a charm. Every man of Co B went up to the Battle House & got a magnificent supper. Some had money, some had not, but he that had paid for him that had not. This spirit of generosity was proverbial in our army. Even the boys that would gamble & win every cent a comrade had would readily spend every cent for that or any other penniless comrade.

Just as we marched into the supper room the first person we met was Col Trabue who was in command of the Brigade. He ripped out an oath saying he had given strict orders that not a man should leave his command & he said, "What in –H– are you doing here?" Lt Benedict replied that his Col had told him to bring a detail into town to look for stragglers. "Yes," said Col Trabue, "you are looking for straggling oysters. I know what you are up to. Now get your suppers quick & get back to the regiment or I'll put forty b[a]yonets through you." He had not confined himself to eating but had already done a little more than his share of drinking.

We reached Knoxville Tenn Oct 3d 1862 & were joined by the 2nd Ky Inftry & Graves battery who had just returned from prison as the result of Fort Donaldson [Donelson]. Col Hanson[17] now being the senior Col of the Brigade was put in command. Our Regiment & the 6th Ky had originally enlisted for 12 Mos & our time was up & every man of us wanted to join John Morgan but Genl Breckinridge formed the Brigade on dress parade & explained that the needs of the country were such that the war department could not spare us from the infantry service & urged upon us the necessity of reenlisting in the same arm of the service. Some boy cried out, "Lets reenlist for thirty years or during the war," & it

17 Roger W. Hanson (1827-1863) was born in Winchester, Kentucky, the son of Samuel Hanson, a prominent attorney. After serving in the Mexican War as a lieutenant of volunteers, and after an excursion to the California gold fields, he returned home and practiced law in Winchester, and later in Lexington. He was active in politics both as a Whig and as a Know-Nothing. At the beginning of the secession crisis he was strongly for the Union. Gradually his position changed; for a time he became an advocate of neutrality for his state, but later his sympathy swung to the Confederacy. He was commissioned colonel of the Second Regiment, Kentucky Infantry, was sent to Donelson and became a prisoner of war upon the surrender of that fort. After his exchange he was commissioned brigadier general and given command of the Brigade. He commanded it at the battle of Stone's River, where he fell mortally wounded, in the charge of January 2. He died two days later. Thompson, *Orphan Brigade*, 375-79.

was met with a shout of approval from almost every throat. The papers were made out for three years or during the war because that was the form adopted by the war department, but thirty years would have been signed for by the boys, such was their earnest devotion to the cause.

On the morning of Oct 15th 1862 we set out to march through Cumberland Gap over the old Wilderness road. Our hearts beat high with hope that we would join Genls Bragg & E Kirby Smith[18] & redeem our state from the hands of the despoiler. But fate was against us. On the morning of the 17th just as we had formed in line to begin our march, a courier galloped up to Genl Breckinridge who was in command of the detachment & handed [him] a dispatch. It bore the news that the battle of Perryville[19] had been fought & that Genl Bragg was falling back from Kentucky & we were to hurry around to Murfreesboro Tenn as soon as we could get our forces to-gether. We were on the Taz[e]well road 3 miles beyond Maynardsville Tenn. So we did not get to press the sacred soil of Ky under our feet. With sad hearts we turned from our cheerished hope & with stern determination to manfully do our duty returned to Knoxville & on the evening of Oct 20th camped on the same ground at Knoxville which we had left on the 15th. Thence we went by rail to Shell Mound on Oct 23.

We moved toward Murfreesboro crossing the river at Bridgeport with much trouble as the R R. bridge at that point had been burned; reached Murfreesboro on Oct 28th just eight months after having left it on our way to fight the

18 Major General Edmund Kirby Smith was at this time commander of the Department of East Tennessee. In co-operation with Bragg's invasion of Kentucky he had advanced through Cumberland Gap and defeated the Union forces at Richmond, Kentucky, August 30, 1862. He then proceeded to a junction with Bragg, but his army was not present at the battle of Perryville.

19 The battle of Perryville, fought October 8, 1862, was the climax of Braxton Bragg's campaign to "liberate" Kentucky. Both sides claimed a victory in the battle, but Bragg withdrew through Cumberland Gap to East Tennessee, from whence he had started with high hopes two months before. *O.R.*, Series 1, XVI, pt. 1, 1087-94.

Battle of Shiloh. In this time we had consecrated with the blood of Ky's sons the Southland's soil at Shiloh, Corrinth, Vicksburg, & Baton Rouge, & the 2nd Ky had freely shed their blood at Fort Donaldson [Donelson]. The troops which had been captured at Fort Donaldson were now back with us ready for duty. Col Roger Hanson in Consideration of gallantry in that battle was made Brigadier General & placed in Command of our brigade.

General Buckner had asked for a court of inquiry into his conduct in the siege & surrender of Fort Donaldson. The court was held & found that he had performed the part of a wise & galant officer & he was forthwith promoted to Lieutenant General & assigned to an important command.[20] General Hansons staff was now composed as follows: Ast' Adjutant Genl, Capt John S. Hope;[21] Ast Inspector Genl, Thos E Stake[22] (Capt) ; Chief Qr Mastr, Capt John R. Viley; Chief Coms'ry, S. M Moreman;[23] Lt Presley Trabue,[24] Ordnance officer; & Lt Joe Benedict Aid-de-camp.

[20] Buckner was not promoted to the rank of lieutenant general until the fall of 1864. He was commissioned major general on August 19, 1862 (*O.R.*, Series 1, XVI, pt. 2, p. 766). Buckner did ask for a court of inquiry concerning his conduct in the surrender of Fort Donelson. If it was granted, there is no report of it in the *Official Records*. However, the propriety of his conduct on that occasion was never questioned by anyone save himself.

[21] John S. Hope was one of the few non-Kentuckians in the Brigade, he being a Virginian. He left in 1863 to serve with General Richard Taylor in the Trans-Mississippi Department. Thompson, *Orphan Brigade*, 593.

[22] Thomas E. Stake of Louisville was a first lieutenant at this time but was made captain in February, 1863. He fought in all major engagements except Missionary Ridge, having been wounded seriously two months before at Chickamauga. Thompson, 581.

[23] S. M. Moorman was from Daviess County. Thompson, 1018.

[24] Presley Trabue was from Union County. Thompson, 644.

4 MURFREESBORO

Through the fall and early winter of 1862 Bragg's army occupied Murfreesboro in central Tennessee, and Rosecrans, who had succeeded Buell after the battle of Perryville, was at Nashville some thirty miles to the northwest. "Guard duty and dress parade" were the daily routine, sometimes enlivened by a cavalry skirmish, as at Edgefield, or a "hit and run" operation, as at Hartsville.

Rosecrans was feeling his way out from Nashville and the bloody battle of Stone's River was soon to come. Johnny Green and his comrades, fresh from their brilliantly successful coup at Hartsville, were pleased with themselves and were looking forward to the Christmas season. But the tragic affair of poor Lewis cast a pall over the army. The incident gives some insight into the character of Bragg and offers some explanation of why he never commanded the affection of his troops. When he lost their confidence as well some months later, his failure was complete. Even Johnny Green, who was intensely loyal to all his superiors, remarked after the execution, "Surely clemency might have been used in this case with good effect."

*N*OV. 4TH 1862. Genl Breckinridge's whole force took up line of march in battle order moving towards Nashville. At night we were permitted to lie down for a short rest. At 9 oclock P.M. we fell into line again marching towards Nashville, we supposed to make an attack at day light.

At dawn on Nov 5th Forrest[1] drove in the enemies picketts & we were formed in line ready to advance & followed up to the sound of the guns until ordered to halt. The cannons were booming but fighting in our front was only skirmish fireing. We now learned that our advance was only a feint to cover a movement by Genl John H. Morgan who had ridden around to the other side of Nashville to destroy at Edgefield a number of stores & supplies, our purpose being to keep the enemy engaged sufficiently to prevent their moving in force against him. He met with partial success, but they had too many men for both of us to risk a general engagement. When the cannonading on the other side of Nashville ceased we knew that Genl Morgan was through with his expedition & we withdrew to Harts spring & encamped for the night. The next day we returned to Murfreesboro.

[1] Nathan Bedford Forrest, the renowned cavalry leader, was on several occasions attached to the Army of Tennessee and thus saw service with the Orphan Brigade.

December 5th, 1862. Orderly call was sounded at about 2 oclock P.M this afternoon. Sergeant Thos Ellis[2] of Co B came back from orderly call loaded down with cartridges & percussion caps & began to issue 40 rounds to each man. He said to me, "Johnnie you dont need any for you are too lame to march & the orders are to fall in ready for action. You had better stay & watch our tents as I have to leave some body in charge of the camp."

I had a severe boil or rising on my heel so that I could not put my shoe on; I could only stick my toe in my shoe & tie the shoe to my foot but I could not stand the thought of the regiment going into action & not to be with it. So I said, "Sergeant this is not my turn on detail. I am going with the regiment."

It was snowing fast but in a few minutes the regiment was formed & off we started. Indeed the whole Brigade was in line of march towards Bairds Mills. Genl Cheatham[3] & Genl Wheeler[4] moved up towards Nashville as far as Lavergne. We marched 18 miles that afternoon & night & stopped about midnight at Bairds Mills. The ground was covered with snow fully four inches but we were tired & told to lie down & sleep for we had more work before us. We found some wood to make a fire, scraped the snow off the ground, spread our blankets down on the frozen ground & went to sleep. Rations of Bacon, flour, sugar & coffee were issued to us on the morning of the 6th & we were instructed to cook two days rations & cary [them] in our haver-sacks. At 1-30 this afternoon we took up the line of march for Harts-

2 Thomas H. Ellis of Bardstown fought with the Brigade throughout the war. In February, 1863, he was commissioned a lieutenant. Thompson, *Orphan Brigade,* 816.

3 Major General Benjamin F. Cheatham commanded a division in Polk's and later in Hardee's corps. He fought with the Army of Tennessee from Shiloh through the battle of Nashville in December, 1864. After the disastrous Tennessee campaign he joined Johnston's army in North Carolina.

4 Major General Joseph Wheeler was chief of cavalry of the Army of Tennessee and thus saw much service with the Orphan Brigade. The Brigade became part of his command when it was mounted after the fall of Atlanta in September, 1864, and served with him until the close of the war.

54

ville Tenn (this we found out later, for until we crossed the Cumberland river we knew not where we were going) . Our two regiments of Infantry to-gether with Cavalry & Artillery amounted to about 1400 men.[5] The weather was very cold & about four inches of snow [were] on the ground.

We marched until about 10 oclock at night when the cavelry halted & we marched up beside them, they then dismounted & we mounted their horses to ride but the snow had wet our feet & we almost froze on those horses & before we had ridden five miles we were shouting for the cavelry men to come & get their horses. Their feet by this time had gotten wet & cold walking in the snow so we both suffered more than we would if we had stuck to our own arm of the service from first to last.

The infantry & artillery crossed Cumberland river at Purcell's Ferry in two small flat bottom boats which we had to pole across. The boats were very leaky & the restlessness of the horses nearly pushed a plank off the bottom of the boats & we had to bail out the water for life & death. Before we got to the ferry we had fearful roads to travel. One long hill was up rocks like stair steps, each step being about two feet rise. The infantry had to take hold of each wheel of the artillery & almost lift it up that hill.

The cavalry had to ford the river at a point about two miles lower down. The most of our forces were over by five oclock A M & General John H. Morgan commanding the expedition ordered the regiment of cavalry not yet over to hurry up & join us as soon as possible & with the main force he pressed forward to attack the enemy. Their pickets were discovered & shot down but this firing allarmed the camp so we did not take them by as much surprise as we hoped to. They had their breakfast just being cooked but they hurriedly fell into line & their artillery was in position ready & opened on us as soon as we came in range.

[5] Morgan reported his force as "about 1300." *O.R.,* Series 1, XX, pt. 1, pp. 66-67.

Our Cavalry pressed forward & drove in a few skir-mishers they had thrown out. Our artillery galloped up & took position & opened on them. Their battery replied with great effect. Our infantry double quicked to the attack. Just as we double quicked past our battery, they [the enemy] sent a shell into one of our caisons, blew it up & killed several of our men & wounded Craven Peyton,[6] a little courier on Genl Morgan's Body Guard, a gallant little fellow only 16 years old. He died from his wounds.

Col Hunt soon had us in line of battle & began the attack in earnest. Morgans men found them strongly posted on our left in a skirt of woods & the artillery & infantry in our front were strongly posted on the brow of a hill with a deep ravine between us; they evidently were much stronger than we, but the river was behind us; we were 25 miles from our friends [while] they were within six miles of a division of 8000 reenforcements which the artillery fire had already notified to come to the relief of their friends;[7] we *had* to whip them & do it quick. A general advance was ordered [and] our infantry dashed forward with a yell. The cavelry was equally as gallant [and] the artillery belched forth death & destruction to their ranks. Their line was thinned by our fire. Col Hunt called out, "Boys kill a man with every shot."

Their line wavered; the command came to us, "Charge bayonetts! Forward march!" We rushed fo[r]ward, their line broke & we pressed them hard; here & there some gal-lant man in blue half hidden behind a tree or rock would stubbornly hold his position & fire at us.

One man raised his gun to fire at Jim Burba running towards him while placing a cap on his gun. Jim called to him, "Surrender or I'll kill you!" The fearless hearted

---

[6] Craven Peyton of Hartford, Kentucky, had fought through the battles of Shiloh, Vicksburg, and Baton Rouge. Thompson, *Orphan Brigade,* 828.

[7] Two brigades of Union troops were encamped at Castalian Springs within nine miles of Hartsville but knew nothing of an impending attack until they heard the artillery firing. They marched to the relief of their friends but arrived too late. *O.R.,* Series 1, XX, pt. 1, pp. 44-45.

56

Yankee heard his threat with scorn & fired point blank at Jim; by some mysterious intervention he missed him, though not ten feet from him. Jim at once executed his threat & sent that poor fellow beyond all the cares of this world.

It was now a rout but we had them surrounded & they surrendered to our 1400 men their entire command numbering over 1800 men which together with those we had killed & wounded amounted to over 2000 men.[8] They were bountifully supplied with every thing a soldier could wish. In our campaigns at Shiloh & Vicksburg & Baton Rouge we had used up or lost nearly all our clothes so we ransacked their camp for good clothes. It was Dec 7th & I had no over coat. I rushed into the tent of Col Moore[9] & found his over coat on his cot & at once put it on & helped my self to some good flannel shirts in his valise; just then he came in & said, "My good fellow dont take my clothes."

I gave him back his shirts & he said, "Oh! do give me my over coat," but I drew the line at the over coat. I said, "No you wont need it; you will be kept warm in prison & I'll need it."

He replied, "Do give me my over coat & get the Major's in the next tent; he was killed in the fight."

But I was hard hearted & replied, "You may have the Majors; I'll keep this."

We now had to hurry to get the prisoners & cannon & guns & all the stores & munitions which we had captured across the river before that column of 8000 men which was

[8] The Union losses were 58 killed, 204 wounded, 1,834 surrendered. *Ibid.,* 45.

[9] Colonel A. B. Moore, One Hundred and Fourth Illinois Volunteers, was in command of the Thirty-Ninth Brigade, Twelfth Division, which was stationed at Hartsville. The Confederate attack was a complete surprise. The Confederates approached within four hundred yards of the Union camp and wheeled into line before being discovered. The Union troops behaved very badly. Only two companies of skirmishers turned out to face the Confederates; the remainder fled ignominiously. Even the two companies broke in confusion as soon as the Confederate artillery opened on them. Halleck recommended that Moore be dismissed from the service for neglect of duty in this affair, but he was permitted to resign. *Ibid.,* 43, 45.

coming after us from Castalian Springs could catch up with us, as we were 25 miles from reenforcements. The cavelry sent out skirmishers to meet that colum & delay it as much as they could. Some of our cavelry each took an infantry-man behind him & ferried him across the river, as it was fordable here. The rest of the infantry had to ford it & the water was waist deep; it was still terribly cold but victory had raised our spirits so that we could stand any thing. I dont believe a single man was made sick by the wetting. We marched hurriedly back to Bairds Mill reaching there the night of Dec 7th having marched in the thirty hours since we left there (in the snow) 50 miles, crossed & recrossed the Cumberland River, lifted the artillery over two miles of almost impassable road, fought a battle with thoroughly armed, gallant troops that outnumbered us by 1/3, captured them & brought off all the fruits of our victory in the face of a column of pursuers more than five times our numbers. We deprived the yanks of their breakfast & kept them on the jump all day so they had nothing to eat that day until at night; when we halted we divided our rations with them & they had appetites to relish them you may be sure.

The next day we marched back to Murfreesborro 18 miles & occupied our tents, well supplied with yankee sut-tlers stores & in good humor to prepare for a joyous Christmas which was only 17 days off. Christmas was drawing nigh with all its sweet memories & longings. We had hoped this joyous season would find us on kentucky's soil, with the in-vaders of our state (for neither the legislature nor the Gov-ernor had asked for federal troops to be sent into the state) driven north of the Ohio River.

We had tents & each mess had built a chimney to their tent. Genl Rosecrans was gradually drawing nearer & cavelry skirmishes were of daily occurrence but we prepared to enjoy ourselves as long as we might; guard duty & dress parade were the extent of our daily duties and we prepared for a good Christmas dinner.

A supply of liquor had been captured at Hartsville & from this source or some other those who wanted whiskey had it & some of the boys were good naturedly full I regret to say. I had gone to some of the farm houses in the neighborhood & bought some eggs & onions. I made a long hunt for a turkey but I was too late; all the turkes in the country had been sold, but I bought a goose & we proceeded to prepare mr goose. He was reported to be young but we were suspicious of his age so Dave Caruth who undertook to cook him first par boiled him, then stuffed him & roasted him. I made & cooked the biscuit & thought I was about to establish a reputation as a pastry cook for I made a pound cake which looked to be a complete success until I took it out of the oven & let it cool, then it sank in the centre & had a very depressing sadness in it, but we enjoyed it very much & talked of the loved ones at home & the pleasure we would have in recounting our experience to them when this cruel war was over.

A most sad occurance has taken place here at Murfreesborro. A young fellow by the name of Lewis,[10] a member of the 6th Ky Regt., who was an only son, learned a few months ago of the death of his father since he left home, his mother being left alone & in rather poor circumstances. His term of enlistment has expired; he like the rest of us enlisted for only one year. But when the Confederate congress passed the law setting forth the fact that the necessities of the Confederacy were such that all soldiers were required to reenlist in the same arm of the service, he asked the privilege of reenlisting in Morgans cavelry but was refused, so he reenlisted as did the rest of us in our old regiments; but he

10 There were a number of men by the name of Lewis in the Orphan Brigade. The official history of the Brigade relates this incident but identifies the victim merely as a corporal of the Sixth Regiment (Thompson, *Orphan Brigade,* 201-202). The register of the Brigade lists a Corporal Asa Lewis, Company E, 6th Kentucky, who was from Barren County, who "displayed more than ordinary gallantry" at Shiloh, and who is recorded as "killed at Stone [*sic*] River, Dec. 26, 1862" (Thompson, 774). This was five days before the battle began.

asked for a furlough to go home to see his mother, but the enemy were threatening us very actively & the furlough was refused. He applied again explaining that he had gotten a letter from his mother saying she needed him sorely. He promised to come back promptly if the furlough was granted, but General Brag[g] refused it, saying discipline must be enforced with all alike.

Young Lewis said he would go without leave as he could not get a furlough; he was captured & brought back, but the circumstances were so appealing that he was not court marshalled but severely rebuked & told to return to his company & sin no more. He soon went again without leave & was captured outside our lines & brought & tried for desertion & sentenced to be shot. A petition was sent up to have his sentence commuted to some less severe punishment but Genl Brag[g] said discipline must be enforced & Genl Breckinridge was ord[er]ed to have him shot in the presence of the division.

The whole division was formed in three sides of a square. Poor Lewis was brought from prison in a wagon riding on his coffin [and] a detail of twelve men was made to shoot him. These twelve men stack their guns unloaded & then march away. A sergea[n]t loads all the guns with deadly load except one; in this one gun (he must not know whose it is) he puts a blank cartridge. The guns are all stacked again & the twelve men detailed as executioners come back, take their guns & are marched fifty feet in front of Lewis who is kneeling facing them. He had been granted the privilege of dieing without being tied or fettered in any way, [but] he consents to be blindfolded because he said he did not wish to recognize any of his comrades who were forced to perform this duty.

All was ready. He asked Genl Breckinridge for permission to say only a few words to the detail. He said, "Comrades I know you are all grieved to do this work but dont be distressed; none of you will know who kills me for you know one of your guns has no ball in it. Each man may think his was the harmless gun. But I beg of you to aim to kill when

60

the command 'fire' is given; it will be merciful to me. Good bye."

The Lieutenant in comma[n]d of the detail of executioners gave the command, "Ready-Aim-Fire!" All was over & a gloom settled over the command. Surely clemency might have been used in this case with good effect.

5 STONE'S RIVER

The city of Murfreesboro is about thirty miles southeast of Nashville. On its western border Stone's River flows in a northerly direction, and the highway and railroad from Nashville form an acute angle with the river as they cross and make their way into the city. The terrain to the west of the railroad and highway is rough and at this time was heavily forested. This region was the scene of the heavy fighting on December 31, 1862.

To the east of the river and directly north of Murfreesboro the land is generally clear and rolls smoothly to the river, which was fordable here at several points. In this locale, about two miles directly north of the city, a hill commanded the surrounding fields. This is the hill which Johnny Green calls "the key to the situation." Its strategic importance was early seen by the Confederates, for a Union battery, if located there, could enfilade the Confederate lines across the river.

Bragg divided his army into two wings; the right, commanded by Hardee and including Breckinridge's division, to which belonged the Orphan Brigade, was placed east of the river; the left, commanded by Polk, was west of the river. Bragg had planned to contain the Union front with Polk while his right, crossing the river at the fords, rolled up the Union left flank.

But the massing of Union troops on his own left convinced Bragg that Rosecrans was planning an attack there. Consequently, he altered his own plans by withdrawing Hardee's corps, except Breckinridge, from the east bank and placing it on Polk's left so that his new line overlapped the Union right. His altered plan called for an attack along his front starting at his extreme left and being taken up in turn by each unit until Hardee's and Polk's entire corps were engaged. Breckinridge on the east bank was to be ready for a surprise attack from that direction.

Hardee launched his assault as soon as the fog lifted after daylight on December 31. It was brilliantly successful, and by noon the Union right, under Major General Alexander McDowell McCook, had been rolled back until it formed a line perpendicular to the original front. Here reinforcements from Generals George B. Thomas and Thomas L. Crittenden stabilized it, and the Confederate assault was stalled. At this point Bragg ordered Breckinridge to send two brigades to spearhead an attack on a Union stronghold called "the Round Forest." Breckinridge, erroneously informed that a large Union force was threatening him, begged and received reinforcements himself. This may have been the fatal Confederate error of the campaign and was one which Bragg did not permit to go unnoticed in his report.

On the next day and through the forenoon of January 2 there was no fighting, both sides contenting themselves with watchful waiting.

After noon of January 2 Bragg, convinced that Rosecrans was in retreat, ordered Breckinridge to attack the Union left flank across the river from Breckinridge's position. This was a tragic blunder. What Bragg had interpreted as preparation for retreat had been a regrouping on the Union *left preparatory to an attack on the Confederate right. Rose-crans had concentrated more than sixty guns on the bluff on the west bank of the river in a position to enfilade Breckin-ridge's line when it moved to attack the several brigades which had appeared in its front.*

Breckinridge moved out promptly at 4:00 p.m., with the Orphan Brigade on his left closest to the river. The Union infantry fell back as the Confederates drove forward. Down the slope went pursued and pursuers approaching the river ford. But as the gray line came within range, the Union batteries across the river opened a heavy, accurate, and de-structive fire. At the same time large masses of Union in-fantry which had crossed farther downstream appeared on Breckinridge's right and opened a withering fire from that direction. Caught in this devastating cross fire, the Con-federate line wavered, halted, then broke in disorder. The action lasted little more than an hour, and in that time the division lost 1,700 of the 4,500 who had launched the attack. The Orphan Brigade alone suffered more than 400 casualties.

The two armies faced each other throughout the next day in sullen and exhausted silence; then before daybreak on January 4 the Confederate army retired to Tullahoma and Manchester, while Rosecrans occupied Murfreesboro, too crippled to pursue. The Ninth Kentucky, Johnny Green's regiment, was again given the assignment of rear guard as the Confederates moved off.

For several months Bragg was unmolested save by the bickerings which developed between him and his subordi-nate commanders, practically all of whom frankly admitted that they had no confidence in him as their leader. Mean-while, the army rested, and the rank and file enjoyed the hospitable activities of the civilians, which Johnny Green so charmingly relates.

$\mathcal{D}$EC 28TH 1862. The cannon's boom has for the past two days told us that the cavelry are constantly skirmishing with the Yankies & that our boys are being pressed back, for the firing gets closer & closer every day & to-day the whole army is formed in line of battle to meet Rosecrans. Col Thos H Hunt who was just last week granted a thirty days leave of absence has returned to us. He learned the enemy were advancing & he hastened back to join in the fight. Our boys were delighted to see him ride in & take command & gave him a spontaneous cheer.

The weather is a cold drizzle [but] we are not permitted to have fires for Genl Bragg does not wish the ennemy to be able to locate our line. Beef & corn meal issued to us un-cooked & fires not permitted! Col Hunt ordered a detail sent back to the wagons from each company to cook the rations & bring them to us. We got our supper about 12 at night, but in the mean time the yankees drove in our pickets & came with a rush at us in the dark. One volley from our line drove them back however; but our volley brought forth a volley of oaths from Mike McClarey, a gallant Confed' from Erins Isle who was out on the picket line when our boys were driven in. His comrade was wounded & to bring him home through a corn field where the stalks had not been cut down & take care of his gun at the same time was a difficult task, but with this comrade on his back Mike came swearing at us most vociferously. "Sure are you trying to kill your own men?" But his digust was immense when upon laying his wounded friend down he discovered that a second ball had gone through his head & killed him, whereupon he remarked, "I thought you said it was your leg you were shot in."

After eating our rations we laid down in line of battle with our guns in our hands to catch a few hours sleep. We were arroused before day the next morning just in time to advance to the brow of the hill from which we had driven the yankies & which was the key to the position & from which our artillery did much to decide the Wednesdays battle in our favor. Monday & Tuesday had been spent skirmishing between our pickets, & frequent cannonading showing that the enemy had gotten our range to a degree to make it extremely uncomfortable for us, frequently wounding some of our men.

Wednesday Dec 31st the battle was terrific on our left & centre but after fearful carnage we drove the enemy's right wing & centre back almost to a right a[n]gle with his left.[1]

Thursday, heavy artillery fire. Lieutenant Curd[2] killed by a cannon ball almost severing his body at the belt.

Capt Joe Desha[3] we thought was killed. A cannon ball

[1] Actually each commander was preparing to attack his opponent's right flank, but the Confederate attack got under way first and was so fierce that the Union right was forced back and Rosecrans had to withhold his offensive on his left in order to support his crumbling right. *O.R.*, Series 1, XX, pt. 1, pp. 192-94.

[2] Lieutenant Henry Curd was adjutant to Colonel Hunt. Thompson, *Orphan Brigade*, 194.

[3] Jo Desha was born in Harrison County, Kentucky, May 22, 1833. His grandfather, Joseph Desha, was one of the early settlers of the state, had risen to the rank of major general in the War of 1812, and had served as governor of the state. In the spring of 1861 Jo Desha raised a company for the Confederacy which served in Virginia until May, 1862, when it was mustered out of service upon the expiration of its term. He returned to Kentucky and for a time served with John Morgan. When Bragg invaded Kentucky, Desha resigned from the cavalry and raised a company of infantry which became

passed through our earth works, struck him on the head &
tore a great gash in his scalp. He was carried to the rear for
burrial but by the time the ambulance driver had gotten
there & called for some one to help him lift out the dead
body the Captain sat up & told them to bring the Surgeon.
He had his wounds dressed & made the ambulance driver
take him back to the regiment & he took command of the
picketts that night.

Friday. Gloomy & cloudy, developing first into a drizzle,
then a sleet. We cant have fires because the enemy's artillery
fire & sharp shooters keep us in the trenches. About 2-30 we
are called to attention & receive orders to charge the enemy.[4]
There is some little delay in arranging the attack & bringing
up the other forces that are to join us in the attack (the Briggades of Genls Preston,[5] Pillow[6] & Adams[7]). About 4 oclock

---

Company I, Ninth Regiment, First Kentucky Brigade. He was wounded at
Stone's River, Chickamauga, and at Dallas, the last time so severely he was
retired from the service. In April, 1865, he returned to the unit for the last
few weeks. At the war's end he returned to his farm in Cynthiana. Thompson, 491-97.

[4] This order and its consequences are almost as controversial as the more
celebrated order for the charge of Pickett at Gettysburg. On January 2
Rosecrans had advanced a force from his left across to the east bank of Stone's
River to threaten the Confederate right stationed there perpendicular to the
river. Bragg ordered Breckinridge, commanding the right wing, to attack
this Union force. Breckinridge protested that an advance by his forces in
this sector would bring them under an enfilade fire from Union artillery
stationed on commanding ground on the west bank. Despite the protest,
which Breckinridge's subordinates endorsed, Bragg peremptorily ordered the
advance. It resulted in disaster. At first the Union force was driven across the
river, with the Orphan Brigade in pursuit. But, as Breckinridge had forewarned, the Union artillery riddled the Confederates. They were repulsed
with heavy losses, and the pursuers became the pursued. The next night
Bragg retreated. *O.R.*, Series 1, XX, pt. 1, pp. 195, 450-51, 675, 784-87; Stanley
F. Horn, *The Army of Tennessee* (Indianapolis, 1941), 207.

[5] William Preston was born near Louisville, Kentucky, October 16, 1816,
the descendant of wealthy pioneer forebears. He attended college at St.
Joseph's in Bardstown and Yale, and was graduated in law at Harvard in
1838. While practicing law in Louisville he was active in politics, serving in
the legislature and in the United States Congress. In 1858 he was appointed
Minister to Spain and was in Madrid at the outbreak of the Civil War. He
resigned at once, and after reporting to Secretary of State Seward in Washington, he made his way to Bowling Green, Kentucky, where he was given
a place on the staff of General Albert Sidney Johnston, his brother-in-law,

the advance is ordered. We are ordered to fix bayonetts, to move forward at double quick, to reserve our fire until within 100 yards, then to take good aim & fire & then immediately to rush upon them with fixed bayonetts.

A more gallant charge was never made; we drove them before us, captured 400 prisoners & followed the fleeing enemy closely, but they waded across the river & their batteries & reenforcements on the other side of the river about 100 yards away poured a deadly fire upon us; we could not reach them & it was certain death to remain where we were, so a retreat was ordered. Our gallant General Hanson was killed, or rather mortally wounded. We brought him back & reformed upon the position we occupied before the attack. But we had over 400 killed & wounded in this charge lasting one hour & twenty minutes; this falling upon our briggade alone, the other three briggades lost not so heavily, but their loss was appalling.[8]

---

with the rank of colonel. He was present when Johnston died on the field at Shiloh. Thereafter he was made a brigadier general and was with Breckinridge at Vicksburg in the summer of 1862, was later ordered to join Bragg in Kentucky, and was present at the battle of Perryville. After the retreat from Kentucky he was given command of a new brigade in Breckinridge's division and was once more closely associated with the Orphan Brigade, although not a part of it. In August, 1863, he was given command of a division in Buckner's corps. He drew praise from General Longstreet for his handling of the division at Chickamauga. After this battle he was sent on an important diplomatic mission to Mexico. He did not return to the Confederacy until the spring of 1865. At the end of the war he underwent a self-imposed exile for more than a year, but in 1866 he returned to Kentucky and took up his residence in Lexington. He was active in the Democratic Party until his death in 1887, but was never again a candidate for public office. Thompson, *Orphan Brigade*, 364-75; *O.R.*, Series 1, XXX, pt. 2, pp. 289-90.

[6] Gideon Pillow's chief claim to notoriety is based on his career as a "vain, ambitious, quarrelsome, and unsuccessful soldier" (*Dictionary of American Biography*). He was second in command at Fort Donelson, where his conduct brought a censure from the Confederate Secretary of War. He commanded a brigade in subsequent battles of the Army of Tennessee.

[7] Daniel W. Adams, a native of Frankfort, Kentucky, entered the war as a lieutenant colonel of Louisiana infantry and fought with the Army of Tennessee from Shiloh to Chickamauga, where he was seriously wounded. After his recovery he served as a cavalry commander in north Alabama and Mississippi. His brigade at this time was in Wither's division of Hardee's corps.

[8] Casualties of the four brigades on January 2 were: Adams', 159; Pillow's,

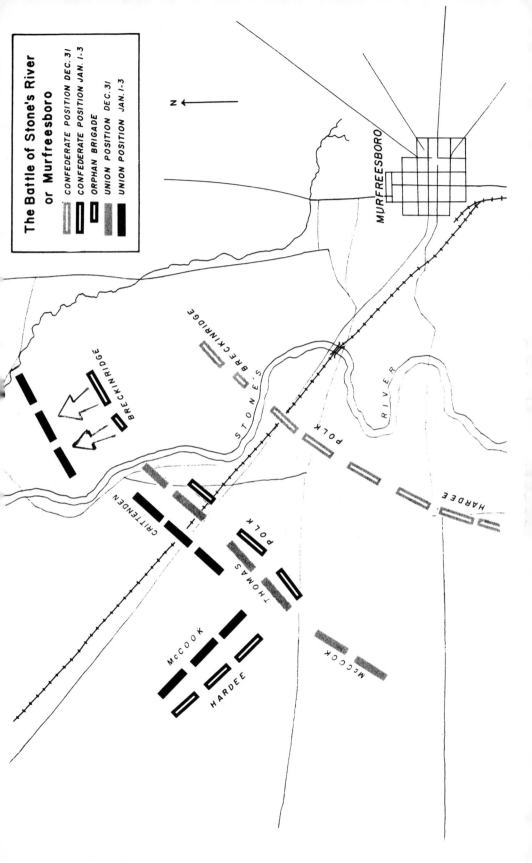

The Battle of Stone's River
or Murfreesboro

CONFEDERATE POSITION DEC. 31
CONFEDERATE POSITION JAN. 1-3
ORPHAN BRIGADE
UNION POSITION DEC. 31
UNION POSITION JAN. 1-3

N

MURFREESBORO

BRECKINRIDGE

BRECKINRIDGE

STONE'S

RIVER

POLK

HARDEE

CRITTENDEN

POLK

THOMAS

McCOOK

HARDEE

McCOOK

This night of sleet & discouragement was trying but never a man faltered. With meager rations, loaded guns & quick eye they went out on picket duty that night to watch lest the enemy, encouraged by our repulse, should attempt to over power us. But they [the enemy] had received severe punishment & did not relish the idea of trying to drive men who seemed determined to sell their lives at such fearful cost to the enemy who dared approach them.

Saturday Jan 3d 1863. A cold sleet fell all last night [and] our wet clothes are frozen on us. Our suffering is so great that the men have gotten out of the trenches & made fires out of such wood as they can find. Being in view of the enemy they open their batteries upon us, to which our batteries & sharp shooters reply. After a fruitless interchange of shots, finding we were increasing each others suffering without satisfactory results, by common consent the firing ceased & we assembled around our fires & they were soon standing arround fires they had built. This day was one of great trial. We learned that our gallant Genl Hanson died during the night. In this cold weather standing pickett is terrible, wet to the skin & clothes freezing, but we take great care to keep our cartridges dry.

Sunday Jan 4th 1863. Just before day light we left our trenches & evacuated Murfreesboro. Rosencranz [Rosecrans] has received reenforcements[9] and is preparing to pass around our flank, so we were forced to fall back to Duck River. The roads are terriffic; time & time again we had to march through liquid mud which came way above our knees. We have fallen back to Manchester Tenn on the south side of Duck River. I waded in the icy cold river to wash some of the mud off my clothes & my skin. We made roaring fires & laid down on the

---

402; Preston's, 376; Hanson's, 401 (*O.R.*, Series 1, XX, pt. 1, p. 675). It should be noted that Adams', Pillow's, and Preston's brigades had been heavily engaged on December 31 and had suffered heavy casualties there while the Orphan Brigade was unengaged. *Ibid.*, 678-79.

9 Rosecrans was not receiving reinforcements, but Bragg as well as Johnny Green thought he was. Horn, *The Army of Tennessee*, 210.

ground feet to the fire & slept soundly; some one getting chilly during the night would get up & renew the fire.

Jan 5th. Our wagons have come up & we have pitched tents. The boys are building stick chimneys to our tents. Dave Caruth is cutting the sticks, some of the others are mixing the mud, & Gus Moore[10] & I are the mechanics who are building the chimney. We have gotten brick bats enough to make the Jambs & the inside of the chimney we have to line well with mud to keep it from catching fire. We are getting quite comfortably fixed.

Later—Guard mounting, drill & dress parade are kept up but we are finding ways to divert ourselves; the people are very kind & cordial. They come in droves to witness dress parade & visit the camp. Every soldier is welcome to any house.

The citizens gave a party at the tavern; all soldiers were welcome. We had ham sandwiches, pies & cakes. You were expected to go up to any girl who was there, tell her your name & be sure of a cordial welcome. She would tell you her name & give you some pie or cake or some thing to eat & tell you how she admired a Confederate soldier who could stand all that we had stood. We could not eat all the time, so some of the boys found a violin & wanted to have a dance but the girls all belonged to the church & would not dance but they would play Weavely Wheat, which meant that you took your stand on the floor with your partner the same as in a virginia reel. Everybody then is expected to begin singing, "I will not have your weavely wheat, I will not have your barley, I will not have your weavely wheat to make a cake for Charley," & a verse or two more of it. To this music you dance the virginia reel or sometimes a cotillion for variation. At any rate we had a good time & I dont know for how many matches the foundation was laid this evening.

10 A. J. Moore of Bardstown, Kentucky, fought in all engagements of the Brigade until he was captured at Atlanta in July, 1864. Thompson, *Orphan Brigade*, 821.

70

We determined that we must in some way reciprocate. So Gus Moore & Phil Vicaro [Vacaro] proposed that we give a theatrical performance in the paper mill which was near this town. So the play selected was the Farce "Bombasties Furioso." We had no book of plays but Gus Moore wrote out the entire play from memory. Gus & Phil were to furnish the histrionic talent & finish out the troup with such material as they could select from the regiment. I was selected to act the part of Distifena, the young lady in the play. Of course it was necessary to provide female attire for so fair a young lady & this task fell to me, so I picked out the finest looking house in the neighborhood to bestow my attentions upon with the hopes of finding among its inmates a young lady whose clothes would fit me. Fortune favored me; this family had two daughters about grown & I began to try to make myself agreeable. Of course I had to cultivate their acquaintance a while before asking for the loan of a suit of the young ladies clothes, especially as crinoline was expensive.

Upon the occasion of my next call I took John Jackman[11] with me to entertain one sister while I tried to gain favor in Miss Sukey's [Miss Sukey Hickerson] good graces. We had come away from camp without leave & the hour for roll call at Tattoo was near. We had nearly a mile to go to camp, a sleet had set in & we had to cross the creek on a log incased in a sheet of ice. So hurried was our pace that when I got half way across the creek I slipped off & went cosouze in the water up to my waist. This made Jack so nervous that he sat straddle of the log & cooned it across. After all we missed roll call & had to serve an extra term of guard duty for it, the only time during the war that I was not present or accounted for at roll call.

But at my next call upon Miss Sukey the ludicrus ac-

11 John S. Jackman of Nelson County was assigned duty as regimental clerk because he was deemed physically incapacitated for service in the ranks. Despite this, he would leave his desk and take active part in all battles. He was seriously wounded at Pine Mountain in June, 1864, and was unfit for service thereafter. Thompson, 820-21.

71

count I gave of our experience & our punishment so much excited her interest & sympathy she consented to lend me the necessary outfit for our play. Gus More & Phil Vicaro [Vacaro] had their hands full in making the flys for scenery, equiping the stage & drilling the actors, but finally the great event came off. We wrote to Mobile for oysters, Fransois Jervis cooked the oysters, we had coffee & cake & gave the guests quite a feast after the play & all the ladies in the town & country came & enjoyed it. Colonl Hunt brought the Belle of the county, a Miss Huggins, & it was a mirthful occasion for every body.

I undertook to procure the oysters for this feast; so I wrote to my cousin Cornelius Fellowes, then living in Mobile, asking him to send us half a barrel of oysters & in responce he sent us a barrel of oysters in the shel and being very cold weather they kept well. At the same time I asked Cousin Cornelius to lend me $25 to buy some shoes & stockings. The next mail brought me one half of a $100 bill issued by the Canal Bank of New Orleans with the information that on the succeeding day he would send me the other half of the same bill & it came to hand all right & when pasted together gave me $100 of the best money in the south, for this bank redeemed all its notes in gold or silver. After the war when I told my dear old cousin that I wanted to begin to pay him back in installments, he answered in very forcible if not polished language, "You damned little rebel you, dont you ever talk about paying me. Dont you know if I had not given it to you it would all have gone in the final crash as all my fortune did go!" He was a generous patriotic soul & I loved him very much.

We had a comfortable winter at Manchester, with only one interruption. Col R. P. Trabue commanded the Brigade from the time Genl Hanson received his death wound until we reached Manchester. While here Genl Marcus J. Wright was placed in command but he was soon succeeded by Genl Ben Hardin Helm who soon became the Idol of his men.

While at Manchester an outpost which we established at McMinville was attacked by the enemy (Mar 25th 1862) .[12] A sharp skirmish resulted in our losing some men. Our whole regiment except the detail already there made a forced march through sleet & snow & muddy roads which made us resigned to the icy bath when we had to wade duck river, for it washed off the solid coating of mud with which we were literally covered.

The enemy however retreated upon the approach of our skirmishers who got an opportunity to fire only a few rounds at them, but they captured some of our pickets however. From here we marched to Ho[o]vers Gap where we did much demonstrating & marched & counter marched. It was here a sad piece of news came to us. It was that Col Hunt had tendered his resignation; he left us & Lie't Col John W. Caldwell was promoted to the rank of Col & soon had fast hold upon the hearts of all the men & officers.

[12] Colonel John Kennett, 4th Ohio Cavalry, led a reconnaissance raid into Shelbyville, McMinnville, and Tullahoma, March 25-30, 1863. *O.R.*, Series 1, X, pt. 1, pp. 46-50.

6 VICKSBURG

After the battle of Murfreesboro, Bragg's army remained in the vicinity of Tullahoma and Manchester throughout the spring and early summer of 1863, while Rosecrans employed tactics of maneuver designed to force Bragg out of Tennessee. For almost five months the Orphan Brigade enjoyed relative inactivity, enlivened only by a small engagement at McMinnville and by competitive drill against Adams' brigade of Louisianians for the championship of the Army of Tennessee—a contest which the Kentuckians won.

Meanwhile, Grant's brilliance and energy had placed Vicksburg again in peril, and Joseph E. Johnston had been belatedly dispatched to its relief. On May 9 when Johnston was ordered to Mississippi, Grant had already moved his flotilla down the Mississippi River past Vicksburg's guns (April 16) and had landed his army at Bruinsburg, south of Vicksburg. Temporarily bypassing Vicksburg, Grant moved directly on Jackson, driving out Johnston, who had gathered a small force there, and severing communication between Jackson and Vicksburg. Having accomplished this, Grant moved on Vicksburg, defeating Pemberton en route. Then, *placing Sherman in a position to watch Johnston, Grant set his army down before Vicksburg.*

The outnumbered Confederacy was finding it difficult indeed to muster troops sufficient to repel all Union thrusts— the Army of the Potomac in Virginia, Rosecrans' Army of the Cumberland in central Tennessee, and Grant's force in Mississippi. Johnston was able to gather together 20,000 men, including Breckinridge's division, which Bragg was willing to part with—surprisingly, in view of his own difficulties in resisting Rosecrans' pressure.

Breckinridge's division, with the Orphan Brigade, arrived in the vicinity of Jackson on June 1, 1863, and remained there throughout the month inactive, while Johnston's main force was camped twenty miles northwest at Canton.

Johnston had sent repeated and specific orders to Pemberton to evacuate Vicksburg and move to form a junction with him. Pemberton did move as far as Baker's Creek, but departing from Johnston's instructions, waited there, where he was overtaken and defeated by Grant at Champion's Hill. Then again departing from Johnston's instructions, he moved back into Vicksburg, where his doom had already been predicted by Johnston.

Despite Pemberton's refusal to co-operate, Johnston now resolved on desperate measures to try to save him. On July 1 he put his entire force in motion toward Vicksburg, planning to attack Grant's rear in the vain hope that a well-timed attack from opposite sides by his and Pemberton's armies might permit the Vicksburg garrison to escape. But even here Pemberton failed him by surrendering his army of approximately 20,000 on July 4.

Learning the next day of Pemberton's surrender, Johnston hurried back to Jackson, where he was pursued by Sherman on July 9. Johnston fought a holding movement here for a week, but as Sherman's force was being reinforced, he crossed the Pearl River on July 16 and abandoned the state capital to the enemy.

Johnny Green never got into Vicksburg on this expedition. But he was in the fruitless campaign from Jackson to the Big Black and back, and he fought through the battle of Jackson from July 9 to 16.

From Jackson the army retreated to Camp Hurricane near Morton, Mississippi. After four weeks in idleness at this place Johnston's force was broken up, and Breckinridge's division was sent back to Bragg, who was to find employment for it along the banks of the Chickamauga.

First National pattern battleflag of the Fifth Kentucky Infantry, later known as the Ninth, presented to Col. Thomas H. Hunt by Mrs. B.J. Adams at the beginning of the war. The embroidered inscription "CG" refers to the "Citizens Guard," the name given to the Kentucky State Guard troops, which Johnny Green eagerly sought to join in 1861. The silk flag, well known by Green, was used by Colonel Hunt as his headquarters flag throughout the early years of the war.
Courtesy of the Museum of the Confederacy

Gen. Simon Bolivar Buckner. Born and raised in Hart County, Kentucky, and a graduate of West Point, Buckner commanded the Kentucky State Guard on the eve of the war. Buckner, who organized the Orphan Brigade's forerunner around the nucleus of the State Guard, directed Johnny Green to Colonel Hunt's camp outside of Bowling Green, Kentucky.
Library of Congress

Gen. Albert Sidney Johnston. Commander of the vast Department Number Two and of the Army of the Mississippi at the Battle of Shiloh, Johnston engineered the rout of General Grant's surprised Union Army of the Tennessee on April 6 only to fall mortally wounded in the early afternoon. "If Genl Johns[t]on had lived," recalled Johnny Green, "he would have pushed forward and we would have captured them all." To Green, Johnston was "matchless" as an army commander.
National Archives

Gen. John Cabell Breckinridge. Probably no one was
more admired by the soldiers of the Orphan Brigade
than General Breckinridge, a United States
Congressman, Vice President, and Senator before the
war. A Lexington, Kentucky, native, Breckinridge
commanded the Orphan Brigade very early in the war
and then proudly led the men as the commander of
the division to which the brigade was attached at
Shiloh, Vicksburg (1862), Baton Rouge, Stone's River,
Chickamauga, and Chattanooga. He is buried in the
Lexington Cemetery.
Library of Congress

Col. Thomas Hart Hunt. Born in Lexington, Kentucky, Hunt moved to Louisville to engage in business before the war. He recruited what became the Ninth Kentucky Infantry and led it through the battles of Shiloh, Vicksburg (1862), Baton Rouge, and Stone's River before resigning from the army in 1863 due to family obligations. Colonel Hunt praised Johnny Green at Shiloh, calling him "bloody as a butcher," and appointed him color corporal of the Ninth Kentucky. Hunt settled in New Orleans after the war, where he died and was buried in 1884.
Courtesy of Mrs. H.L. Minter

Col. Robert P. Trabue. Three-time commander of the Orphan Brigade, Trabue hailed from Columbia, Kentucky; before the war, he practiced law in Natchez, Mississippi. He entered Confederate service as commander of the Fourth Kentucky Infantry, but, because of losses of brigade commanders, actually commanded the Orphan Brigade at Shiloh and Baton Rouge, as well as after Stone's River. He died of a "violent illness" while in Richmond, Virginia, in 1863.
Ed Porter Thompson, *History of the Orphan Brigade*, 403

Shiloh Church, April 6–7, 1862. Johnny Green and the Orphan Brigade attacked the Union lines just west of the log Shiloh Church on April 6 but were hurled back on the next day to the church grounds. Green and the Orphans made their final stand there and buried many of their dead in the woods around the church.
Rossiter Johnson, *Campfire and Battlefield,* 103

Gen. Braxton Bragg. Commander of the Army of Tennessee from the close of the Shiloh campaign to Chattanooga, Bragg was most unpopular in the ranks. His execution of Corp. Asa Lewis of the Sixth Kentucky Infantry at Murfreesboro was never forgotten by the Orphans. When Bragg was replaced by Gen. Joseph E. Johnston in December 1863, Johnny Green noted, with considerable understatement, that the army was "enthused."
Library of Congress

Gen. William Preston. Born in Louisville, Kentucky, and a Lexington lawyer before the war, Preston served as an aide to his brother-in-law Gen. Albert Sidney Johnston at Shiloh. He briefly served as commander of the Orphan Brigade at Vicksburg in 1862 before being assigned to command another brigade in Breckinridge's division. He fought alongside the Orphan Brigade, who always regarded him as one of their own, at Stone's River, Chickamauga, and Chattanooga. He is buried in Cave Hill Cemetery, Louisville. Library of Congress

The charge of Gen. James S. Negley's division across Stone's River against
Breckinridge's attacking brigades on the afternoon of January 2, 1863.
The Orphan Brigade forms the first line of the Confederates in the
distance. No battle cost the Orphans more casualties or was remembered
with greater sorrow than Stone's River.
Rossiter Johnson, *Campfire and Battlefield,* 202

Gen. Roger Weightman Hanson.
Born in Winchester, Kentucky,
Hanson practiced law in
Lexington before the war. He
raised and commanded the
Second Kentucky Infantry and
surrendered it at Fort Donelson.
Returning to the army after his
release from prison, Hanson
commanded the Orphan
Brigade at Stone's River, falling
mortally wounded after being
struck by a shell fragment. He
died two days later and is buried
in the Lexington Cemetery.
Library of Congress

Capt. Joseph Desha. Born in Harrison County, Kentucky, and brother to Maj. Ben Desha, Captain Desha was a county surveyor before the war. He raised in his home county what became Company I, Ninth Kentucky Infantry, which he led at Stone's River, Chickamauga, Chattanooga, the Atlanta campaign, and the Carolinas. At Stone's River, recalled Johnny Green, "a cannon ball passed through our earth works, struck [Desha] on the head and tore a great gash in his scalp." Everyone thought Desha was dead, but he "sat up . . . had his wounds dressed and made the ambulance driver take him back to the regiment. . . ."

Ed Porter Thompson, *History of the Orphan Brigade*, 491

Lt. Henry Curd. Born in Lexington, Kentucky, Curd became a first lieutenant and then adjutant of the Ninth Kentucky Infantry in 1862. He died in battle at Stone's River on January 2, 1863. Johnny Green remembered that Curd was "killed by a cannonball [that] almost sever[ed] his body at the belt." Curd was the brother-in-law of Lt. Col. John Cripps Wickliffe of the Ninth Kentucky and is buried alongside him in the Lexington Cemetery.

Confederate Veterans Ass'n of Kentucky, *Bylaws and Constitution*, 119

ON MAY 24TH 1863 we marched to War-trace Tenn. Orders to have three days cooked rations in our haversacks made us all fear that we were to go back to Mississippi, which proved to be true. Bragg had tried to sholder the responsibility for the failure of our charge on Friday at Mufreesboro upon Genl Breckinridge, saying that he should have made it on the previous Wednesday when the Yankies on our left were almost in a rout. But Breckinridge had asked Bragg for permission to charge on that day & Bragg after taking some of his troups from him to reenforce another part of the line told him if he was certain of success to charge. Breckinridge sent him word that he had faith that he could carry the position but asked for positive orders & he would make the attack, but Bragg just sent the same reply as before, leaving all the responsibility upon Breckinridge, who was unwilling to take upon himself the responsibility which rightfully belonged to the Commander in chief.[1]

1 When Hardee's attack on the Union right at Murfreesboro was doubling back McCook's corps, Bragg ordered Breckinridge to send two brigades from across Stone's River to support the attack. Ill advised that he was being attacked by the Union left, Breckinridge pleaded that he should be reinforced. Bragg, persuaded by Breckinridge, reversed his original plan and ordered Breckinridge reinforced, thus preventing Hardee from securing a complete victory. Later, when Breckinridge's alarm proved unwarranted, Bragg was

Because of this feeling Breckinridge was sent to Mississippi just when the army was preparing to march into Ky. Breckinridge obeyed [the] orders without a murmur, but knowing it would suit the men much better to send Mississippi troops to their own state & give our Ky boys a chance to come to Ky asked Bragg if such an arrangement could not be made & Bragg again threw an unpleasant responsibility upon Breckinridge to choose what troops he wanted to take to Mississippi. Whereupon Breckinridge addressed the Brigade & explained to them, saying there could not be a moments hessitation as to what troops he preferred to have with him but he felt it would be selfish & unkind in him to take us a way from the chance of going into our native state & he therefore asked the men to choose whether they should go to the burning sands & scorching sun of the far south with him or stay where they had a chance of seeing again their own beloved land. They felt that to stay with Bragg while others were sent with Breckinridge would be taking part against their beloved Breckinridge & they said where thou goest there we will go also. On May 25th 1863 we were loaded in Cattle cars & flat cars & freight cars to hurry to Joseph E Johnston at Jackson Miss who was trying to gather together troops enough to relieve the beleagured garrison at Vicksburg under Genl Pemberton.

Railroad travel was at this time tedious & hazardous. There had been a good deal of rain & in going around a curve the rails spread & our whole train rolled over & over down a thirty foot embankment. Many of the cars were utterly demolished. Several men were killed & many wounded.

We met with so many delays & difficulties that it was the 1st of June before we reached a point six miles from Jackson, Miss; here Genl Grant had torn up the track & burned a tressel so we remained there a few days while the rail road was repaired. Near this place when we arrived the train

---

bitterly critical of him in his report. *O.R.*, Series 1, XX, pt. 1, pp. 665-66, 778, 790-91.

seemed to have stopped in the midst of a swamp & apparently on a single track. It was night & we were lying around, some on the floors of the cars & some on top of the cars, when we heard a whistle blow & heard a train coming at a rapid rate; we had had one R.R. accident & were rather suspicious of recklessness on the part of the train hands; nearly every one jumped to his feet & looked first to one side & then to the other to see if there was a track for the fast approaching train to pass on & it was so dark that we could not see any track so we all jumped off & came sprawling in a ditch with mud & wauter in it up to our middle & just then the other train passed by in safety on the other side of our train for the road at that point was double tracked & we could not see it, but we counted ourselves lucky that it was not a catastrophee.

We went into camp near a lagoon just outside of Jackson; here we had rare sport catching fish. There was a canoe on the lagoon & at night the boys would take a torch in this canoe & pull along the banks near the bushes & sein with a blanket & we caught a number of fish.

I tasted my first eel here but I suppose if it had been a snake & some one else had said it was good to eat, I would have tried it. We were fully prepared for a change in diet.

Some prisoners captured early in the war were exchanged about this time & some of them joined us here. We remained at Jackson nearly one month while Genl Johnston was trying to assemble force enough to relieve Vicksburg.

On July 1st 1863 we marched towards Vicksburg. We knew our force was small to attack Grant in his entrenched position around Vicksburg but we had such confidence in Joseph E. Johnston that we had no doubt we could do whatever he planned for us to do. We marched only about 14 miles this day but it was about the most trying march we ever made, [for] we had three days cooked rations, forty rounds of cartrages, & the sand was shoe mouth deep & so hot it actually blistered our feet. More than half the regiment fell by the wayside that day but I was one of the fortunate ones who managed to stand it & come in to camp with my regiment. We nearly perished for wauter.

We camped near Clinton. About 2 oclock on the morning of the second we resumed the march & camped near Bolton's Station. Here we stayed until the afternoon of the 5th when we marched about Six miles & bivouacked near the Big Black River expecting that night to throw a pontoon bridge across the river & cross over & attack Grants forces. I had a terrible stomach ache & went to the hospital steward Jim Bemis[2] & told him I wanted something for my pain. He told me to go to his surgeon's knapsack & I would find a bottle of Jamaca Ginger & help myself, which I did, but I got the wrong bottle in the dark & took a swallow of Iodine Tincture. Fortunately I threw it up immediately but the vomiting seemed to relieve my pain.

About three oclock we were awakened with great silence. We supposed we were to cross over the Big Black & endeaver to supprise the enemy. But soon we found that the whole Army was in full retreat & learned that we now had a foot race before us to beat a colume of Grants forces back to Jackson for we now learned that Vicksburg had fallen on July 4th. The march back to Jackson was very trying owing to the intense heat & lack of water, but we beat Grant there & immediately began entrenching.

On the morning of July 8th 1863 we sent a detail up into Jackson to press into service such negroes as could be found to relieve us in the laborious duty of entrenching. They brought back a sufficient number to use all the entrenching tools we could find so we layed around & took it easy while the negroes used the picks, spades & axes under the superintendance of our company officers.

Dave Caruth & I went bathing in Pearl river, on the banks of which the left of our regiment rested. Dave could

2 James Bemis was from Bloomfield, Kentucky. Thompson, *Orphan Brigade,* 817.

80

swim a little & I next to none but I learned a little & got out beyond my depth & into the current which was carrying me further from shore; but Dave managed to get a foot hold on a sand bar & reached out & caught me by one foot & dragged me in but his hold upon my foot threw my head under the water so that I was half drowned when he got me right end up again, but I think he saved my life for I could make no head way against that current.

The enemy appeared in our front on July the 9th. The next morning the fireing between the opposing forces was quite brisk but they made no charge upon our works. July 11th some pretty sharp fiting. The artillery being pretty active [and] the extreme right of our line being pretty hard pressed we went to Lorings[3] assistance & repulsed the ennemy.

The line of battle ran right through the yard of Col Withers, an old man, probably near 70. One of the soldiers was killed & the old gentleman buckled on the dead mans cartridge box & took his gun & began deliberately to pick off the enemy. Our boys would lie down & load & then rise to their knees & fire at the enemy, but he stood erect in plain view of them, loading & firing with deadly aim, completely ignoring our calls to him to lie down to load. He was fighting for his fire side & the fire of battle was in his eye but in a few minutes the deadly bullet felled him & he expired with the remark, "There they've got me." We repulsed this charge & burried him & the others who were killed in his yard & returned that night to our rifle pits on the extreme left.

July 12th. Fighting again brisk. Our good commisary Seargent Henry E Hughes brought to us the days cooked rations. We had hardly broken our fast before the enemy made a furious attack on our Brigade but we were fixed for them & when they were in close range we opened Capt Cobbs

---

[3] Major General W. W. Loring had commanded a division of Pemberton's army in Vicksburg. At the Battle of Baker's Creek or Champion's Hill (May 16) his division was cut off from the rest of the army, whereupon Loring led it to Jackson, where it became a part of Johnston's force. *O.R.*, Series 1, XXIV, pt. 1, pp. 38, 242.

battery on them, which to this time had been masked, & the slaughter was dreadful. We killed two hundred & fifty of them in less than a half hour.[4] They had been repulsed in every attack thus far.

July 14th. A truce has been arranged to bury the dead, [for] the stench has become terrible. All Our dead have been burried as the deaths occured, we having held our lines without fail; it is therefore their dead we are helping to bury.

July 15th. Brisk musketry & artillery fire.

July 16th. More quiet today. Some sharp shooting but no charge & only occasional artillery fire; at midnight we are ordered to fall into line & be very quiet; we soon find out we are in retreat for we cross Pearl river. Great quiet was preserved until we got across the river, when the pontoon bridge was burnt. It was important to keep the enemy in ignorance of our movements, otherwise they would have rushed upon us while we were crossing the river & caught our forces divided. Genl Johnston found they had gotten heavy reenforcements & were preparing to flank us.

Our Brigade covered the retreat in such a soldierly manner as to receive the praise of Genl Johnston. We marched 14 miles & bivouacked near Brandon Miss.

July 18th. We marched only about 10 miles as we had to stop whenever a wagon got stuck in the mund [mud] while the sappers & miners helped pry the wagon out & so get the column in line of march on the road. The day alternated between intense burning sun shine & torrents of rain. Every little gully which crossed the road was flooded until it was waist deep for us to ford & the other parts of the road nearly knee deep in mud. We went into camp by the road side while the rain was coming down in torrents. I stretched my blanket over a young pine sapling bent down, making a dog tent of it, & crawled under to sleep on the pine boughs piled

4 This was probably inflicted on General Jacob G. Lauman's division of Ord's corps, but is undoubtedly exaggerated, since Lauman's total killed in the entire siege of Jackson was only 68. He also suffered losses of 302 wounded and 149 captured or missing. *Ibid.*, pt. 2, pp. 547-48, 575.

under there (they were to keep me out of the water which saturated the ground) .

I had hardly disposed my wet carcas in these comfortable quarters when an orderly came from head quarters saying I was ordered to report at Genl Breckinridges Head Quarters. I went at once. A big marquee had been stretched for the Generals Head Qrs & in there were Genl Breckinridge & his Staff & Col Caldwell my regimental commander who said to Genl Breckinridge, "This is one of my best men; this is Johnnie Green."

Genl Breckinridge, after saying to me, "Johnnie I am glad you were not washed away to-day," turned to my cousin Cornelius Fellows & said, "Cornie is this your boy?"

There much to my surprise sat on a camp stool Cousin Cornelius Fellows, a man considerably over sixty years old. In my surprise I said, "Why cousin Cornie how came you here & what are you doing exposing yourself to hardships like this in camp?"

His reply was, "I am a volunteer aid on Genl Breckinridges staff."

To which I replied, "O cousin you cant stand exposure like this; you cant be any aid."

He indignantly & rather jocularly replied, "The hell I cant; look under that cot."

There I saw safely stored two Jugs of whiskey & a basket of Champaigne.

"Dont you call that aid?" he said.

He thereupon related to me that some time before Head Quarters was suffering to a deplorable degree from lack of *spiritial* aid & comfort & he sat down & wrote to his old friend Cuth Bullitt, whom Lincoln had appointed Collector of the port of New Orleans, saying, "Dear Cuth; You no doubt are wallowing in ease & luxury with all things good to eat & drink while John Breckinridge & I & a multitude of your other friends are barely keeping alive on Bull Beef & corn bread & are actually dying for something to drink.

"And dont you know the dear old Yankee sent me all that good stuff. There is no doubt that I saved Genl Breckinridges life. Now dont you boys know that I am the greatest aid on his Staff? Cuth Bullitt is a fine fellow. What a pity it is that he cant see that Lincoln & his crowd have violated every principal of the Constitution & it is this which has destroyed the Union.

"Well this liquor he has sent me is a life saver & we are all about to have a drink & I thought a drink would do you good so I asked the Genl to send for you."

I certainly appreciated his interest in me but declined the drink as I had never taken one except when prescribed by the Doctor.

We bivouacked here until July 28th, rain every day. We marched about 4 or 5 miles & camped in a pine forest near a fine spring. We built Arbors for quarters & arranged sleeping huts thatched with pine boughs to protect us from rain. We would live under the Arbors until the rain would run us into our huts. This was called Camp Hurricane. We stayed here some time & there being no good place to drill we were permitted to rest except for guard & police duty about camp.

A number of the boys established near the spring a regular gambling station. They had poker & keno & a few were raking in the money of many & Genl Breckinridge ordered the gambling broken up. John B. Pirtle was Provost Marshall & he raided the dens & gained for the time great unpopularity. Whenever he would pass by the Brigade the cry of "Keno" would start & follow him from one end of the line to the other, but when battle was on he was game to the bone & the boys would forget all old scores & say, "He is little but he's plucky."

Some people would bring vegetables & watermelons to sell to the soldiers. Our mess paid $40 for a good big watermelon.

Aug 21st. Still at Camp Hurricane. This day has been

appointed by Pres Davis as a day for humiliation & prayer. Our reverses at Vicksburg & at Gettysburg were severe blows, but not to our faith. Our cause is just & will surely prevail. We must have been a little too puffed up with pride & confidence in our own powers; justice may be delayed but it will come; we have enlisted for thirty years or during the war. I trust we may gain our independance in less than 30 years but if we have to fight the whole time we may remember that others have struggled that time to gain their independance. We need scarcely hope to achieve our independance in less time than our Revolutionary Fathers had to struggle for freedom from Great Britain. The boys are all of one mind. Fight on until death.

Aug 26. Left Camp Hurricane & marched to Morton, took cars on 27th at Morton, arrived at Meridian Miss at 8 P.M & changed cars for Mobile piled inside & on top of box cars. The boys who could get a place to stretch out full length on top of a car were fortunate because it is so much cooler up there than inside. It does seem strange that a fellow can lie down & go to sleep there with no danger of rolling off but we dont roll off. Arrived at Mobile Aug 28th [and] embarked on the steamer Natches. Steamed out in the bay & up the Tensas river to Tensas landing. There we took the Mobile & Montgomery RR. for Montgomery [and] arrived at Montgomery at day light.

Aug 30th 1863 Sunday. Went to Church.

Aug 31st. Took train at Montgomery this morning for West Point. Very hot. Traveled in flat cars [and] arrived at West Point about 4 P.M. Had to march across town & wait for transportation to somewhere near Chattanooga. Fished in Chattahouchee river, caught a turtle, boiled him with rice, potatoes & a piece of bacon & had a soup fit for a king. Got the cars late that night & landed at Tyners Station Sept 2nd 1863.

7 CHICKAMAUGA

In early July, Rosecrans by a series of well-planned maneuvers forced Bragg from his fortified position at Tullahoma. Bragg thereupon crossed to the south of the Tennessee River and took refuge in Chattanooga, a railroad junction of great strategic importance.

Three distinct parallel ranges, separated by narrow valleys, run in a southerly direction from the Tennessee River almost due south of Chattanooga. These ranges, from west to east, are Raccoon Mountain, Lookout Mountain, and Missionary Ridge. A fourth ridge, Pigeon Mountain, is actually a spur of Lookout Mountain, branching off twenty-five miles south of Chattanooga and running in a northerly direction almost parallel to Lookout. The region enclosed by these latter two ridges is known as McLemore's Cove, and from it the west branch of Chickamauga Creek flows north to its junction with the Tennessee eight miles above Chattanooga.

With Bragg strongly entrenched in the city, Rosecrans, rather than make a frontal attack, again determined to maneuver him out of position. To do this he had to get across Bragg's line of supply which ran southeast from Chatta-

nooga to Atlanta. *Accordingly, by September 4 he had moved his army across the Tennessee at Caperton's Ferry, thirty-five miles below Chattanooga, crossed the defiles of Raccoon Mountain into Lookout Valley, and rested his troops on the western slope of Lookout Mountain. Here he separated his three corps. Leaving Crittenden in Lookout Valley to watch Chattanooga, he sent Thomas through a pass in Lookout Mountain and into McLemore's Cove twenty-five miles south of Chattanooga, and McCook crossed at Winston's Gap twenty-four miles farther south.*

As these movements unfolded, Bragg, in order to safeguard his supply line, evacuated Chattanooga September 8, and two days later Crittenden moved in. Mistakenly concluding that Bragg's retreat was a headlong flight, Rosecrans separated his three corps by even greater distances, while Bragg lay in hiding, waiting to fall upon them one at a time and defeat Rosecrans in detail. But Bragg's reconnaissance was faulty, and although Rosecrans bared the vitals of his army again and again in a week of reckless marching and counter marching, Bragg hesitated and dissipated each opportunity.

Finally sensing his danger, Rosecrans hastily concentrated his three corps along the west bank of the Chickamauga extending from Crawfish Springs north to Kelly's Farm, a distance of about five miles.

Meanwhile Bragg was reinforced first by Breckinridge's division returned from Mississippi in early September and on the eve of the battle by Longstreet's famed corps from the Army of Northern Virginia. By September 19 he had concentrated his army along the east bank of the Chickamauga opposite Rosecrans. Bragg planned a concentration on the Union left in order to swing around that flank and gain control of the road to Chattanooga, cutting Rosecrans off from that line of retreat and from his base in case of a Confederate victory. For this purpose he moved Breckinridge from the extreme left to the extreme right of his line

87

on the night of September 19, so that Breckinridge partly overlapped the Union left.

Breckinridge was to start the assault at daybreak on the twentieth, and the attack was then to be taken up division by division from right to left. Through poor staff work, orders for the attack were not delivered until breakfast rations were being issued to the men, and so the attack did not get started until 9:30.

Thomas, who commanded the Union left, had thrown up a breastwork of logs during the night, and these were to prove an impregnable barrier to frontal assaults. The Orphan Brigade, which was the left of Breckinridge's division, struck the extreme left of Thomas' breastwork and suffered a bloody repulse. Most of Breckinridge's division, however, overlapped the Union line and thus was able to swing around to the rear, where they threatened to take Thomas in reverse. Thomas, hard pressed by Breckinridge, sent urgent pleas to Rosecrans for reinforcements.

To succor Thomas' flank Rosecrans withdrew Major General James S. Negley's division from the right and sent it to Thomas. But Negley got lost in the woods and was later found at Rossville, four miles north of Thomas, after the issue had been settled.

When no reinforcements reached him, Thomas again applied to Rosecrans for support. Rosecrans, thinking that Negley was with Thomas, concluded from these calls of distress that Bragg must be concentrating the bulk of his forces against Thomas and that there was, therefore, no danger on his own right. Acting on this belief he withdrew the divisions of Brigadier General Jefferson C. Davis and of Major General Philip H. Sheridan from the right center and ordered them to report to Thomas. In these movements faulty staff work played a fateful part, for a gap of a division's front was left in the Union right center.

Meanwhile, Longstreet had massed his entire corps in columns of brigades in the woods opposite the gap, waiting

88

for the order to attack. By coincidence the order was given precisely at the moment it would have the most effect. John B. Hood's division was in front, and as it poured through the gap in the Union line, it instinctively turned to the right and ran upon the rear of Davis' division en route to Thomas. This division was broken and fled in panic, carrying its panic in turn to Sheridan's division, which it was following. Down the Union right Longstreet's victorious corps dashed, sweeping everything before it. McCook's and Crittenden's Union corps were hopelessly broken and isolated. They fled in panic down the road to Chattanooga, carrying Rosecrans with them, for he, too, concluded that the day was lost.

But Thomas, ignorant of the collapse on the Union right, had bent his two flanks back along a horseshoe-shaped ridge. To him rallied such remnants of the broken corps of Crittenden and McCook as could make their way to him. Here Thomas battled valiantly throughout the long afternoon, repulsing the entire Confederate army, which now concentrated its fury on him. Finally nightfall came, and under its protection Thomas retreated in order to Chattanooga, having earned that day a new title, The Rock of Chickamauga.

After the brilliant initial victory, Bragg's subordinates, notably Longstreet and Nathan Bedford Forrest, urged him to pursue the fleeing enemy at once. Such a pursuit could have annihilated the two corps in flight and would have cut off Thomas from his line of retreat into Chattanooga, leaving him no alternative but surrender. But Bragg, who stubbornly refused to recognize the extent of his victory, would not permit his troops to follow the fleeing enemy in the approaching night. Instead he permitted the Union army to reach and entrench itself in Chattanooga, thereby committing perhaps the supreme blunder of his ill-fated career as a commander.

$\mathcal{T}$HE BRIGADE camped in a woods near Tyners station. Rations very scarce & very poor [with] the coarsest kind of meal which seemed to have been ground in a cob crusher, for actually a good deal of the cob was ground up in the meal, & the poorest kind of blue beef. This is beef packed in barrels of brine & shipped up to us, and is certainly very poor eating.

Some of the boys killed some hogs in the neighborhood, and as the citizens had hard times to feed their families many complaints were made to head Quarters about the lost hogs. Lieutenant Buchanan[1] was officer of the day & was instructed to examine every mess just at breakfast time & see if he could find any fresh hog meat & report the offender if he found any; but he had too much sympathy for the poor half starved boys to report them. He found in one mess a nice roasted ham & in an other spare ribs & all through the regiment fresh hog meat in unmistakeable form but he invariably pronounced it beef just drawn from the commisary. The boys in my mess had their share but as I would not help steal the hog I would not eat the stolen meat, but when Dave Caruth cooked our rations of sweet potatoes which we were fortunate enough to get that day in the skilit with the stolen

1 Sam H. Buchanan of Louisville.

hog meat I would not let them beat me out of my share of the potatoes with the argument that it was no worse to eat the Devil than to drink his broth & that was what I was doing, Dave said, to eat my potatoes which had been cooked with the gravy of the stolen hog. This however was drawing too fine a moral point for my appetite.

We thought we were to go into winter quarters here & having no tents we built a hut. Booker Reed[2] who was at this time in our mess dug a cellar in our hut big enough to store away any luckless hog that might be captured by any of the mess. Our beds were made of straw laid down on the floor & his cellar was covered over & the bed spread over it. We found a deserted house & took the boards off that roof to cover our cabin. They were not nailed on & when we go away if the owner wants them he is welcome to come & get them. At any rate we are in greater need of them now than he is for he is either dead or gone away.

Before day light Sept 10th we received orders to hurry to Stevens Gap & attack Genl Thomas' corps which was detached from the Union army & so far from support that it was thought we could whip & perhaps capture them before any help could reach them.[3] We had our long march for nothing however; Genl Thomas became aware of his exposed position & got away before we got there.

Genls Bragg & Rosecranz [Rosecrans] seem to be playing a game of chess among these mountains & valleys. On the 12th we chased down to LaFayette starting about day light & then turned around & marched all night towards Ring[g]old, then slept half the day & moved a few miles in the afternoon, formed line of battle on the side of a mountain overlooking

2 P. Booker Reed of Louisville fought with the Brigade at Shiloh, but was then temporarily assigned to Morgan's Cavalry. He returned to the Brigade in time to fight at Jackson and all other engagements. After the war he was a successful businessman and mayor of Louisville. Thompson, *Orphan Brigade*, 822, 1055.

3 Thomas' corps was indeed isolated from the rest of the Union army and should have fallen a helpless victim to an aggressive movement by Bragg. Bragg's performance here, as elsewhere, left much to be desired. Horn, *The Army of Tennessee*, 249; *O. R.*, Series 1, XXX, pt. 2, pp. 26-31.

the road expecting to surprise Crittendens corps[4] if they retreated from an attack to be made by Polks corps. Genl Polk, however, was a little slow & Crittenden slipped away through an other gap in the mountains. We remained in line of battle all night; the sun was quite hot in the day but the night was really cold.

On the 17th we marched towards Lee & Gordons Mill on the look out all day for the enemy. Cavalry skirmishing & cannonading. On the 18th we moved towards Glass Mill [and] began skirmishing. Early next morning Sept 19th 1863 we were moved across the creek closer to the enemy & placed in position to support our battery which was hotly engage[d] in a duel with two yankee batterys & threatened with attack from Beattys[5] & Stanleys[6] brigades. They were out of reach of our muskets so we were ordered to lie down & wait for them to come closer. The enemys shells played great havoc in our ranks. One shell killed one man next on my left & the man on the other side of me & their next shell killed one of the battery horses & wounded three of our men; but Cobb fought them gallantly & dismounted one of their guns & put them out of business to such an extent that they withdrew their remaining guns & left us. We were ordered to another part of the field where the fighting was fierce. This was about three miles south of Lee & Gordons Mill. While in the fight at Glass Mill Genl Breckinridge recd an order to hurry us to this second position south of Lee & Gordons Mill

4 Major General Thomas L. Crittenden commanded the Twenty-First Corps of the Union army. Crittenden was the son of United States Senator John J. Crittenden of Kentucky and the brother of Major General George B. Crittenden of the Confederate States Army. On September 11 Bragg had ordered Polk to fall upon Crittenden's corps at Peavine Church. Crittenden was not at that location, having moved the preceding night to Lee and Gordon's Mill. Even here, however, Crittenden was isolated and was extremely vulnerable to any energetic attack by Polk, who along with Bragg failed to take advantage of a great opportunity. Horn, *The Army of Tennessee,* 253-54; *O.R.,* Series 1, XXX, pt. 1, p. 604; pt. 2, pp. 30-31, 44-45.

5 Brigadier General Samuel Beatty, commanding the First Brigade, Third Division, 21st Army Corps. *O.R.,* XXX, pt. 1, pp. 808-809.

6 This was Colonel Timothy R. Stanley of the Eighteenth Ohio Infantry, who commanded the 2nd Brigade, 2nd Division, 14th Army Corps. *Ibid.,* 379.

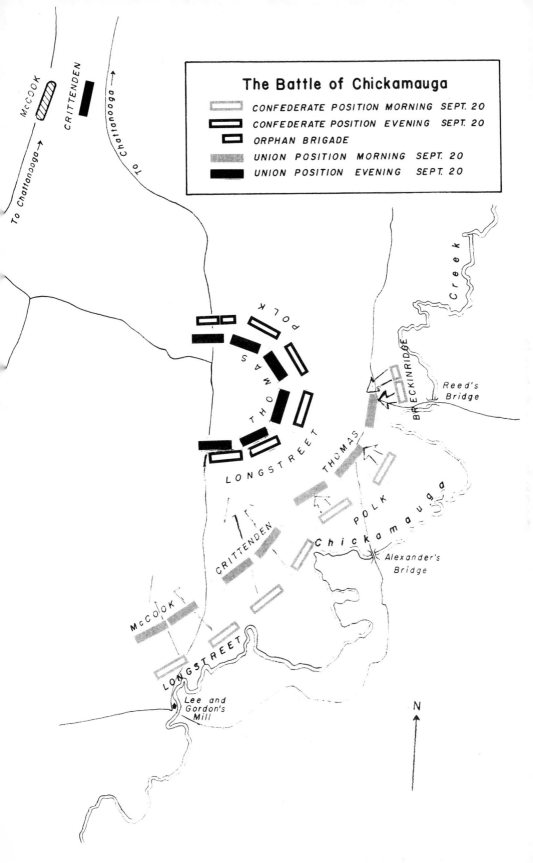

The Battle of Chickamauga

- CONFEDERATE POSITION MORNING SEPT. 20
- CONFEDERATE POSITION EVENING SEPT. 20
- ORPHAN BRIGADE
- UNION POSITION MORNING SEPT. 20
- UNION POSITION EVENING SEPT. 20

McCOOK

CRITTENDEN

To Chattanooga →

To Chattanooga →

To Chattanooga

POLK

THOMAS

THOMAS

LONGSTREET

BRECKINRIDGE

Reed's Bridge

Creek

THOMAS

POLK

Chickamauga

Alexander's Bridge

CRITTENDEN

McCOOK

LONGSTREET

Lee and Gordon's Mill

N

but we could not withdraw until we drove the enemy away, which we did, & hurried to the point indicated.

From this point we advanced to Lee & Gordons Mill to relieve Genl Patton Anderson[7] who was desperately pressed. Our arrival here turned the tide of battle in favor of Genl Anderson & we were almost immediately ordered to move further down the Chic[k]amauga, cross over, & occupy a position to be indicated by an officer of Genl Polks staff. We marched about four miles & crossed the Chicamauga at Alexanders Bridge. Here we bivouacked in line of battle with our arms in our hands about 11 oclock at night. The moon had gone down but the heavens were studded with stars. The terrific roar of artillery had ceased, the continuous roll of musketry was hushed, no sound was heard save the groans of the wounded & the wheels of the Ambulances & the sullen rumble of the artillery wheels as the batteries were moving into position to do their deadly work on the morrow. The night was very chilly but no fires were allowed as both armies lay in sight of each other exhausted from the sanguinary struggle of the day trying to regain their breath, as it were, for the death struggle as soon as day should dawn. It is the only time in the war that I thought I had a presentiment, but fatigued & worn as I was, I did not drop off immediately to sleep; I knew the next day would bring us into one of the bloodiest battles the world had ever witnessed. I remembered that the men at my elbow on each side of me had both been killed by the same shot & that many of my friends had met their death that day & I could not shake off the conviction that I would meet my death in the next days battle. I offered up a prayer that the Lord would guide me & strengthen me & that when death came to me it would find me gallantly doing my duty, that my first desire should be not that I might escape death but that my death should help the cause of right to triumph.

[7] Brigadier General Patton Anderson commanded a brigade in Hindman's division of Polk's corps. *Ibid.*, pt. 2, p. 314.

I soon dropped off to sleep & did not wake until day when we were all ordered to fall in line of battle. We had no breakfast. The canteens were all filled from Chicamauga river & we were moved forward & to the right of our line of battle when orders came from Genl Leonidas Polk to move forward & attack the enemy. Just then our commissary came up with our rations & Genl Hill[8] ordered that we throw out skirmishers & eat our rations before making the attack.[9] Lt Colonel Wickliffe was placed in command of the skirmish line & we halted long enough to eat & then we were ordered to wait for the line on our left to get in position.[10] Finally at about 9-30 the order was given to advance & attack the enemy. Soon we were up with our skirmish line. They fell into their position with the regiment & the fighting began. We were in range of the enemys small arms, [and] the artilery was sending a regular hail of shot & shell at us. We had been ordered to reserve our fire until we were in close range. A perfect shower of grape shot tore through our ranks. The enemy were pouring a voley of minnie balls upon us; we fired a volley & rushed upon them; they were posted behind breast works made of longs [logs] & there was

[8] Lieutenant General Daniel Harvey Hill had gained fame as a division commander in Lee's Army of Northern Virginia. In July, 1863, he was sent to Bragg's army in Chattanooga to command Hardee's corps, Hardee having been temporarily sent to Mississippi. He thus commanded the corps to which the Orphan Brigade belonged and led them in the battle of Chickamauga. *Battles and Leaders,* III, 638-39.

[9] Bragg had given Polk, who commanded the right wing of the army, orders to attack at dawn. About midnight on September 19-20 Polk had sent orders to Hill, who commanded Cleburne's and Breckinridge's divisions, but Hill could not be found and the order was not delivered. After daylight Bragg sent to Polk to learn why the attack had not begun. Polk then sent orders direct to Breckinridge and Cleburne, but Hill, who by that time had come up, instructed them to delay until the men were breakfasted. Thus the attack was not begun for several hours after the time planned. After the battle Bragg charged that this delay deprived him of the fruits of victory, since night fell and he could not pursue the fleeing enemy. He removed Polk from command and preferred charges against him, but the charges were dismissed by President Jefferson Davis and Polk was given command elsewhere. *O.R.,* Series 1, XXX, pt. 2, pp. 35, 47, 52, 53, 55-70.

[10] Actually the line was in position, but Hill mistook a line formed by a supporting brigade on his left as the line of battle and delayed action further under this misapprehension. *Ibid.,* 47.

so much undergrowth in the woods we were charging through that our artillery could not get in position to fire upon them.

On the left of our line[11] the Confederate forces had not come up, so the enemy to our left poured their fire into us as did those directly in our front. We would load our guns as we advanced & fire but our men were falling fast. Capt John H Weller[12] was shot just under the eye & the ball came out just behind the ear. Every one thought the wound must soon take him out of this life & he thought so too & called out to his men (as he lay ebbing out his lifes blood as all supposed) "Forward men, tell my friends I died bravely doing my duty."

About this time it seemed to me a bushel of grape shot from a battery just in front of us came pouring down upon me, cutting down the bushes & tearing up the ground all around. I was running towards the enemy, as was our whole line, [when] a grape shot struck me in the groin; it in some manner whirled me clear around & threw me flat of my back. I thought my entire leg was torn off, but I looked down & saw my leg was not gone. I felt with my hands & found no blood, but there was a grape shot in my pocket. It had force enough to tear through my pants, but struck the steel clasp of a pocket book which I had in the pocket of my pants & this stopped it. The clasp was doubled around the ball. I found I could limp along & soon caught up with the regiment which was now within thirty yards of the enemy's breast works giving & taking death blows which could last but a few minutes without utter annihilation. To rush upon them with our decimated ranks would mean to rush into sure captivity for they had at this point two men to our one.

---

11 Not the left of the entire army but the left of the right wing. *Ibid.*, 199.

12 John H. Weller was born in Larue County and was reared in Louisville. He joined the Orphan Brigade at its formation, was elected first lieutenant, and was promoted to captain in December, 1862. He participated in every engagement in which the Brigade took part and was twice wounded. After the war he returned to Louisville, where he was active in business and local politics. Thompson, *Orphan Brigade*, 487-91.

Here it was that Major Hewett[13] was killed, & the gallant Rice Graves[14] offered up his life upon the altar of his country's liberties at this point. Capt Pete Daniels,[15] than whom no braver soldier ever lived, fell at the head of his Company within a few yards of the enemy's works & Our Beloved & Gallant Genl Helm here fell mortally wounded leading his brigade, which he knew would never falter but at his command would dare & do whatever mortal man could accomplish. But besides the Field & General officers named who had been killed, in our regiment alone we lost right here One Hundred men killed and wounded. Col Caldwell was so desperately wounded he had to be taken from the field & we must reform our line, so the retreat was sounded & we fell back about 200 yards over a little hill where we could reform out of range of most of the enemys infantry fire, & plans could be perfected for a concerted & more desperate charge.

We went into this charge with only two hundred & fifty men & now one hundred of that number had been killed or wounded.[16] The enemy held great advantage over us as they were protected by heavy logs piled up & they had batteries posted which wrought great havoc in our ranks, while the underbrush, the timber & formation of the ground prevented our batteries from giving as much assistance as usual. But our line was soon again formed & being ordered to lie down so as to be a less prominent mark for the enemy we laid down to await the plans of our generals.

[13] James W. Hewitt was at this time a lieutenant colonel, having been promoted after the battle of Hartsville, December, 1862. He was the son of a wealthy cotton factor and commission merchant in Louisville. Thompson, 438-40.

[14] Rice E. Graves was commander of a famous battery which bore his name. He had been a member of the Brigade since its founding and had distinguished himself in every engagement. Thompson, 860.

[15] Peter V. Daniel of Hardinsburg was elected first lieutenant in September, 1861, and was promoted to captain in February, 1863. He had fought in all engagements of the Brigade thus far. Thompson, 837.

[16] The Ninth Regiment entered the battle on September 20 two hundred and thirty strong. Its casualties were 102. *O.R.*, Series 1, XXX, pt. 2, p. 214.

96

While waiting I took several of the canteens of my comrads & went back about one half a mile to refill them. The fireing on our part of the line had quieted down, but just as I got to the spring the yankie batteries broke loose with a terrific cannonading & the spring was the target that most of their guns seemed to be trained upon. It was any thing but a comfortable experience to fill those canteens, with a wicked shell every minute cutting off a limb just above your head or plowing in the ground just behind you or exploding almost in your face. I was never more relieved of an uncomfortable feeling than when I got back to the regiment with my full canteens, for while shells & minnie balls were flying thick over their heads, I felt if I was shot here every body would know I was at my post of duty.

Reinforcements were now brought up & Genls Gist & Ector[17] with their two brigades advanced against the breast works which we had unsuccesfully assaulted. They soon found that they could not move the enemy, who had reinforced this position which was already defended by two lines of battle behind breast works. They halted & we were then ordered up & passed over them as they laid down. We rushed against the enemy but their batteries had full play upon us, while our batteries could not fire for fear of fireing into our own line. Their several lines of infantry poured volley after volley into us & again we were forced to retire.

We fell back to about the same point we had previously taken to reform & when our lines were again mended Genl Breckinridge & Genl Cheatham & Genl Polk rode along our front & stopped to tell us that Longstreet & Buckner were driving the Yankees before them on our left. Genl Cheat-[h]am said, "Now boys soon you will up & at 'em & give em Hell." Genl Polk, who commanded our wing of the army,

17 Brigadier General States Rights Gist, commanding Walker's division, had just arrived from Rome, Georgia, and was thrown into the battle at this point. Brigadier General Matthew D. Ector commanded a brigade in Walker's division. *Ibid.*, 245-46.

97

said, "Boys! You are going at them again. Now when the command forward is given, go at them & give what Cheatham said."[18] Genl Breckinridge now called us to attention, told us to fix bayonetts, hold our fire, rush upon them until within ten yards of them, then fire & rushing on them give them the bayonett.

The very air soon became full of shot & shell. Here Flying cloud[19] (our Mohawk Indian Chief), who enlisted in Co H of our regiment, had the half of his face shot away & Mick Clary[20] (for that was the only name by which he was known in the regiment) was fatally shot in the forhead with a minnie ball & Jim Hunter,[21] the wit of the regiment, was shot through the heart. Dick Taylor[22] was shot on top of the enemies breast works. John Fightmaster,[23] Nat Hedger[24] & Benj F. Butler[25] were all killed almost at my elbow & here Norborne Gray,[26] Lute Collins,[27] Lieutenant Wagoner,[28] Thos Ellis, Jim Ford,[29] Jim Yonts[30] & many others were wounded.

The struggle was to the death but our bayonetts were

18 Polk was, of course, a bishop in the Episcopal Church.

19 Konshattountychette, or Flying Cloud, was a Mohawk chief who became attached to the Brigade in November, 1862, and remained with it throughout the war. Thompson, *Orphan Brigade*, 853.

20 John B. Cleary was from Harrison County. Thompson, 832.

21 James Hunter of Bardstown. Thompson, 820.

22 Robert K. Taylor, a native of Scotland. Thompson, 847.

23 John Fightmaster of Harrison County. Thompson, 833.

24 N. F. Hedges of Harrison County. Thompson, 833.

25 Benjamin F. Butler of Logan County. Thompson, 809.

26 Norborne G. Gray of Louisville enlisted in the Brigade in November, 1862. He fought at Hartsville, Stone's River, Jackson, and Chickamauga. He was appointed second lieutenant for his gallant conduct at Chickamauga, but a wound he received there kept him from active service thereafter. Thompson, 819.

27 J. L. Collins of Hartford fought in every engagement the Brigade participated in. He was wounded at Shiloh, at Baton Rouge, and at Chickamauga. He was awarded a medal for gallant conduct at Stone's River. Thompson, 825-26.

28 Leslie Waggoner of Russellville was badly wounded at Shiloh and was discharged as disabled. He recovered and re-enlisted, and was elected second lieutenant in November, 1862. He fought in every engagement thereafter. Thompson, 815.

29 James W. Ford of Hartford fought in all the engagements of the Brigade. He was elected second lieutenant in March, 1864. Thompson, 825.

30 James W. Yountz of Paradise. Thompson, 826.

fixed & our onslaught was irresistable. Cleyburn[31] had carried their works on our left & their line broke & fled precipitately; many seeing escape was impossible surrendered. We persued the others about half a mile & shot down many as they ran.

Night was now on us; we had captured many of their cannon (all that were in the front of our division) & we were ordered to take rest with our accoutrements on & our arms in our hands. We were so inspirited & elated over our victory that we wanted to press right on for it was one of the most beautiful moon light nights I ever beheld. Certain it was "the pale moon rose up slowly & calmly she looked down on the red sands of the battle field with bloody corses strewn." But our Generals thought it best not to persue the flying foe,[32] as they had fled to the woods & the ground was not familiar to us.

We had gained a complete & glorious victory & we boys in the trenches upon waking the next morning supposed we would press right on & capture all of Rosencranz [Rosecrans'] army who had not already made good their escape across the river. But nothing was done but to issue to us rations & have details made to bury the dead & others to gather up the arms off the battlefield which had been dropped by the killed, wounded & prisoners. Here we loitered until Sept 22nd. In the afternoon of this day we marched to within five miles of Chattanooga.

On the 23d we marched over Mission Ridge & down in the valley approaching near to Chattanooga. The yankees had been hard at work repairing & enlarging the breastwords

[31] Major General Patrick R. Cleburne commanded a division in Hill's (Hardee's) corps. It was on the immediate left of Breckinridge's division on September 20 and fought valiantly. Cleburne was an unusually capable and aggressive officer.

[32] It was indeed a "flying foe." Charles A. Dana, Assistant Secretary of War, who was with the Union army at Chickamauga, reported that night to his chief, "The lines of Sheridan and Davis broke in disorder, borne down by immense columns of enemy. . . . Before them our soldiers turned and fled. It was wholesale panic. Vain were all attempts to rally them." *O.R.*, Series 1, XXX, pt. 1, pp. 192-93.

here. We thought surely we were to assault the ennemy behind his works, but night was approaching & we were ordered
to throw out a line of picketts & bivouack in line of battle.[33]

[33] For his dilatory and indecisive tactics after Chickamauga, Bragg was
severely criticized by the generals of his army, who signed a round-robin
letter to Jefferson Davis asking that Bragg be replaced as commander of the
army. *Ibid.*, 65-68. See also, *ibid.*, pt. 4, pp. 705-706, 728.

100

8 CHATTANOOGA

After his defeat at Chickamauga, Rosecrans had retreated to Chattanooga, where he was besieged by Bragg. The Confederate lines extended from the northern tip of Missionary Ridge, a steep and rugged mountain to the east of the city, south to Rossville at a pass through the ridge. Thence the line turned west across Chattanooga Valley to Lookout Mountain, another rugged peak south of Chattanooga which rose abruptly from the river bank opposite Moccasin Bend. The Confederates thus had encircled Chattanooga on the east, south, and southwest, and controlled Rosecrans' most accessible line of supply along the lower Tennessee from Bridgeport, the terminus of the railroad from Nashville. This forced Rosecrans to transport his supplies by wagon sixty or seventy miles over miserable mountain roads with starving draught animals.

The Union army was in a precarious situation when on October 19 Rosecrans was replaced by Thomas, and then Grant, who had been appointed commander of the newly created Department of the Mississippi, moved his headquarters to Chattanooga and assumed active charge of opera-

tions. Immediately Grant ordered Sherman up from Mississippi with his Army of the Tennessee. Meanwhile, General Joseph Hooker had been sent from the Army of the Potomac with two corps and had arrived at Bridgeport in early October. From there on Grant's orders he had marched down Lookout Valley west of Lookout Mountain and seized Brown's Ferry, a few miles below Chattanooga. Grant was now able to establish a steamboat line from Bridgeport to Brown's Ferry, thus removing the threat of starvation.

While Grant was shortening his line of supply and bringing up reinforcements under Sherman and Hooker, Bragg was doing worse than nothing. He was dividing his strength by sending Longstreet with his corps and part of Buckner's to drive Burnside out of Knoxville. Possibly his willingness to diminish his own strength at this critical juncture was influenced by his desire to rid himself of Longstreet, who had been brutally frank in his criticism of Bragg's incapacity for command.

When Sherman arrived at Brown's Ferry on November 20, Grant had him cross to the north of the river there and march under the cover of the hills to a point on the river opposite the northern tip of Missionary Ridge. From here on the morning of the twenty-fourth Sherman crossed the river again and launched an attack on Bragg's right flank.

At the opposite end of the Union line, Hooker at the same time attacked Lookout Mountain. Hooker's attack was supposed to be a diversion, but succeeding beyond expectations swept the Confederate force from Lookout, and by evening Hooker had rounded the tip of the mountain, had occupied Chattanooga Valley, and was in a position to threaten the Confederate left now withdrawn to Missionary Ridge in the vicinity of Rossville.

Bragg's forces were now all concentrated on Missionary Ridge east of Chattanooga in a strong position, and the Union army was arrayed in the valley to the west. Command of the Confederate army was subdivided, with Hardee

102

on the right and Breckinridge on the left. The Union left was commanded by Sherman, the center by Thomas, and the right by Hooker.

It had been Grant's plan to have the main blows struck by Sherman on the left and Hooker on the right. But after a brilliant beginning both those commanders were bogged down as a result of stout Confederate resistance and their own unfamiliarity with the terrain. Disturbed by the failure of his two flank movements to make headway by mid-afternoon of the twenty-fifth, Grant ordered Thomas to make a diversionary movement on the center, but cautioned him not to move beyond the base of the ridge without special orders. Thomas' men moved out and took the first line of Confederate entrenchments at the base. Then without orders and in the face of a galling fire from the crest they ascended the ridge and threw the Confederate left-center into panicked confusion. But let Johnny Green take up the story and tell it as he saw it.

ON THE MORNING of the 24th [of September] we thought we surely now would move against the enemys works & as their position was a strong one we pittied ourselves that we had not pressed upon them the day after the drubbing we gave them at Chic[k]amauga. It was after noon however before we were finally called to attention; the hour apparently had arrived for action; but instead of being ordered forward to attack the enemy we were ordered to fall back to the foot of Mission ridge. Here we attempted to build breast works, but the ground was so full of big unmovable rocks that we could construck nothing but very poor defenses.

Here however we bivouacked in line of battle until Oct 21st 63. The weather was bleak, chilly & for the most of the time very rainy. We frequently had the most dense fogs one could conceive off; they would seem to originate at the Tennessee river & then come rolling along the valley & up the mountainside like a moving mountain & it seemed to approach as fast as a man could walk; when it reached us you could not even see a horse twenty feet away; indeed you could not tell at that distance that there was any object there & it occurred so often that I wondered that the yankees did not come at us along with the fog, for in this way they could get right upon us before we would know it unless the noise of their coming should betray them.

Our rations were nothing but beef pickeled in a very strong brine & corn bread & our supply of this was so meager that we actually suffered from the pangs of hunger. I have actually gone where the officers horses were fed & picked the grains of corn out of the dirt where left by the horses, washed it & parched & ate it with great relish.

When the fog was not hanging over us we could look down upon the enemy & see them plainly; indeed our long range cannon could reach them easily but we shelled them seldom because it could not effect any real good while the battle was not on.

To live out doors in this bleak rainy weather with insufficient food & no shelter put our patriotism to the test but we made a joke of it & professed to enjoy it; really this made it much easier to endure. On Oct 21st we were withdrawn from Mission ridge & marched about ten miles to Tyners station & were permitted to go into camp. We were brought here to guard commissary & quartermaster stores & to protect the rear of our army, as the Yankees were now beginning to show considerable activity; but all except the daily details on guard set to work to build huts with chimneys to them & to make ourselves very comfortable.

Our army was accumulating large Commissary & Quartermaster supplies at Tyners Station & also at Chic[k]amauga station & we had heavy guard duty to protect them & to keep watch in our rear to see that no raiding Yankees threatened our base of supplies. Some Alabama troops shared this duty with us. They were almost daily cheered & comforted by boxes received from their homes; but every body was not so fortunate as to receive these marks of loving remembrance & the pangs of hunger & want caused some to develope a willingness to help themselves to whatever they could find not closely guarded.

One night some of our Kentucky boys who permitted

their desires to obscure their moral perception slipped
through the guards & stole a box of very munificent appearance which they found in tempting position at the RR.
depot; but they were perplexed as to how they could carry it
off as it was too heavy for the two of them to carry it further.
The Alabama boys were on guard & our fellows bargained
with one of these boys who had just been relieved from duty
that if he would help carry it down into the woods they would
divide with him. It proved to be a rich haul indeed, three
hams, delicious pickels & preserves, nice warm wollen socks,
two coats, a pair of shoes, & various other good things. The
Ky boys each took a coat & as the shoes just fit Alabama they
said, "Here Yellowhammer you may have the shoes."

The socks & other things were pretty fairly divided but
finally they came to a letter at the bottom of the box & Kentucky said, "Yellow hammer as we sort of got you in the
division of coats & socks you may have the letter."

He threw some fresh wood on the fire to make a good
light to read the letter by while the other two stretched themselves to rest awhile. Alabama soon grew serious & he turned
to the end of the letter to read the name when he exclaimed,
"Look here boys, dern my fool skin! This box is from my
mother, sent to me. Now look here, youens aint going to
keep my things is you?"

But the Kentuckians told him they were surprised at
him. "Did'nt we keep our bargain with you & divide fair?
Surely you aint going to back out on your bargain when we
acted so fair with you. Why look here, there are two of us
to your one, [and] we need not have given you any of the
things if we had not been gentlemen of our word."

He replied, "Now look here boys, these things all belong
to me & youens aint got no right to em."

But the only compromise he could get out of them was
to give him back the two coats. They said that after a Yellowhammer's trying to go back on a bargain like he had done

106

they would not wear an old Coperas Jeans coat for fear they would run away from the next battle they went into.

They do tell that the next night this same Yellowhammer tried his hand at stealing a box. He had to get some help to carry off his prize but when the box was opened it proved to be a dead soldier who was to be Shipped home for burial.

The guard duty here was very heavy & the weather very disagreeable. Col Lewis here received his commission as Brigadier-General & was assigned to permanent command of our Brigade. He is a brave, kind man but we feel that no one can fill our Ben Hardin Helm's place. Sam Buchannan has been made Capt & Adjt & Inspector Genl of our Brigade. Every body is so devoted to Capt Fayette Hewett[1] that we hope both he & Capt Buchannan will continue with our command. I will here state they both served to the day of surrender on Genl Lewis' staff & every boy & officer in the command loved & admired them.

On the night of the 22nd[2] of Nov we marched back to Missionary ridge & took our position in line of battle close to the same point we occupied before we moved back to the rear.

The enemy are making active preparation to attack us & we begin to try with the very poor tools we have to construck rifle pits, but being on almost a solid rock we can do but little in the way of building defences. The ascent is so

1 Fayette Hewitt was born in Hardin County, Kentucky, the son of a schoolteacher. He was a clerk in the United States Post Office Department at the outbreak of the war. He resigned at once, and after serving briefly in the Confederate States Postal Department, he entered the army in December, 1861. After a year in the Trans-Mississippi Department, he was transferred to the Orphan Brigade in February, 1863, and commissioned captain on the staff of General Helm. He fought with the Brigade in all engagements after that date. After the war he practiced law for a time in Elizabethtown and served as state auditor from 1880 until 1889, when he resigned to accept the presidency of the State National Bank of Frankfort. Thompson, *Orphan Brigade,* 474-79.

2 The Orphan Brigade was first moved on November 23 from Chickamauga Station to a position at the base of the western slope of Missionary Ridge in the left center of the Confederate line. They were not engaged during the twenty-fourth, but at night were moved back to the crest of the Ridge. *O.R.,* Series 1, XXXI, pt. 2, p. 739.

steep however that we feel we can kill all they send after us, notwithstanding our line is so thin that we are two yards apart.

On the 23d Genl Grant learned from a deserter[3] from the Confederate army that Buckner's Division had been sent to Knoxville & he thought Bragg was evacuating & thereupon ordered Thomas to advance, which he did; we had a sharp fight with him & he drove our troops from Orchard knob. Our brigade had a beautiful view of this fight, but it did seem useless to sacrifice any men there for it was really only one of our outposts. After our troops there were driven back by force of numbers they fell back & Joined our main line & fighting ceased for the day.

I took the cantee[n]s of four of our boys & went back down the hill to find some water to drink. Down near the foot of the hill I came upon a log cabin & I heard a moan inside. I looked in & saw a sick soldier lying on a bunk. I said, "Friend what are you doing here all alone?"

He replied, "I have small pox & my nurse has gone after rations and I am *so* thirsty."

I saw his canteen lying beside him & said, "Have you no water in your canteen?"

He said no; I took his canteen & said, "You tell me where the Spring is & I will fill your canteen as well as my own." He directed me to a point a short distance down the hollow & I filled all the cantee[n]s & brought his to him & gave him a drink. He seemed to me to be broken out with some eruption. I asked him if his nurse would be back soon & he

---

[3] Grant in his official report stated that a Confederate deserter came into the Union lines on the twenty-second and reported Bragg was falling back. Grant believed the deserter was honestly mistaken, but Bragg has been credited with making "exceptionally good use of propaganda spread by carefully coached 'deserters' who sifted into the Federal lines with high-class cock-and-bull stories" (Horn, *The Army of Tennessee*, 248; *O.R.*, Series 1, XXX, pt. 2, p. 32). Grant does not state that the spy told him that Buckner had been sent to Knoxville, but on the contrary states that this fact was not learned until later. He ordered Thomas to drive in the Confederate pickets in order to test the accuracy of the deserter's report that Bragg was retreating. *Ibid.*, 33.

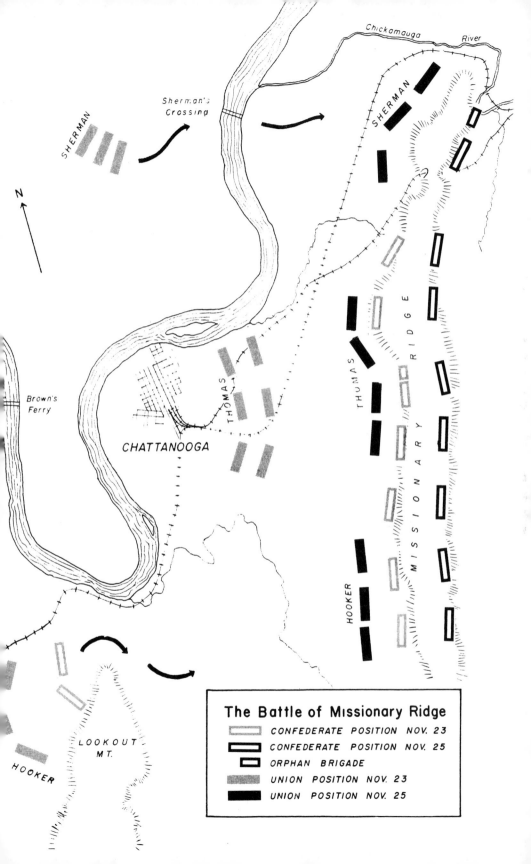

Chickamauga River

SHERMAN

Sherman's Crossing

SHERMAN

N

THOMAS

RIDGE

Brown's Ferry

THOMAS

CHATTANOOGA

MISSIONARY

HOOKER

HOOKER

LOOKOUT MT.

The Battle of Missionary Ridge

CONFEDERATE POSITION NOV. 23
CONFEDERATE POSITION NOV. 25
ORPHAN BRIGADE
UNION POSITION NOV. 23
UNION POSITION NOV. 25

replied that he would. I wished to know how long he had been sick [and] he said about ten days. He repeated, "You know I have the small pox."

This information did not give me any real peace of mind & I thought if there was no duty calling for my continued presence at this humble cabin that I might be able to make myself useful elsewhere & I at once said to him, "If there is nothing else I can do for you I will go," & I went.

During the battles of the next few days there was one consoling thought. I knew if I should be killed on the field I would not have to suffer the pain of small pox. But as I was not killed I may have small pox yet, but I dont expect ever again to have as good a chance to get it.

Nov 24th 1863. The yanks have begun the attack in earnest over on lookout mountain. The rocks & the under brush & the broken country prevent our seeing the line of troops on either side. We see them here & there & we trace them by the smoke of their guns; they fought nearly all day without seeming to move our boys until nearly night. Then a colum of yankies came up the Tennessee river & got on our general Walthals[4] flank & forced our boys to fall back, higher up the mountain; the fighting continued until late in the night (up to about 10 Oclock). The flash of the guns made a beautiful sight but it saddened us to see the yankees had gotten so high up the mountain side.

Our part of the line was not engaged except [from] the long range batteries which sent frequent shells at us doing but little damage.

To-night it is discovered that the Yanks have gotten possession of the road coming in the rear of Look out moun-

4 Brigadier General Edward Cary Walthall of Mississippi commanded a brigade which was stationed on the western slope of Lookout Mountain. It was driven from this position by Hooker's advance of November 24. Slowly withdrawing around the northern slope of Lookout, Walthall was unable, in an all-day engagement, to stem the Union advance. That night he took position on Missionary Ridge and participated in the battle there next day. *O.R.*, XXXI, pt. 2, pp. 692-97.

109

tain so we evacuated Look out mountain this night the 24th of Nov 1863.

We laid down in line of battle & slept until about 2 Oclock. We were then ordered to fall in & we thought we were to make a night attack upon the yanks. It was a beautiful night, the stars in myriads were shining above, the atmosphere was clear & crisp & very chilly, the enemies camp fires in the valley below were almost as numerous as the stars above but not a gun was heard & the sleeping valley seemed a picture of peace instead of the valley of death.

We took up the line of march after first being ordered to load our guns; quick step was ordered & we were hurried along for about two miles where we reached the extreme right of our line of battle. Genl Sherman had been ordered to occupy a position here so as to attack us in the flank but Genl Brag[g] discovered from his movements that this was his purpose & hurried us to this point in advance of him. So on the morning of the 25th when his troops advanced against this point we met them with a deadly volley & after a short sharp fight they withdrew out of sight & we did not persue, as our duty was to hold this point to prevent the enemy from flanking our line of battle on the right.[5] The battle raged all along the crest of Missionary ridge from day light until sun down. Cleyburn [Cleburne] occupied the ridge just above us & occasionally I would go up to their line. They had swept their front clean of Yankies; indeed, when I went up about sun down the side of the ridge in their front was strewn with dead yankies & looked like a lot of boys had been sliding down the hill side, for when a line of the enemy would be repulsed they would start down hill & soon the whole line would be rolling down like a ball, it was so steep a hill side just there.

---

[5] Green's narration would indicate that Sherman's attack on the right flank was begun on November 25. Actually Sherman had moved his three divisions across the Tennessee during the night and morning of November 23-24, and had launched a full scale attack in the afternoon of November 24. *Ibid.*, 572-73.

At our part of the line we thought the battle had all gone our way, but soon we were ordered to fall in & we took up the line of march to the rear & then we learned that the effort to flank our line on the left had been more successful than the effort made on our end of the line.[6] The enemy had sent a strong force to attack our extreme left at the gap at Rossville about six miles distant. Our small force there was soon over come & then the enemy came along the ridge on our left flank & at the same time attacked our thin line (the men being two yards apart) in front. Thus they broke our line in many places, but Genls Bate[7] & Genl Breckinridge, from whose command we were this day temporarily detached, formed their men across the ridge & extending to a spur of the ridge in the rear & thus the rest of the line was held in tact until night when we retreated giving up the field to the enemy.

Nov 26th 1863. We are still operating with Cleyburn's [Cleburne's] brigade, covering the retreat. We Camped at Chic[k]amauga station last night. The roads are very heavy & the wagon trains are falling back very slowly.

Great quantities of commisary stores are being abandoned at this place [and] the boys are filling their haversacks with sugar & hard tack. We had a sharp skirmish with the yanks here. We had to keep them back until the wagon train got out of the way. We were deployed in line of battle on a

---

[6] The Union break-through came on the right center and the extreme left of the Confederate line, apparently simultaneously. Panic soon seized the entire left, and only prompt action by Generals Hardee and William B. Bate prevented annihilation of the army. Bragg himself said, "A panic which I had never before witnessed seemed to have seized upon officers and men, and each seemed to be struggling for his personal safety, regardless of his duty or his character." The artillery, he said, was "shamefully abandoned by its infantry support." *Ibid.*, 665.

[7] General William B. Bate and his brigade had been transferred from Stewart's to Breckinridge's division on November 12, 1863. Bate was the senior brigadier general of the division, and since Breckinridge was in command of a corps, Bate was temporarily commanding the division of which the Orphan Brigade was a part. The Orphan Brigade, however, had been sent to the extreme right on the morning of the twenty-fifth to aid Cleburne in resisting Sherman. *Ibid.*, 661, 739.

111

wooded ridge & the yanks advanced across a wide field about
one mile away. Our artillery opened on them & though they
outnumber us ten to one we deterred them from advancing
for an hour or more; finally they advanced against us in
force & we, having dclaycd them as long as we could, fell back
through an open field. We had first to climb a high staked
& rider fence. George Granger,[8] a fat short leged boy in Co.
H who was a good deal handicapped by a big supply of sugar
& hard tack which he had just gotten at the station, was
pressed pretty hard & had a close shave when he had to climb
the fence. Before he had gotten well over a mr yank fired
at him but mised him. He was making his best speed across
that open field when an other yank blazed away at him which
helped Granger along a good deal & enabled him to increase
his speed by about double. When the second yank fired &
missed him he yelled at him, "Run you scoundrel of a rebel!"

Granger called back at him, "You blamed fool you, dont
you see I am doing my best."

We all made fine time across that field & had no body
killed; but Granger over took one of the boys who was shot
in the leg & though he had a decided longing for the cover
afforded by the timber on the other side of that field he
stopped & helped that poor wounded fellow along, and they
both got safe across.

We had to form line of battle several times that day to
give them a volley which should check ardious pursuit but
we lost no men killed that day & only one wounded. The
Yanks seemed determined to keep company with us just when
we did not want to have them around, and it was determined
by Genl Lewis to give them a hint. The road went up a
wooded hill & then turning around followed its crest for a
short distance. Our infantry was formed at the foot of the
hill in the woods & the artillery was put in position on the
top of the hill. The enemy could not see our line of infantry

---

8 George Grainger of Louisville had fought in all engagements of the
Brigade through the Chattanooga campaign. He was transferred to the navy
a few months later. Thompson, *Orphan Brigade,* 851.

[and] when the artillery opened on them they made a rush for the battery. When they got near we surprised them by giving them a volley from our infantry & just then an other piece of our artillery somewhat on their flank opened on them & they took the hint & hurried back out of the reach of our guns. We had only one man wounded.

This gave our wagon train time to get a good start but we now learned that there was another column of Yanks coming out from Rossville trying to cut us off where our road came into the Lafayette & Chattanooga road. Orders were sent to the wagon train & to the artillery to hurry up, but the road was terribly muddy & it seemed to us they were creeping along. It had grown dark & the road ran through the woods. We took no time to think of being tired. It was twelve oclock at night & we were drawing close to the junction of the two roads where we expected the attempt would be made to ambush us. Vidett[e]s marched ahead of our column, flankers were thrown out on each side of us & instructions were given to load & no body was to speak a word. If we were fired upon the flankers from that side were to fall back immediately upon the regiment & the regiment was to face in that direction & wait for the flankers to come in & then fire at the flash of the enemies guns. We reached the junction without allarm save once or twice when a twig would break under the foot of one of the flankers who were walking through the woods.

Our course now turned at right angles to the left. Colonel John W Caldwell riding at the head of the regiment had made the turn & the first company of the regiment had turned when crack, crack, r-o-o-l came a volley of musket shots from a skirt of woods across an open field about fifty yards wide. Col Caldwell's horse became unruly, being startled by a flesh wound. The Col had his pistol in his right hand & his bridle reins in his left & the wound he had received at Chic[k]amauga in his left elbow had so disabled him that it was with great difficulty that he could manage

113

his horse who dashed across this open field directly towards the ennemy. Several more shots were fired directly at the Col. He finally stopped his steed within a few yards of the yanks & fired his pistol into the bushes from which their shots had come & they evidently believeing that he was leading a charge against them skurried off to the rear. Our men had hurriedly formed in line facing the ennemy but did not fire because the Col was in front & we might have shot him. He rode back to the regiment & sent out the flankers on the skirmish line to see that the road was clear & finding it was we hurried on to Ring[g]old, waded the East Chickamauga River which was waist deep & halted.

Here we rested, ate & took a short nap. The Yanks were following us up pretty close & as this is naturally a strong position Genl Cleburn[e] determined to teach our friends the ennemy a lesson. Our forces were posted with the infantry on each side of the Gap & the cavelry on the level ground in advance of the Gap. They [the cavalry] were to bring on the fight & it was hoped the yanks would rush after them & when they got in the Gap our infantry on both sides would give them a dose that they would remember for some time. And so it came out; our cavalry, infantry & artillery slaughtered them. Their loss was about eight hundred & ours only 20 killed & 190 Wounded. This gave the enemy such a lesson they persued us no further & Genl Cleburn[e] ordered our Brigade to fall back to Dalton & join our Division commander Genl Bate.

114

9 DALTON

After Major General Pat Cleburne had checked the Union pursuit at Ringgold, thus saving the Army of Tennessee, Bragg retreated to Dalton, about twenty-five miles southeast of Chattanooga in northwest Georgia. Bragg, now thoroughly discredited, asked President Davis to relieve him, and the command devolved temporarily on Hardee and then on Joseph E. Johnston.

The Union strategy did not envisage an aggressive movement in north Georgia, and the brilliantly victorious team of Grant, Sherman, and Thomas was broken up. Grant went temporarily to Nashville before he was called to Washington as commander in chief of all the armies of the Republic, Sherman was sent with part of the army to Mississippi for a time, and Thomas with the remainder assumed an unthreatening attitude in Chattanooga. Save for one demonstration made by Thomas against Dalton in late February, Johnston was given from December to May to rebuild the morale of his shattered army.

When Johnston assumed command, his army numbered about 37,000 infantry and artillery and about 5,500 cavalry.

Drills, sham battles, and some frolicking, including a mammoth snowball battle between divisions of the army, did much for the morale. Sergeant Green tells of the camp life and the drill during the winter of 1863-1864.

$\mathcal{W}$E REACHED Dalton late in the afternoon of Nov 27th 1863. This is almost a mountainous country. Rock[y] Face Ridge looms up as a young mountain; the dirt road & the Rail Road find their way through this range by way of Mill Creek Gap & here we go into camp just out side of the Gap. It is drizzling & cold, & such a piercing wind blowing that it chills the marrow in our bones. Our wagons soon reach us in which each mess has an axe, a frying pan, a camp Kettle & a skillet & we were fortunate enough to have a tent fly. We immediately began to cut pine saplings to make us a hut over which to stretch our tent fly. Some went for water, some built a fire & some set to work to sift our meal, make corn bread, toast the meal husk & make coffee from it & fry our bacon, for we were fortunate enough to have a small piece of bacon. We thought it a fine supper & counted ourselves almost comfortable notwithstanding the wind blew through our hut so. But we got our blankets partially dry & soon went to bed.

The morning of the 28th much to our disgust we were ordered to fall in ready to march. We broke camp & marched through the Gap nearly 2 miles & began again to make ourselves comfortable for winter quarters. John Jackman the Adjutants clerk, & I will build a hut for the Adjutants office

& to serve as our own quarters. Jack is pretty good at such work if he was not so lazy. At home he was first a carpenter, then a school teacher & now a rather lazy soldier, but a christian gentleman. I have to keep at him though to get him to do any of the dirty & hard work.

We have however finally finished a very nice hut with pine poles, a tent fly for a roof & a stick chimney. The Jambs & the back of the fire place are built of rocks which are plentiful here. John is a good forager after reading matter & we have had from his efforts in that direction Jean Van Jean [Les Miserables], the Three Guards Men [Musketeers] & the Bride of Lammermore [Lammermoor].

The army has been enthused by the fact that Genl Joseph E. Johnston has been placed in command in lieu of Genl Braxton Bragg, relieved at his own request. Genl Johnston took command Dec 27th 1863. I saw him at the Episcopal church last Sunday, or rather at church where an Episcopal preacher conducted the service & preached. Genl Johnston is not a large man except in brain & ability but is every inch a soldier in fact & in appearance. A number of us stood on the pavement & lifted our caps in salute as he passed. He saluted in response & said, "Good morning my men, I am glad to see you at church."

The army has made itself very comfortable winter quarters here at Dalton. They have built log huts, with chimneys. The roof in most cases is made of boards which some of the men have rived from pine timber, a froe having been provided by the quartermaster for each regiment.

Rations however are very short; the only meat we have had since the first few days since we arrived at Dalton has been blue beef. The cattle are slaughtered somewhere down south, cut up & put in barrels of very salt brine & shipped up here. I fear the cattle came near starving to death before they were slaughtered, the meat is so poor & tough; but we are glad to get it for they are not able to give us even that more frequently than 3 times a week. Last week we had

118

none. They gave some days corn meal & sweet potatoes & some days corn meal & peanuts in lieu of meat. Yesterday they had not even these substitutes & issued instead Whiskey. I let my old mess in Co B divide my share among them, & even then none of them got enough to get very merry.

Soldiers often seem much more to desire the thing which they can secure by stealth & strategy than that which comes in the regular way. Orders have been published strictly prohibiting the bringing of any whiskey into camp by the men, & Col Cofer,[1] who has been made provost marshall of the town of Dalton, has strictly prohibited the sale of liquor except for medicinal purposes in the town or about the camps. He has posted guards on all the roads leading out from the town & every body caught with any whiskey, unless it be only a small dose accompnied by a doctors certificate that it is for a sick patient, has to see it confiscated; it is taken from him & sent to Col Coffers [Cofer's] Head Quarters where it is added to the medical stores of the department. There was a good deal caught in this way & some of our boys thought they could catch a little of it for their own use; so one of them put on his accoutrements, took his musket & posted himself on the same road that the most frequent captures were made upon and at a post that he would capture the contriband before it got to the regular guard. Dusk had hardly set in before he had stopped two citizens & three Georgia Soldiers with bottles & canteens full of whiskey & took them away from the lawless purchasers saying the orders were very strict that all liquor must be confiscated & brought to Head Quarters.

[1] Martin H. Cofer, lawyer of Hardin County, Kentucky, helped organize a battalion of the Sixth Kentucky and was elected lieutenant colonel November 1, 1861. He took part in all engagements of the regiment except Stone's River. He was promoted to colonel September 30, 1863. Shortly before this he had been made provost marshal general of the Army of Tennessee. He served in this capacity through the battle of Nashville and the retreat to Tupelo. He then joined Johnston in North Carolina before his surrender to Sherman. After the war Cofer returned to the practice of law in Elizabethtown and was elected judge of the Court of Appeals in 1874. He died in this office May 22, 1881. Thompson, *Orphan Brigade*, 423-28.

After having captured a good lot this enterprizing soldier arranged to get into camp past all the guards without having his captures taken from him as contraband. He had taken the precaution to have near his "self assumed post" a big pumpkin. He opened one end, took out all the insides & put his cantee[n]s full of whiskey inside, closed the end up again & passed all guards, saying he had gone out to hunt squirrels but found none, but had gotten a good big pumpkin & intended to have a nice mess of stewed pumpkin. His entire mess were mellow for several days after that.[2]

Drill, dress parad[e] & Guard mounting filled up a good deal of time. Our Kentucky brigade challenged Adams brigade for a championship drill. The judges were chosen; we drilled regiment against regt & then a brigade drill & we carried off the prize, which was a complimentary order nameing us as the prize brigade.[3]

The winter was very cold but the health of the army was good. We were camped near a very bold [cold?] spring which afforded water amply sufficient for the whole brigade —& ran off waste water in a branch about four feet wide & fully two feet deep. Once a week throughout the winter I took a bath & a good plunge in this branch & many times the water a few feet farther from the spring was hard frozen.

The rivalry between the troops in drilling seemed a little later to extend to a rivalry of interest in the religious services for we had quite a revival in all the churches & a great number of the soldiers joined the church. We had

[2] The official historian of the Orphan Brigade relates another manner in which the soldiers outwitted Cofer in smuggling whisky into camp. They would inform him that friends in Atlanta or other points would "at such and such a time" send them a package of food and request that he take charge and safeguard it until they could call. Being thrown completely off guard by this conduct, Cofer would receive and hold the packages and turn them over to addressees, not suspecting that they contained liquor. Thompson, 236.

[3] According to Ed Porter Thompson this event took place April 23 of the preceding year while the army was in the vicinity of Tullahoma, Tennessee (pp. 205-206). Thompson states that Green's regiment, the Ninth, did not compete because the army moved before the day scheduled for its competition.

taken the prize in drilling & Lieut Col Wickliffe told the men that he would not be satisfied for his regiment to be beaten in any thing; he said if we did not send in as many recruits to the church as any other regiment in the army he thought he would be compelled to have details made to Join the church, for our regiment must not be outdone in any way.[4]

We had a good deal of spare time in the five months we camped at Dalton because much of the time was sleeting & very rough weather. The most of the top of my cap had been shot away during the fight at Missionary Ridge & when our Quarter Master Capt Mort Perry[5] got a new coat I told him if he would give me the tails from his old coat I would make him a new cap & make one for my self also. My proposal was accepted & my success was such that I was beset by several in the regiment to make them caps. The scarcity of the material however prevented my being worked to death in the cap industry.

Mar 22 1864. When we awoke the ground was covered with snow & it continued to come down for some time. When it ceased our boys began snowballing each other & had quite a battle. The Florida boys began hallowing to our combatants, whereupon our boys began a snow fight with that

[4] A great religious revival started in the Army of Northern Virginia in the spring of 1863 and by the next winter had spread to the Army of Tennessee. Many Confederate leaders, among them President Davis and Generals Ewell, Bragg, and Hardee, joined the church during this time. The movement was at its height at Dalton in April, 1864. From there a member of the Tenth Texas wrote repeatedly of the spiritual enthusiasm and the mass conversions. "I have never seen," he said, "such a spirit as there is now in the army. Religion is the theme." Again he wrote, "The good work still goes on here. Thirty-one men were baptized at the creek below our brigade here yesterday. . . . This revival spirit is not confined to a part only, but pervades the whole army." Other days he reported seeing eighty-three, sixty-five, and forty baptized in the creek. He likened the army's religious zeal to that of Cromwell's Roundheads. T. J. Stokes, quoted in Henry Steele Commager (ed.), *The Blue and the Gray*, 2 vols. (New York and Indianapolis, 1950), I, 415-16.

[5] J. Mort Perry of Russellville was elected first lieutenant in September, 1861. He fought at Shiloh with Company A, Ninth Regiment, but shortly thereafter was assigned as regimental quartermaster and promoted to captain. He settled in Louisville after the war and died there in 1885. Thompson, *Orphan Brigade*, 808.

121

brigade & soon each brigade including the commanding officers were hotly engage[d] in a snow ball battle, charging, flanking & reinforcing until we had them driven to the further confines of their camp. They had captured our color bearer & part of our flag staff but we had captured their camp; so we made peace upon the terms that they should release our color bearer & we should evacuate their camp.

As I have previously mentioned many of our boys were much impressed by the eloquent truths of the Gospel as presented by the Chaplains of our regiments & the preachers in town but about Feb. 23 1864 I was struck with the missionary influence of the enemy's cannon. Genl Hardee was sent about the 18th of February with his corps to Mississippi[6] & Genl Thomas on Feb 23d pressed forward thinking he would find Genl Johnston weakened & not fixed for him. The cannonading was first heard out front. It grew more vigorous & I observed several squads of card players who were proverbial gamblers soon lose their interest in the game. The fireing came nearer. The games entirely stopped, the decks of cards were thrown upon the ground & soon these gamblers were discovered in their cabins or behind a big tree reading their testament. The fireing kept up [and] we were ordered to fall in & marched out Mill Creek Gap towards Ring[g]old where we were to support the Cavelry. There we had sharp skirmishing on the 24 & 25 of February repulsing the enemy. On Feb 26 we were back in our winter huts & the gamblers had hunted up their various decks of cards; the missionary influence was prompt but not lasting.

On the morning of the 23d of February I awakened

6 Hardee was sent to oppose a contemplated offensive by Sherman (who at this time was in Mississippi) against Meridian and possibly against Mobile, Alabama, to take that important Confederate port in reverse. Sherman was to be supported by 7,500 cavalry under General W. Sooy Smith. Smith was defeated by Forrest and retreated to Memphis, whereupon Sherman destroyed the railroads around Meridian and returned to Vicksburg. Hardee's corps, which had reached Demopolis, Alabama, was then returned to Dalton. *O.R.*, Series 1, XXXII, pt. 1, pp. 173-78, 333, 336-68; Horn, *The Army of Tennessee,* 315-16.

with a severe tooth ache & went to Dr Smith of the 2nd Regiment to have the tooth drawn [because] our Surgeon Dr Byrne said he had no forceps. Dr Smith cut the gum & took several pulls at the tooth but he could not move it, so we let her stay. While he was making his unsuccessful efforts the cannonading began & I said to him we might as well let it alone for it sounded as though a fight was coming on & the tooth might be shot out or I might be killed, either one of which occurrences would save me the trouble of having the tooth pulled; so we let it alone.

But now the fight is over the tooth wont let me alone; so to day the 28th of Feb I appealed to a dutch man, "Jake brown," in our regiment who was a barber, leacher [leecher], tooth drawer & blood letter in New Orleans, who has an old fashioned pair of pullikins. He sat me down on a stump & wrestled with that tooth as though he was trying to pull up a gate post. He got her out however at last & would not charge me any thing. He said he really liked to pull teeth & would be glad to pull some more for me, but did not see any more that needed it.

10 RETREAT

After Grant was appointed commander in chief of the Union armies and summoned to Washington, almost at once a grand strategy was developed whereby great pressure was applied to sensitive areas of the Confederacy. Early in May, Union armies were on the move from the James River front, across northern Virginia, up the Shenandoah Valley, through southwest Virginia, in north Georgia, and toward Mobile. It is with the north Georgia phase of this grand strategy that Green's account is now concerned.

Sherman succeeded Grant as commander of the Division of the Mississippi and moved to Chattanooga to direct operations against the Army of Tennessee now commanded by Joseph E. Johnston. By May, Johnston had built his army to a strength of approximately 50,000, and there can be no doubt that its morale was remarkably improved. This army came to regard Johnston with the respect, if not the devotion, which the Army of Northern Virginia held for Lee. As Green said, "The boys ... feel sure they can do just what Marse Joe says they can." Johnston had been urged by Davis, Beauregard, and Bragg (who was now a personal adviser to Davis in Richmond) to take the offensive against Thomas during the winter months, but Johnston, who has been accused of being allergic to offensive movements, refused. Consistently he remained on the defensive throughout the ensuing campaign, always waiting, he explained, for an opportunity to strike when he found the enemy overextended. Ironically, that time arrived simultaneously with orders for him to turn the army over to Hood.

Sherman faced Johnston with about twice his numbers. His force was made up of three formerly distinct armies: the Army of the Ohio commanded by General John M. Schofield, the Army of the Cumberland commanded by Thomas, and his own Army of the Tennessee, now commanded by General James B. McPherson. On May 6 the combined armies launched the offensive against Dalton. But Johnston had strongly fortified his position, and Sherman hesitated, even with his overwhelming force, to make a frontal attack.

It is here that the nature of the ensuing campaign began to unfold. Instead of making the frontal attack, Sherman sent McPherson by the right flank through Snake Creek Gap, threatening Johnston's rear, and on the thirteenth Johnston retreated to Resaca. Here there was some hard fighting, but with Union cavalry again threatening his rear by a flank movement, Johnston retreated to Kingston.

As Johnston retreated, he tore up the railroad, which Sherman would rebuild as he moved forward. This, together with damages in his rear by the Confederate cavalry raids under Joseph Wheeler, delayed Sherman's progress some, but it is surprising with what speed the Union engineers rebuilt bridges and relaid rails.

By late May, Johnston had taken a strong position at Allatoona. A Union movement by the right flank toward Dallas attempted to nullify this position, but this time Johnston had anticipated Sherman and there was a week's hard fighting at New Hope Church. Thereupon Sherman began extending his left, threatening to hem Johnston in.

Johnston then fell back to Marietta and Kenesaw Mountain, which were strongly entrenched. Pine Mountain and Lost Mountain, mentioned by Green, were integral parts of the general battle fought in this sector. It was at Pine Mountain that Bishop–Lieutenant General Leonidas Polk was killed on June 14.

Sherman, here departing from his previous tactics, made a frontal assault which the Confederates repelled with heavy casualties. Even here, however, Schofield gained around Johnston's right flank, and again the Confederates were forced back—this time to the Chattahoochee. Here Sherman seized bridgeheads above and below Johnston, and once more threatened his rear. On July 9 Johnston crossed his army over the river and stood with his back to Atlanta.

This was the end of the line for Johnston. Apprehension in Richmond had been mounting as Sherman forced his way ever closer to Atlanta. A cabinet crisis developed, and Davis, with much more reluctance than is commonly believed, ordered Johnston to turn his command over to Lieutenant General John B. Hood.

Johnston is a controversial figure. Hood, not an impartial witness, was later to excoriate his campaign as a series of blunders. And even Secretary of War James A. Seddon, who had formerly championed Johnston, was convinced that he had not managed his campaign with that brilliance that might have been expected of him. On the other hand, as distinguished a critic as Ulysses S. Grant said, "For my part I think Johnston was right" in his strategy of retreat. But regardless of how these distinguished critics felt, Johnny Green and his comrades loved and trusted Joe Johnston.

$\mathcal{M}$AY 1ST 1864. To-day we heard artillery firing at the front; the cavelry report that the enemy are getting ready to move forward.

May 2nd. General inspection to day. Every thing is ready for an engagement.

May 7th 1864. Our wagons all sent to the rear, & we move from our winter quarters & take position in line of battle on Rocky Face Ridge near Mill Creek Gap. The yanks came up about noon & the fighting began; pretty brisk skirmishing every day until the night of May 12th. Our sharp shooting corps was organized here & did most effective work. They were armed with Kerr rifles, english guns, I believe, brought in through the blockade. They were of long range and in the hands of good marksmen did dreadful havoc in the enemy's ranks. There were but eleven in the brigade, three of them from our regiment, chosen for their expert markmanship. They became a great terror to the enemy's artillerymen, for they could kill at much greater range than the infantrymen. They would crawl up within range, conceal themselves & when the cannonneers would attempt to load they would shoot them down. Several of this corps were killed during the campaign & every one of them was at some time wounded; but whenever needed there were numerous volunteers.

The night of 12th we made a hurried march to Snake Creek Gap where we had a sharp skirmish but none of our regiment were wounded.

I believe it was at Dug Gap that one of our men on the skirmish line was killed. Where two of them were posted to-gether they were so tired & worn that one would take a nap if there was no fireing on the line, while the other watched. The yanks opened fire & the man on look out punched his comrad to waken him; he sat up & gaped & immediately fell back dead. A yankie ball had entered his mouth while open & came out the back of his head, killing him instantly.

On 13th took position in line of battle at Resaca [and] began immediately to build rifle pits. Slight skirmish in the afternoon.

Morning of the 14th, the enemy having come up in force, about 9 A M sharp skirmishing began & was very vigorous, accompanied with heavy artillery fireing. About noon they assaulted our line with five lines of battle. Our infantry reserved their fire until the enemy were in close range when we opened on them, almost every shot killing a man. So terrible was the slaughter that for a time they were hurled back, but rallying, they charged again & again when being utterly discouraged they fell back in great disorder, but they so greatly outnumbered us it was not prudent to leave our breastworks to pursue them. At 3 oclock in the afternoon they made another attempt to carry our works but with no better result & again late in the afternoon they made another assault but were driven back with great loss.

After every repulse their artillery would be used against us with terrific effect. We had but few cannon which could equal theirs in range; they therefore could post some of their batteries out of range of ours & damage us much more than we could them. Between their 3 oclock attack & the

128

later one they opened a terrific cannonading on us & completely enfiladed our regiment. They shot right into our trenches & the boys got out & laid on the ground in rear of them. The next shell that came cut Lieut McLain's[1] leg off & exploding killed two of our men. Lieut McLain thus dreadfully wounded called to his men, "Be steady men; dont let them see any confusion; they will know they have our range & make it worse for us." Another shot came before the litter bearers could carry him off the field & cut him almost in two, killing him instantly & wounding one of the litter bearers.

The men got back into the trenches & crawled up to the right leaving that portion of the works which their [the enemy's] fire enfiladed unoccupied. But as we crept along the rifle pits the movement could not be observed by them. When the last assault was made as the assaulting line got within range of our rifles their annoying artillery ceased fireing upon us for fear of hitting their own men, so we ran back to our rifle pits & drove back their attacking line.

That night, after burrying those gallant men of ours who were killed, we evaccuated Resaca, crossed the Oostanaula River & marched about 5 miles to about Calhoun. This move was made necessary because the enemy had such superior force that while engaging us in front by numbers about double our own, they were moving a large flanking column across the Oostanaula River to get in our rear.

In all my experience I dont believe I ever knew an instance of more heroic courage & greater presence of mind than this act of Lieut McLain's. Almost in the agonies of death thinking only of the success of his cause & the spirit of his corps.

May 16th 1864. We formed line of battle near Calhoun & with light skirmishing held our position until about 2 P.M. when we fell back towards Adairville. The march was slow

---

[1] Thomas A. McLean of Logan County. Thompson, *Orphan Brigade*, 808.

129

but very tedious. Marched all night stopping every now &
then for we knew not what—some broken down wagon or
small bridge or mud hole possibly. But we were so tired &
sleepy that when halted we would lie down in the road &
catch a few minutes nap. We reached Adairville early the
17th & laid down to rest.

About 2 P.M. rations [were] issued & before we had more
than swallowed our food & filled our cantee[n]s the cannon
began to boom; the enemy are up with us & we form line of
battle. Light skirmishing. After dark we are started of[f] to
Kingston. It seems we are to guard the wagon train. This is
another tiresome nights march, so terribly pooky [pokey]!
We halted near Kingston, had rations & took a nap. Formed
line of battle about 11 A.M. on the 18th. The enemys advanced guard came up & [we had] light skirmishing.

May 19th 1864. The entire army is here & about Cassville. Genl Joseph E. Johnston has issued a battle order &
tells us he is to day ready to fight the ennemy. We did no
entrenching last night [for] Genl Johnston is going to attack
the enemy. This certainly means we have got him just
where we want him. Genl Joe knows what he has been
watching for & the boys are all delighted; they feel sure
they can do just what Genl Joe says they can. It seems the
yanks have divided their forces here; part are on the Kingston
road & part on the Cassville road.

We moved forward, threw out skirmishers, found the
enemy, & received from them a few shells, when we almost
immediately were ordered back & marched tow[ar]ds Cassville. It seems that Polk & Ho[o]d were to bring own [on]
the engagement but Hood having heard some report that the
enemy were approaching in our rear did not press forward
to the attack & as the whole plan was to take the enemy
unawares & as this delay had let the opportune moment pass
Genl Johnston changed his plan & took up position at Cassville there to await the attack of the enemy but Genls Hood
& Polk insisted that their position could be so badly enfiladed

130

they said they could not hold the position & hence after slight exchange of shots we rested on our arms until night but that night we evacuated Cassville & passed over the Etowah.[2] The enemy made it very uncomfortable for us because they discovered we were evacuating & shelled the bridge over the river all night; fortunately however but few of our men were hurt.

We camped on the Allatoona road near the Etowah Iron works about three miles from the bridge over which we had crossed; here we remained resting May 21st & 22nd. At about 2 P.M. on May 23d we took up the line of march towards Dallas & bivouaced on the Allatoona & Dallas road. About midnight we were ordered to move to New Hope Church to guard the right flank of the army; here we had a sharp skirmish & drove the enemy off. We then moved to Powder Spring where we found a small detachment of the enemy, attacked them & drove them off, following them to the Burnt Hickory road where they made a stand & we had a Sharp fight with them here. Smith's[3] Brigade & the Florida Brigade[4] came up & reenforced us & we dislodged the enemy & drove them for nearly a mile towards Dallas. This was May 24th 1864.

May 25th. Last night we marched a few miles, came to this position near Dallas & began entrenching. Before we

[2] This decision not to attack the enemy at Cassville but to continue the retreat was later the subject of bitter controversy between Hood and Johnston. Johnston stated in his official report that the attack was about to be launched when Hood erroneously reported Union troops on his right flank and rear. When the error was established, Johnston said "the opportunity had passed." He then arranged his lines in a strong position to receive the enemy's expected attack, when Hood and Polk reported to him that their positions were untenable because of the Union artillery. Years later Johnston still maintained that there were no Union troops on Hood's flank and that Hood and Polk had caused him to order retreat when he should have stood and fought. Hood took issue with this and stoutly affirmed that Union troops were in force on his flank at the time he was to attack. He also denied that he and Polk had advised retreat. *O.R.*, Series 1, XXXVIII, pt. 3, p. 616; Horn, *The Army of Tennessee*, 328, 471.

[3] Brigadier General James A. Smith of Cleburne's division.

[4] Probably the brigade of Brigadier General Mark P. Lowery of Cleburne's division.

had our breastworks completed the enemy came up & attacked us but we repulsed them. They however got a lodgement on a commanding hill which very much annoyed our line on the right.

The morning of May 27th Genl Bate our Division Commander determined to drive the enemy from that hill. The word was passed along the line to have every gun loaded & ready to charge. The word was given, every man was on his feet, [and] the command "forward march" was given. "Reserve your fire until within forty yards of their line, then fire, each man taking careful aim & then rush upon them & give them the bayonet," the Genl Said.

They poured a volley into us almost as soon as our advance began, but we pressed steadily forward until so close that we could count the buttons on their coats. We poured a volley of deadly fire into them, then rushed upon them with fixed bayonets; they stood by their works pouring their leaden hail into us until we got within thirty feet of them, when they fled & left the field to us. It was then our turn & those who got their guns loaded before the enemy got out of sight caused many of them to bight the dust.

May 28th 1864. The enemy as well as ourselves have become so expert in fortifying that both of us are well entrenched. So close are we that from our trenches we can often pick off the enemy from our regular line of works & they, having longer range guns than we, annoy us more than we can them. Our pickets are relieved & posted in the dark before day light in the morning & after dark at night. Almost constant skirmish firing was kept up this morning but this afternoon the enemy responded but little & kept so quiet that our Corps commander suspicioned that the enemy had left but a small force in our front & was massing the most of their army in some flank movement. We were ordered to move forward in line of battle & develop their true position [and] if they had but a small force to rush it & capture them [but] if however they were in strong force simply to

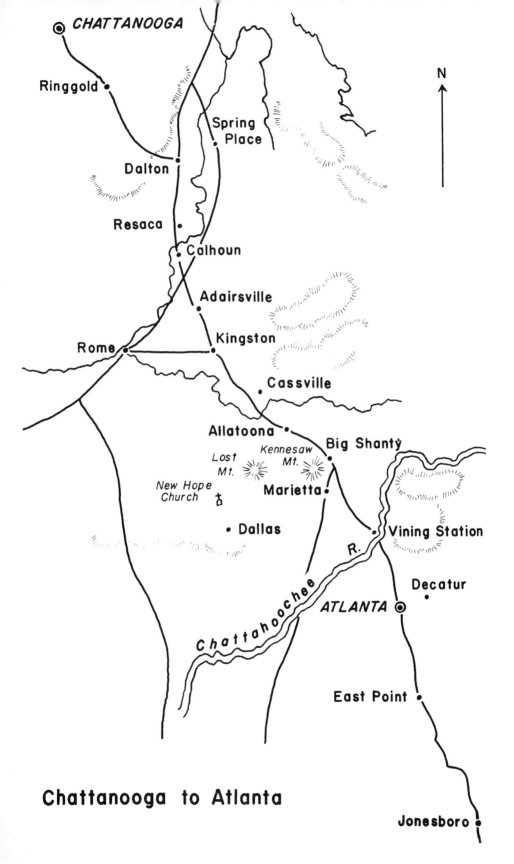

Chattanooga to Atlanta

ascertain that fact & retire. Armstrongs[5] brigade was to begin the attack & if he drove the enemy & found them in Small force Smith was to advance his brigade & fire four guns in quick sucession, whereapon the rest of the divisn was to assault & capture the enemy if possible.

Armstrongs brigade advanced with such fierceness that they drove the enemy before them, captured their works & one piece of Artilery but the yanks brought up heavy rein-forcem'ts, showing they had withdrawn none of their troops. Smith seeing this did not advance nor did he fire the Signal 4 Guns in quick succession but the rest of the division mis-took Armstrongs guns for the agreed signal & rushed in a charge against greatly superior forces strongly entrenched. We carried their first & Second line of works but were again confronted with greatly superior forces, & by this time Genl Bate, having found that the enemy had by no means with-drawn from our front but were intrenched in great force, ordered us to fall back into our line of breast works. We lost in the one hour that this fight lasted fifty one per cent killed & wounded of the men taken into the charge.[6]

This is the game of war; it was necessary to know whether the yanks were still before us or were they trying to execute some move that would be disasterous to us & we had to pay the price in blood. If however Armstrongs fierce cannonad-ing had not been mistaken for Smiths four Signal guns, Armstrongs brave men would have been the only ones to pay the penalty, for he had already developed the enemy & gained the needed information.

May 29 1864. Both armies are sullenly holding their entrenched lines, each Scowling at the other & watching for an opportunity to catch his opponent at a disadvantage. The Sharp shooting is very vicious & many were wounded.

[5] Brigadier General Frank C. Armstrong's brigade of cavalry.

[6] Losses of the Orphan Brigade at New Hope Church were 20 killed and 177 wounded (*O.R.*, Series 1, XXXVIII, pt. 3, p. 687). The division losses were 47 killed and 345 wounded, which was only 10 per cent of the division effectives reported April 30, and 11 per cent of those of June 10. *Ibid.*, 676, 677.

At night the firing on the skirmish line suddenly became very fierce & soon every yankee battery had opened on us & they had the range of our regiment exactly. We knew they could not capture our works except with infantry & that before the infantry could charge the battery which was playing on us would have to cease fireing. So we laid down in our trenches & a great many of their solid shot & shells passed completely through the earth bank of our works, but very few of our men were hurt. After keeping up this firing for about two hours they ceased.

It is said that some of the Florida boys brought this cannonading & terrific fusilade upon us. The tale is that the Florida boys on pickets mistook the flash of the lightening bug for the flash of a yankee gun & fired at the flash. The ball whizzed over the head of the yankee picket who in turn fired & this started the firing which grew rapidly at every flash, whether it was a gun or a lightning bug, until the yankee pickets ran in & reported that we were making a night attack upon them. This the yankee papers did report. When their pickets ran in their batteries & their whole line of battel opened on us from their rifle pits & some of their pickets got so confused that they ran to our line exclaiming the damned rebels were making a night charge on them. We took in such cases & sent them to our rear as prisoners. After that whenever we met that Florida regiment we would call out, "Boys we will get you some blacking to blacken the lightening bugs lamps, for we dont want you to bring on any more night attacks."

The enemy withdrew from our front at Dallas after the 30th of May & we took up position near Ackworth & set busily to work building breastworks. The rain was almost incessant. The enemies skirmish line entrenched in rifle pits within range of us. We could not even stretch our blankets as dog tents but had to just squat in the trenches or behind trees with our blankets wrapped around us & take the rain & catch what sleep we could in this squatting posture. We then moved, one night marching the most of the night to near Marietta Ga. Had a skirmish near Marietta June 10th 1864. We moved almost every night to some new position in the vicinity of Marietta & Lost Mountain, entrenching & skirmishing, then took up position on Pine Mountain. Gave the Yanks a sharp check here. Intrenched & had daily fights with them [but] their batteries got our range & made it very hot for us.

On June 14th 1864 Genl Leonidas Polk with his staff[7] rode up to our position to inspect, as it gave a full view of the enemies lines & was in easy range. One of the officers of our line walked up to the General & saluting said, "Genl you ought not to sit on your horse in this prominent position here, for they have accurate range of this hill & they will soon kill many of your party."

Just then a shell came & killed John Pirtles horse which fell under him, but fortunately John escaped unhurt. The Genl still sat unmoved inspecting their lines through his field glasses when another shell came from one of their batteries & passed clear through the General, killing him instantly.

We could not show our heads outside the trenches without having a minnie ball come whizzing at us, but the boys would lay around out side notwithstanding. We were sitting around with shells bursting over us when it was evident from the sound that one piece of a shell was coming close to us. Every fellow was holding his breath wondering if that piece would strike him when suddenly it stuck John Jackman who was sitting on the ground near me & Col Caldwell & Dr Hester,[8] our assistant Surgeon, & Jim Bemis, our hospital steward. (Jackman was adjutants clerk). He was just mak-

[7] Generals Johnston and Hardee and their staffs were present with Polk on the mountain. At the first shot Johnston ordered all to seek cover, but Polk, as Green points out, moved too deliberately (Horn, The Army of Tennessee, 331, 332). General Sherman makes an interesting comment on this incident in his Memoirs, 2 vols. (New York, 1875), II, 52-54.

[8] Dr. B. L. Hester, a North Carolinian, served with the Orphan Brigade throughout the war. Thompson, 807.

ing out a report which had been called for by Division
Head Quarters. He was sitting on the ground, [and] the
fragment of a shell struck him on the head & turned him a
complete sommersault. We thought he was killed, but Dr
Hester, Jim Bemis & I picked him up & carried him behind
a tree; by this time he revived & did not seem very seriously
hurt. I poured water on his head from my canteen & Dr
Hester washed & dressed the wound & Jack was so bright by
this time that we had a hearty laugh at the way he had
flopped over, just like a chicken when his head is cut off.
Jack went back to the hospital at Atlanta & got on pretty
well for a few days but gangreen developed in the wound &
he had a very serious time with it.

We remained at this point until the 17th—the time was
spent in skirmishing & Sharp Shooting with frequent artillery
duels, the yanks attacking us first on one flank & then on the
other trying to locate or develope our line, & we would
extend as they would make effort to turn our flank. The
rain & sunshine were freely intersperced.

Our meal rations were the worst I ever saw; it was damp,
musty & almost green with mould when issued to us; the
only way we had to cook it was to mix it with a little water
& salt & then cook it in a frying pan like hoe cakes. My share
gave me such a pain in my stomach that I could hardly walk.

That night, June 17th,[9] we fell back from Pine mountain. It rained terificly; the roads & my pain were both very
bad & I went to our surgeon & asked him to give me some
medicine. He said, "John the hospital stores have all gone
on ahead of us; the only thing I have is some whiskey in my
canteen; here take a drink of that." And here I took my
second drink of whiskey during the war.

We plodded on until about 4 oclock in the morning
with the rain still coming down in torrents & halted near

[9] The Confederate army evacuated Pine Mountain the night of June 14-15.
On June 17 they evacuated Lost Mountain. *O.R.*, Series 1, XXXVIII, pt. 1,
p. 67; pt. 3, p. 708; Sherman, *Memoirs*, II, 54.

Lost Mountain. My pain was keeping up with me all the time & I went again to the Doctor & asked him to give me some paregoric, but we had not yet caught up with the ambulance & the Surgeon's medecines so I took another drink of whiskey, got three rails to make me a bed to lie on so as to keep from lying in the mud & water, spread my blanket over me so as to keep the rain out of my face & slept like a log & woke up the next morning well. I was surprised & pleased that I had so soon recovered.

We formed line of battle near our former position at the base of Lost Mountain in the forenoon of June 18th.[10] Our position was on the side of the mountain in the woods. Entrenching tools were given us & we set to work building earth works. We had gotten pretty well advanced in our labors notwithstanding the rain when we were moved to an other position & had to begin all over again in our work of entrenching. We had scarcely finished when we had a visit from the enemy, but it was a light skirmish. That night we moved near the Marietta & Canton Road [and] skirmished with the enemy on June 19th. That night [we] marched to Ken[n]esaw Mountain & began working like beavers entrenching. The Yanks were on us early next fornoon.

June 20st, 1864. Fighting & entrenching all day. Late in the evening the yanks made quite a determined assault which we repulsed. We drove them back far enough to be able to put out picketts in front of our regular line. The pickets have built defenses with rails known as rail pens. They help a good deal in a fight with infantry but if they bring up the artillery to play upon them they are worse than nothing; if a cannon ball dont hit you, it is almost sure to hit the pen & the pieces of rails will knock you out. That night entrenching tools were sent out to the pickets & they worked for dear life digging rifle pits to protect those on duty for they knew there would be great need of them when day

10 It was on June 19 that this left wing of the army took a position across the Lost Mountain and Marietta Road. *O.R.*, Series 1, XXXVIII, pt. 3, p. 617.

light came. The enemy opened the artillery on us trying to prevent our entrenching but our boys worked hard & had good pits by day light.

The enemy have moved up in force & entrenched in point blank range so that there is constant firing both from our trenches & from theirs. Any one who shows his head above the trenches is sure to have two or three minnie balls come singing around his ears, but we soon got so accustomed to it that the boys grew very careless. I had to pass along the line to give orders for the pickets to be ready to go out after dark to relieve those who had been on duty all day. I noticed Tom Wimms[11] laying on the ground outside of the trenches, [and] I said, "Tom dont lay out there; that ball that struck that tree did not miss you six inches."

His reply was, "I am sleepy for I was out there on picket all last night & I am going to have a good stretched out sleep if they kill me for it." I passed on down the line & came back within ten minutes & poor Tom had received his death wound; a yankee bullit had passed clear through him.

Our position was at a salient angle & the enemy's fire caught us front & flank. Indeed the Artillery & infantry fire was so incessant that we had to keep half the regiment on the watch both day & night & in order that any of us should get sleep we dug a second line of sleeping pits down the hill in rear of our main line but so annoying was the flank fire that even in these rear pits several of our men were wounded while lying asleep in them.

Green Lassiter[12] of Co H in our regiment had a dreadful awakening by a death wound in the abdomen. His suffering was intense. He writhed & called on the Blessed Virgin

11 T. P. Wimms was from Logan County. He had been wounded at Shiloh, and had been wounded and then captured at Hartsville. He was exchanged in time to take part in the Mississippi campaign, in the summer of 1863, and had fought in every engagement of the Brigade from that time until the battle of Kennesaw. Thompson, *Orphan Brigade,* 815.

12 Green H. Lassiter of Louisville had joined the Brigade in November, 1862, and fought in all engagements from that time until Kennesaw. Thompson, 854.

138

& prayed that she should have mercy on him but he died in about fifteen minutes. I suppose the ball ranged upwards near the heart for he seemed to suffocate from internal hemorage.

We had a head Quartr's pit dug immediately in rear of the centre of the regiment where Colonel Caldwell, Adjutant W. D. Chipley[13] & I stayed when duty did not call us elswhere but of course we were outside a great part of the time.

The ladies in the country about sent some fresh vegetables to the soldiers; our share was two simlins & I set to work to cook them. I found one boy who lent me a frying pan & I got to work to stew the simlins notwithstanding the minnie balls & occasional shells which came flying over us. I thought I was getting on splendidly & had our dish almost ready when boom came a shell right in my fire & scattered fire, frying pan & simlins.

We all scampered to the pits for a few minutes. I then yelled over to the yanks, "Stop your foolishness until after dinner," waited a few minutes & as no more shells came I got out of the pit, scraped up all the simlin I could reclaim from the ashes & we all ate it with a rel[i]sh notwithstanding a slight taste of ashes, but I never have forgiven that yank for shooting my knife out of my hand with which I was stirring the simlins for I never laid eyes on it again.

Lieutenant Clay McCay[14] was standing behind Cap't Cobbs battery watching a fierce Artillery duel when he was killed by a piece of a shell.

The yankee's made a fierce attack one afternoon[15] on

13 W. D. Chipley of Louisville was sergeant major from October, 1861, until he was appointed first lieutenant and adjutant March 1, 1863. He was wounded at Shiloh, Corinth, and Chickamauga, and was captured at Atlanta in July, 1864. Thompson, 807.

14 Henry Clay McKay of Nelson County enlisted in the Kentucky Brigade in the fall of 1861 when he was only fifteen years old. He fought in all engagements from Shiloh to Kennesaw Mountain. He was appointed sergeant major in May, 1863, and joined General Lewis' staff the next October with the rank of first lieutenant. Thompson, 749.

15 Probably June 27, when Sherman, departing from his flanking tactics, launched a frontal attack. He was repulsed with heavy losses. O.R., Series 1, XXXVIII, pt. 3, p. 617; pt. 1, p. 69; Sherman, Memoirs, II, 60-61.

139

our picketts [and] they were repulsed with great loss, but getting reenforcements they came again & were driven back
but the position was a commanding one & they seemed determined to dislodge us & made a third attack which Capt
Price Newman who was in command of the picketts succeeded in repulsing. But he had lost many men & after dark
sent back to the regiment for reenforcements to supply the
place of the killed & wounded. Just at this time the enemy
made a fourth attack & rushed with such numbers against
some of our picket posts in which they killed one of the
pickets in each of those pits & the other man saw he would
be overwhelmed & killed or captured so he fell back to the
regiment.

Capt John Bird Rogers[16] was sent out with reenforcements. They recaptured the lost portion of the line, capturing some of the enemy, but Cap't Rogers passed through
our line in the dark & without knowing his mistake rushed
right into the enemys line; amindst the roar it was impossible at the time to tell whether he had been shot or not
but as he was never afterwards heard of it was eveident that
this gallant officer here gave up his life.

We remained in this position having almost constant
fighting, sometimes simply skirmishing, sometimes heavy
artillery duelling & once again a short, sharp & fierce assault
on part of the line which we drove back with but small loss
to ourselves. The night of July 2nd Genl Johnston order[ed]
us to retreat but to be sure to make no noise that would
apprise the enemy of our move. It was very difficult to
withdraw without being seen by the yanks for it was a moon
light night [and] a message must be carried to the officer on
the picket line. I went down a kind of gully until I got really
a little further out than our picket line. The yanks fired at
me but missed me. I then began to crawl up to the post

16 John Bird Rogers of Barren County joined the Orphan Brigade in
autumn, 1861, being elected first lieutenant at that time. He was wounded at
Shiloh, but fought in every engagement thereafter until Kennesaw Mountain,
meanwhile rising to the rank of major. He disappeared, as Green relates,
and his fate was never known. Thompson, *Orphan Brigade*, 469-71.

where the officer in charge of our picket line (Capt John Gillium) [17] was, to deliver to him the order & tell him to stealthily withdraw at 12 oclock & follow the army on the road to Smyrna Church. One of our boys raised his gun to fire at me, taking me for a yank, but discovered the error just in time.

July 4th 1864. Had a skirmish with the yanks at this place (at or near Smyrna Church) and fell back to a position near the Chattahoochee River. Skirmished with the yanks here every day until July 9th 1864. That night we crossed the Chattahoochee River. We did not entrench here but kept strict watch of the enemy. Us Eleven Dollar Generals, as the boys in the trenches called themselves, said, "Now watch Mars Joe fall on Sherman when he crosses this river & eat him up."

But Sherman entrenched on the opposite side of the river & having more than double our force he sent an army fully equaling ours to cross miles away & threaten Atlanta in our rear. We remained here some days picketing, we on one side the Chattahoochee River & the yanks on the other.

For a while the picket fireing was fierce but it being so evident that they were just hurting each other & doing nothing towards winning a battle that the boys yelled at each other, "Lets have armistice," & armistice they had. They soon got to trading tobacco for coffee & had quite a friendly time. Some time yank would swim over to our side & some time Reb' would swim over to yank's side & the barter would be conducted. When the officer in command came around, though, the armistice would have to end but the boys would always keep faith with each other. They would yell out when the officer was discovered approaching, "Hunt your holes," & the visitor was always given time to swim home & get in a safe place & get his gun.[18]

17 John W. Gillum was from Logan County. He took part in all engagements of the Brigade until he was wounded at Intrenchment Creek, July 22, 1864. Thompson, 808.

18 Alexander Hunter, who fought in the Seventeenth Virginia Regiment,

I was dead on my feet here, could hardly mount guard & do my other duties. I had a hard chill last night & fever to-day—got some Calomel & Quinine from the surgeon & laid down on my blanket nearly all day. To night after I had dismissed the old guard Gus More came to me with a tin cup full of hot coffee & said, "I saw when you dismissed the old guard that you were sick & I think this cup of coffee will be good for you." He had been on picket duty all day, had arranged an armistice with the picket in his front, had swum the river (only about 200 feet wide however) & swaped some tobacco for good genuine coffee, & brought me this treat because he thought I was sick. When I messed with Co B Gus & I were in the same mess & we have always been fond of each other.

July 15th. The yanks have crossed the Chattahoochee but because of their overwhelmning strength we have had no opportunity to fall upon & punish them. This fact has caused President Davis to remove Genl Joseph E. Johnston.

July 18th. Genl John B. Hood has been placed in command. The boys have no objection to him but they dont think there is another General in the world eaqual to Genl Joseph E.—except Genl R. E. Lee.

The removal has cast a gloom over the army.

———————
has given a parallel account of fraternization in his *Johnny Reb and Billy Yank*. Cited in Commager (ed.), *The Blue and the Gray*, I, 325-27.

11 ATLANTA

If Joseph E. Johnston had been removed because of what was termed in Richmond his timidity, Confederate authorities would not be able to censure his successor on that score. John B. Hood, given the temporary rank of general to correspond with the assignment, took command of the Army of Tennessee on July 18. In the next ten days he lashed out at the besieging host in three major offensives.

A few miles north of Atlanta, Peachtree Creek ran through steep banks due west, emptying into the Chattahoochee River about seven miles northwest of the city limits. Johnston had prepared two separate lines of defense: the first was two miles south of and parallel to Peachtree Creek; the second encircled the city just outside its boundary. On July 18 and 19 Hood took a position in the outer line facing Peachtree Creek and awaited Sherman's approach.

Sherman crossed the Chattahoochee north of Peachtree and with Thomas as a pivot swung his army on an arc to the east. Thomas occupied a position north of and parallel to Peachtree. McPherson was on the outer flank approaching the city from the east along the Augusta railroad. Schofield was in the center between them. Sherman had made a tactical error in separating his three armies beyond supporting distance, and Hood moved to take advantage of his own position between them.

While General Cheatham was assigned to the task of holding McPherson and Schofield, Hood concentrated Hardee's and Stewart's corps against Thomas. At 3:00 p.m. on the twentieth Stewart and Hardee attacked Thomas while he was crossing the Peachtree. The attack might have succeeded had not McPherson's advance on the east been so precipitate that Hardee had to detach Cleburne's division to aid Cheatham in stopping this threat. Thereupon the attack on Thomas stalled, and Hood withdrew to his inner line of defense.

The failure of the twentieth did not dampen Hood's offensive ardor. With Stewart and Cheatham now ordered to hold Thomas and Schofield, Hardee was sent on a brilliant, Jackson-like movement against McPherson. McPherson had formed a north and south line across the Augusta road several miles east of Atlanta near Decatur. His left, unprotected by cavalry or terrain, hung in the air. If this left flank could be struck unexpectedly by a powerful force, it could be rolled up and McPherson's army captured or destroyed before aid could reach it.

About midnight on the twenty-first Hardee withdrew from the lines and took his four divisions into Atlanta. With Bates' division, of which the Orphan Brigade was a part, leading the way, the corps moved by a circuitous route south, then east. Past the unsuspecting Union flank they marched, until shortly after daylight they were in McPherson's rear. Then, facing to the left, they formed line of battle and prepared for the thrust that, had fate been impartial, might have brought disaster to Sherman's army even at this late date.

Completely ignorant of the Confederate flanking movement and without design other than to add strength to his left flank, McPherson had ordered General Granville Dodge's Sixteenth Corps forward from Decatur. While Hardee's corps was marching east, the Sixteenth was marching in parallel column in the opposite direction, the two columns hidden from one another by a grove of trees. Had McPherson been forewarned, he could not have designed a better defense for the flank movement. When Hardee's attack came, Dodge's corps of veterans by merely facing to the left were in line of battle to meet it.

This battle of the twenty-second was the bloodiest of the entire campaign. Losses on both sides were nearly even —about four thousand each. It was here that the gallant McPherson was killed when he rode unexpectedly into a Confederate skirmish line and then tried to escape. The struggle raged from noon until night, when Hood yielded the field and withdrew.

Sherman now controlled the railroads on three sides of Atlanta, which was being supplied by the one line south to Macon. To cut off this supply line Sherman began to move by the right flank, sliding by Atlanta on the west and feeling for the Macon railroad. Hood sensed this and moved in parallel column to forestall it. The two forces met at Ezra Church a few miles west of Atlanta on July 28. After a struggle of several hours Hood again withdrew, but held the line of the railroad.

During the entire month of August, Sherman edged to the right, southward and eastward. But wherever he advanced he found the Confederate line entrenched opposite. Meanwhile, Sherman had sent his cavalry under Generals Stoneman and McCook to raid beyond the Confederate lines and destroy the Macon road at Jonesboro and farther south. But Wheeler and Alfred Iverson, falling on the Union cavalry, routed it.

On the night of August 25 the Union armies were drawn back from their lines west and southwest of Atlanta and struck for Jonesboro, twenty-five miles south of Atlanta. The

145

corps of Hardee and S. D. Lee were rushed there and gallantly attempted to dislodge the Union army on August 30-31. Their failure made the fall of Atlanta inevitable. Hood retreated hastily to Lovejoy's Station, a few miles below Jonesboro.

Johnny Green was, of course, in the midst of all this bitter fighting. The Orphan Brigade was part of Hardee's corps and participated in the battle of Peachtree Creek on July 20. The next night it was withdrawn from the lines and led Hardee's flanking movement which resulted in the battle of the twenty-second. The Brigade was then moved to the west of Atlanta and was engaged in the battle at Ezra Church on the twenty-eighth. On the next day the Brigade was sent to Jonesboro to intercept Stoneman's raid on the Macon railroad at that point. The Union raiding force, however, avoided Jonesboro, and the Brigade was returned to the vicinity of Atlanta.

On August 28 when the beginning of Sherman's move on Jonesboro was detected, the Kentucky Brigade together with an Arkansas brigade was sent there to protect that important point. From the evening of the twenty-ninth until the morning of the thirty-first those two brigades held off the overwhelming numbers in General O. O. Howard's Army of the Tennessee. About noon of the thirty-first Hardee arrived with his and S. D. Lee's (formerly Polk's) corps, and Hardee ordered a full scale attack on the constantly growing Union force. This attack was repulsed with heavy loss, and the fate of Jonesboro, and thus of Atlanta, was sealed. It was after this repulse that Green, John B. Spurrier, and Thomas Young made the heroic rescue which Green relates in the diary and which is recorded by the Brigade's historian.

On the next day, September 1, Green's regiment, the Ninth, together with Govan's brigade on its left, was engulfed in a Union charge, and Green and his companions were taken prisoner and held for several weeks before they were exchanged.

146

*J*ULY 20TH 1864. A short sharp fight we had at Peachtree Creek to day. Lost seve[r]al men killed & wounded. The army is massed around Atlanta now. We were slowly moving from one position to another nearly all night July 20th & in the afternoon of July 21st set in motion & after marching in a rather aimless way nearly all day were finally placed in the trenches west of the Burkhead road. As we passed by Genl Johnston's old Head Qrs (still occupied by him) so continuous from our men was the call for him that he came out on the porch as we passed by & the cry went up, "God bless Genl Johnston for ever."[1]

The afternoon of the 21st we were set in motion again; we marched through Atlanta & turned towards the right of our line; we now hear the rumor that we are to attack the enemy on his flank. We poke along until nearly day light. We hear that we are to attack the enemy at day light at a point near a little village called Decatur but it is still three miles off. Our guide seems to have missed the road & this makes us late.

Day light comes & we are still three miles from the point

---

[1] In his memoirs General Hood charged that Johnston deserted him at this hour and that "The evening of the 18th of July found General Johnston comfortably quartered at Macon." *Battles and Leaders*, IV, 336. If Johnny Green saw him on July 21, Hood's charge is disproved.

of attack; it has been a terribly tedious march. The sun comes up & makes the heat so oppressive that many of the boys throw away their blankets rather than carry them over their shoulders. We finally reach our appointed position, form line of battle, advance a line of skirmishers & wait for Walkers brigade[2] to come up & go into the fight on our left.

Finally at about 8-30[3] the order for attack is given. It is supposed we have gone far enough to our right to over lap the left of the ennemy & thus turn his flank. Soon our skirmish line has found the enemy. We drive in their skirmishers & our line of battle comes up with our skirmishers. They fall into their position with their regiments & all push forward.

We now discover that the yanks have two lines of battle in front of us, both strongly entrenched. They pour their lead into us [and] their three batteries open on us slaying our men right & left. We give them a volley & push forward through an open woods. We are halted by a staked & ridered fence. The comma[n]d is, "Load boys, then go over the fence & rush on them; when in close range give them a volley & then charge & give them the bayonet."

In some places where the fence is not too strong to be thrown a number of the men take hold of it and throw it down. Just where I was, it was too strongly built to yield to our efforts to throw it, so we climbed over. Unfortunately for me when I got over the top rail my canteen, which was full of water & swung around my neck, stayed on the other side of the fence while I was held on the yankie's side suspended to the top rail by the strap of my canteen. I could not disentangle it & my feet could not reach the ground. Minnie balls & grape shot were splintering that rail & there I was held a fair mark for the yanks. I was making desperate efforts to free myself when much to my delight a yankee bullet that

2 Major General William H. T. Walker commanded a division in Hardee's corps at this time, not a brigade. *O.R.*, Series 1, XXXVIII, pt. 3, p. 680.

3 Brigadier General Daniel C. Govan, whose brigade led the assault, did not move to the attack until 11:40 A.M. and did not make contact with the enemy until 1:00 P.M. *Ibid.*, 737-38.

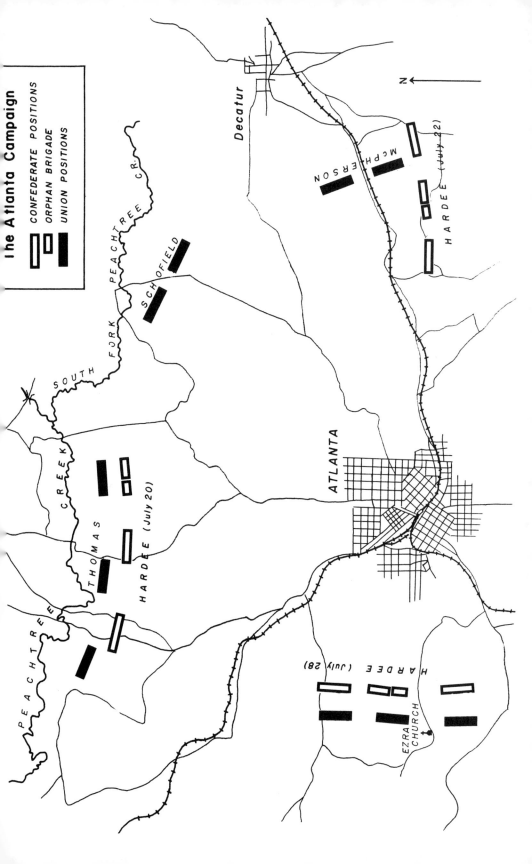

The Atlanta Campaign

CONFEDERATE POSITIONS
ORPHAN BRIGADE
UNION POSITIONS

N

Decatur

McPHERSON

HARDEE (July 22)

SCHOFIELD

PEACHTREE CR.

SOUTH FORK

CREEK

THOMAS

PEACHTREE

HARDEE (July 20)

ATLANTA

HARDEE (July 28)

EZRA CHURCH

stung me on the shoulder cut that canteen strap & left me free to join the other boys in our rush upon the enemies works.

Here General Walker who was to charge the enemy on our left was killed & his men struck a mill pond which they could not get through. After wading in it & getting entangled in briars & brush it was impossible to make their way through, [and] they had to fall back. This left the enemy in their front disengaged & they poured their fire into us. Here a number of our men were killed & many more wounded. Captain Fayette Hewett's horse had been killed under him as we made the charge.

We drove the enemy out of the first line of their works in our front but they fell back upon the second line & rallied in those works & our General [Lewis, Bate, Hardee?], finding that the line on our left could not come up to our support, ordered us to fall back. This was really attended with more danger than to advance if it had not been for the fact that by this time the yanks had brought up so many reenforcements that to advance would have meant certain capture. But so soon as we turned our backs upon them they poured the shot into us & caused many of our dear boys to bite the dust. We fell back over the brow of a hill and reformed and laid down to rest after putting out a line of pickets.

As we were hurrying back with grape & canister & minnie balls pouring in on us & getting some of our men every second I passed by Capt Hewett standing by his dead horse apparently trying to get his saddle off the dead animal & I thought it was the most foolish thing I ever saw for a man to take all that risk for a saddle. That night when we were sitting around Head Qr's I asked Capt Hewett why he took such a risk for a saddle, [for] I expected every minute to see him fall.

He said, "No indeed I would never have stopped there for my saddle but as we were going into the fight one of the boys was about to throw his blanket away saying it was too hot to go into a fight a day like this with a blanket over your shoulder. I told him I would carry it on my horse. I had it tied to my saddle & as we were falling back I did not want him to lose his blanket. I brought it out & gave it to him & he will need it before this campaign is over." Such thoughtful kindness at such a moment shows the coolness & kindness of this dear officer & causes all the men to love him.

We held this position all night (the night of July 22d 1864) & the next day we withdrew & again took position within the breast works around Atlanta.

July 23d 1864. Took position again in the trenches around Atlanta. The men set to work to strengthen our defenses. Chevaux de freze [frise], head logs &, where needed, transverses were built, the yanks in the mean time having their diversion by shelling us. We remained here several days.

Jim Bemis the Hospital Stewart [steward] went to a house to get some water fit to drink, for it was a scarce commodity. He found there a widow with a daughter very sick. He prescribed Calomel & Quinine for the little girl & gave a supply to be used by the patient. When he returned the next day the girl was better & the widowed mother was full of gratitude. She wanted to do something for the soldiers in return, so Jim asked her if she had any thing to read & she gave him The Heart of Midlothian. He & I would sit in the rifle pits with the enemies shells flying over us & read this charming story. Sometimes the bursting shells would make so much noise that the person reading aloud would be interrupted by a request "Read that over again; the blamed fool yanks made so much noise I did not hear that sentence."

One day the yanks tried to take a hill in our front that would enable them to bring their battery closer & in a more commanding position. We opened both artillery & infantry on them & drove them back. This interrupted our reading so much that Jim Bemis said, "The 'Dag Gone Yanks' have no soul for literature."

150

July 29th we made a hurried march towar[d]s our left to intercept a raiding party coming across by way of Fairburn & Fayetteville to strike the Macon road. We had a light skirmish & captured a few stragglers. On the next day we withdrew again into the trenches around Atlanta & took a position nearer our left, some other troups having been placed in the trenches we had previously occupied. Cannonading & light skirmishing until August 5th 1864 when we were moved to the Sandtown road about two miles from our former position.

We were here posted near Utoy Creek to repel an attack expected to be made by a flanking party reported to be moving in this direction. We were given entrenching tools & set vigorously to work but the enemy was soon on us & we dropped the pick & spade & did rapid work with our rifles. The yanks retired & as it was now night we worked diligently & completed our trenches. At day light the enemy began to feel us & skirmishing kept up until about one PM when they made a savage assault but we repulsed them handsomely notwithstanding they made three determined attacks upon us.

A portion of their forces effected a lodgement in some timber on a hill from which they annoyed the line on our right. We were ordered to charge this position, which we did, & drove away all except about thirty of them who fought desperately. These we completely overpow[er]ed & captured. So gallant was this fight that Genl Stephen D Lee issued a Genl Order complimenting our Division.[4] Genl Bate of Tennessee was at this time our Major Genl.

The enemy lost much more heavily in this days fighting than we did; his loss in killed, wounded & captured was estimated to be about 800 men. The next day we retired into the main line of entrenchments, manning the rifle pits. Our line was so extended now that our men were one yard apart.

[4] General Lee's complimentary order is in *O.R.*, Series 1, XXXVIII, pt. 3, p. 765.

The enemy made frequent demonstrations as though they were ready to assault us in our works. They would open their cannon on us around the whole line & advance their skirmishers. We generally laid low & saved our amunition but our sharp shooters were so well posted that their skirmishers were soon repulsed & much damage done amongst the gunners in their batteries. Sometimes they would open every battery along the line at day light. This would hurry us out as we thought now they have determined to make the grand attack, [but] after an hour or so of this demonstration they would quiet down & nothing more be done but a sharp shooter here & there would be killed & another take his place.

One day towards the last of Aug 1864 just before sun down they began a terrific cannonading & kept it up until dark but did nothing else. They then quieted down; not even a picket gun was heard in our front that night. The next morning [August 26] our skirmishers reported they had withdrawn from our left. This was reported to Genl Hood & we were ordered to develope their position. We discovered that their right had been retired & a new position had been taken. It afterwards was learned that part of their force had been withdrawn & sent towards East Point & Jonesboro to flank us & cut off our retreat.

At night on Aug 28th we were started on a hurried march to Jonesboro. The night was very hot & a most fatigueing march we had of it.

Aug 29th 1864. We reached Jonesboro ahead of the enemy & began fortifying with the few tools we had. The Cavelry report to us to-day that a whole Corps of the enemy are pressing on this way. Our regiment is sent out about three miles from town to meet the Yanks. We take up a position in a skirt of woods with an open field in our front. Our Cavelry are skirmishing with them. Soon they open their artillery on the Cavelry & they fall back through our line & will take up a position in our rear & when we find that we can no longer hold back the enemy's advance we will fall back through the skirmish line formed by our Cavelry & thus try to keep back this force of 20,000 yankies until Genl Hardee can get here with reenforcements, but I fear any force he can bring will be greatly outnumbered by the enemy as our latest Cavelry scouts report that the yanks are sending 40,000 men here with the determation to break our lines at this poi[n]t with the hope of capturing Hoods army.

We soon saw the blue coats swarming in the woods on the other side of the field in our front. Our sharp shooters opened with their long range guns on them & we saw several fall & the others begin to seek cover. They posted a battery in position where it was to a degree masked from sight & began to shell us. We laid still as they were beyond the range of our infantry guns but our sharp shooters after a while got sight of their battery & made it so hot for them that they deployed a line of skirmishers & advanced against us. When they got within range of our rifles we gave them a volley that killed many of them & drove back the others. Then they formed in double line & advanced against us. We knew we could not drive them back for theirs was a double line & ours only one line in a single rank & they extended way beyond us on each flank.

We fell back behind the Cavelry & the enemy advanced very slowly, being evidently afraid that we had a great force for a few of our Cavelry would show themselves first in one place beyond our flank & then on the other flank so as to create the impression that our line extended further than theirs. We kept them back until dark & then left the Cavelry to watch them, while we fell back to a point near Jonesboro & began again to entrench & notwithstanding we were marching all last night we had to work with the pick & spade nearly all this night the 29th of August.

Aug 30th. We hear the cavelry skirmishing with them very briskly this morning. We complete our rifle pits & wait, momentarily expecting our cavelry to be driven in & the

153

fight to begin, but the enemy certainly did not realize the fact that we had less than 2,000 men to their 20,000 or more.[5]

Late in the afternoon of the 30th of August 1864 our cavelry was driven in & we gave the yanks a few shots from our battery & our infantry skirmishers opened on them & gave them a check.

We certainly have cause for anxiety—20,000 or more of the enemy in our front pressing us hard & we with not more than 2,000 trying to hold them back until Genl Hardee can get here with reenforcements. Oh! that Hardee or night would come.

Our bold stand seems to have the desired effect; they evidently dont believe that so insignificant a force would defy an army of 20,000. They halt for the night knowing that heavy reenforcements are coming to them. But at daylight on Aug 31st Genl Hardee has arrived with 10,000 Confedertes good & true. But his had been a forced march at night & it was really nearly noon before his entire force had arrived & gotten their rations.

Genl Hardee determines to attack this 20,000 of the enemy with his 12,000 Jaded troops.[6] The yanks have made good use of the past 18 hours. They have chosen a strong position and entrenched within rifle shot of our breast works. But the order to attack & carry their works is given. As soon as we are called to attention & form outside our works they open artillery & infantry on us. "Forward!" is the command.

---

[5] On the evening of the thirtieth General O. O. Howard had deployed the Fifteenth, Sixteenth, and Seventeenth Army corps, totaling more than 25,000 men, in front of Jonesboro. General Jeff C. Davis arrived more with the Fourteenth Corps and attacked by 4:00 P.M. on the thirty-first. This brought the Union forces at Jonesboro to 43,000, and the entire Union army was in supporting distance (*O.R.*, Series 1, XXXVIII, pt. 1, pp. 81, 82, 116). The Confederate forces there on the thirtieth were the three brigades of Lewis, Armstrong, and Govan—about 2,000 men. Hardee's and Lee's corps totaling 22,000 were dispatched to their support, but all did not arrive until about 1:00 P.M. of the thirty-first. Lee was ordered back to Atlanta on the night of the thirty-first, leaving Hardee with about 14,000 to face the entire Union army which was on the field on September 1. *Ibid.*, pt. 3, pp. 682-83, 700.

[6] By 2:00 P.M. when Hardee launched his attack he had approximately 22,000 men. *Ibid.*, pt. 1, pp. 81, 82, 116; pt. 3, pp. 682-83, 700.

"Hold your fire until you get close to them (at a place pointed out which was about 50 yards from their works) then fire & rush on them with fixed bayonetts & give them the cold steel."

Soon our men begin to fall, rapidly and steadily we advance—but horrow of horrows! just as we have fired the volley at them & begin to rush on them we come to a deep gully ten feet wide & fully as deep. No one can jump this gully & at this close range it will be impossible to clamber up the other side of the gully & reform to rush on them with fixed bayonetts. The shot & shell & minnie balls are decimating our ranks. Forward we rush. The order is given, "Jump into the ditch!" for there we will for a time be out of range of their guns & although the walls of this ditch are so precipitious that we cannot climb out on the other side & renew the assault upon them we are forced to take this shelter & then move out by the flank & withdraw to our former position.

Many of our men have been left dead on the field we have just passed over & many wounded. Some who were wounded just as we got to this deep gully rolled down into the gully where they were taken by the infirmary corps & carried out of the mouth of the gully which fortunately ran off away from the yankee line & in going back to our position the road was protected from the enemy's fire except for a short space. But in this short space Maj Ben Desha & several of our men were severely wounded.

Just as I was about to escape from the terrible fire of shells & minnie balls by following our men by a jump into the ditch, I discovered one of our poor boys whose leg had been shatter[ed] by a fragment of a shell about twenty feet from the ditch struggling to reach that point of safety. Great was his agony & slow his progress & when I ran to his side & helped him into the ditch I thought we both would certainly be riddled by the bullits which were pouring down on us before I could lower him down to those who were already in the ditch, but finally we both got within its protecting walls before further calimity came upon us.

We got back to our trenches & the infirmary corps had their hands full with the wounded. The field hospital was located far to the rear because no point of safety could be found closer, therefore the litter bearers had more than they could do.

The enemy continued to fill the air with shot & shell. They seemed infuriated & volley after volley came from their rifle pits. Many of our poor wounded men lay in close range to their works; pitiful cries came for help [and] volunteers were called for to rescue our wounded.

John B. Spurrier[7] of the 6th Ky & Thos Young[8] of Co C Ninth Ky promptly responded & I joined them. We for a moment listened to locate three wounded men, each to run to a certain man & help him in. As we dashed across this open field the yanks just rained bullits at us. The minnie balls were singing in our ears & raising a cloud of dust about our feet but each reached his man & got him so he could assist him into our lines. Fortunately both arms of my man were sound. I helped him into a sitting posture, then had him put his arms around my neck & thanks to the Yanks I got him safe to our lines without further wound. I say thanks to the Yanks because if they had kept up that murderous fire while we were slowly & with difficulty bearing our burdens off the field both the rescuers & the rescued would certainly have been killed. But when we stood up with the wounded and turned to bear them off the field, suddenly the enemy ceased to fire & gave a shout of applaus. They seemed just to have realized what we had come running out there for & cheered us as a sign of their approval of the act. We brought in the rest of our wounded without a shot being fired at us. We got them back to our works & they were carried to the field hospital.

[7] Spurrier was from Louisville. He fought throughout the war, after having been seriously wounded at Shiloh. Thompson, *Orphan Brigade*, 758, 273.

[8] Thomas B. Young was from Bowling Green. Thompson, 830.

156

We occupied our works the remainder of the day & that night for the first time in three days we slept, but of course our pickets had a weary time to keep awake.

All this time the enemy's reenforcements keep pouring in & at Atlanta they have pressed our men more & more closely & it is apparent that we will be surrounded if we do not give up Atlanta but so closely are we pressed there & so greatly outnumbered that Genl Stephen D. Lee is sent back to a point near Atlanta to enable Genl Hood to withdraw the remainder of his army without a total rout. Genl Hardee with a force scarcely 12,000 strong is left to hold in check an army of about 40,000. This point must be held twenty hours longer or Hoods army will be lost, for this is their only road upon which to retreat. The boys with dejected spirits say you would never have caught Genl Joe Johnston in this trap.

Sept 1st 1864. Shells & picket guns waken us at day break. Some Arkansas troops come to take our position in the trenches & we are marched to the Railroad where it is rumored that we will take the cars & hurry to a part of the line near Atlanta where rumor has it that our line is hard pressed. We wait for hours for the cars to come; the yanks catch sight of us & open their batteries on us. There is nothing to do but to lie down & take it; we fortunately however had but one man wounded here. The cars at length came & we began to pile into the flat cars which were to transport us but we were then ordered to get off the cars & hurry on foot to the right of our line at Jonesboro. The enemy were sending an overwhelmning force to flank us on our right.[9]

We hurried to the position shown us & could see myriads of the enemy concentrated in our front already advancing against us. A few picks & spades & axes were given us with instructions to work for dear life to erect some defence to enable us to keep the yanks at bay until night for the remnant of the army had not yet been rescued from Atlanta.

[9] This force was General Thomas' Army of the Cumberland comprising about 47,000 men. *O.R.*, Series 1, XXXVIII, pt. 1, pp. 81, 116.

We must hold the enemy off until night, by which time our forces in Atlanta could be withdrawn & the army reunited about Lovejoy station.

We cut & piled some logs & dug for dear life. The yanks began to shell us but we could not stop. We were two yards apart in our line & we could see them in a large field in our front massing three solid lines of battle to move against us. All the rest of the line on our left was hotly engaged. Just to our left was Govans brigade & to the left of that was Swetts battery,[10] then our line turned to the left at a rather Sharp angle and in the front of that part of our line the yanks were keeping up a furious artillery fire and all the shells that passed over Swetts battery landed right in our midst. There was a good sized tree about six feet in our rear which was cut down by these cannon balls. One shell hit that tree & exploded, killing one man & wounding several. Another shell hit the stump & rolled into the ditch we were digging. The fuse was sizzling, [and] in the next instant it would burst in our midst. Walker Nash[11] had just returned from the rear where he had gone for water, [and] he had a bucket of water in his hand. He saw the danger & dashed the water on the shell extinguishing the fuse & thus no doubt saved the lives of several of our men.

We have done but little in the way of digging rifle pits before the enemy's first line charges upon us. We drop the entrenching tools & seize our guns, fire a volley into them & go at them with charged bayonets. They fall back hurriedly & we as quickly return to our entrenching because we see four solid lines of battle advancing across a wide field against us.

The battery on our left gives us great annoyance as it enfilades us & thus shoots right down our line. We construct

---

10 Swett's Mississippi Battery was commanded by Lieutenant Henry N. Steele. *Ibid.*, pt. 3, p. 674.

11 Walker Nash of Grayson County fought from the beginning to the end of the war, being seriously wounded at Chickamauga. Thompson, *Orphan Brigade*, 845.

as best we can a transverse defence; but a crack is open just where the transverse joins the front works and an occasional minnie ball slips through & brings down one of our men.

A second charge is now made upon us. Two lines coming in Solid phalanx determined to overrun our thin gray line, our men being two yards apart. But with steadiness & deadly fire we meet them. They stagger; they waver. Our fire is so sure [and] so steady we have covered the ground in our front with their dead & dying. They fall back out of this withering fire but a third line advancing to their support presses them on with them. Surely with five times our numbers there is but little chance for us to withstand them. They come as a death wave. Their fire is thinning our slender ranks & surely I never saw men brave death more defiantly than they.

Just to our left, in front of Govans brigade, I saw their color bearers, of which each volunteer regiment had two, one to bear the state colors (theirs was New York) & the other the National Stars & Stripes, rush right up to Govans rifle pits & take their flag staffs & beat our boys in those trenches over the head with the but of the flag staff. Our boys had exhausted their amunition. While I rejoiced to see them both fall the next instant (each with a bayonet run through him) I could not help fe[e]ling those brave men deserved a tear.

But our own men were surely falling like leaves in wintry weather. Fourqueran[12] of our regiment, who had been on the picket line under command of Lieut' Jas McAllen[13] & was now fighting on the left of the regiment, cried out, "Oh I am killed! what shall I do?"

I looked at him & he was sitting down in the trenches trying to pull a bullit out of his forehead. I said, "Fourquin (for that is what we called him) I will pull it out & you then run to the rear & go to the hospital."

12 B. Fourqueran was from Logan County. Thompson, 810.
13 James R. McAllen of Logan County. Thompson, 813.

Just then he got it out & said, "Never mind now, I have
it out."

I just then saw Sam Boutcher[14] fall dead from a ball
which killed J. E. Adams[15] at the same time. The shot came
from a gun poked through the crack between the end of our
front trenches & the transverse. Jim McAllen saw it at the
same instant & grabbed the muzzel of the gun which a yank
had poked through there, fired it off & killed those two men
at one shot. Jim McAllen [had] some one else to help him
bend the gun barrel in there so that Mr Yank could not get
it out & no other gun could be poked in there to do such
murderous work.

Just then Fourqueran, who had again loaded his gun
notwithstanding his desperate wound, cried out, "I got him
but Oh! I cant fight any more my head hurts so." He then
took my advice & went back to the hospital.

Their fourth line has now come up to their assistance;
they have pressed on regardless of our death dealing fire until
they are lying down flat just on the other side of our works.
One great big Yank jumped up on our works & called to
Booker Reed, "Surrender, you dam rebels."

Booker said to him, "The H—l you say," & shot him
dead on the works.

I had my gun loaded, for notwithstanding I as Sergeant
Major carried ordinarily only a sword, I always carried a gun
into a fight with me. I rose from a stooping posture in the
trenches to shoot but just as I looked over our trenc[h]es a
yankee with the muzzle of his gun not six inches from my
face shot me in the fact [face] & neck but fortunately it was
only a flesh wound. It stung my face about as a bee sting
feels but in my knees I felt it so that it knocked me to a
sitting posture. But my gun was loaded and the other fellow had had his shot. I rose & put my gun against his side &
shot a hole through him big enough to have run my fist
through.

14 Sam Boutcher of Hancock County. Thompson, 839.
15 Adams was from Logan County. Thompson, 838.

It was now sullen give & take. The enemy however were lying down & fired only when one of our men loaded & rose to fire & if our man was not killed he took the best aim; indeed we were now placing our guns against the man we fired at, but just as we were taking some hope from this slight advantage the enemy captured our Battery by just swarming over it.

Govans line, seeing this, gave way & Liet Col Wickliffe seeing we would surely be captured gave orders for us to fall back but at this instant a message came, "Hold your ground for reenforcemts are coming."

We again jumped into our pits & resumed our deadly work. Minutes seemed like hours. Would those reenforcements ever come?

Lieut Boyd[16] called out, "Never give up, boys."

Just then a yank jumped to his feet & shot Lieut Boyd dead but Steven Rowan[17] settled the account for he sent a minnie ball crashing through the brain of the man who fired that deadly shot.

Our reenforcements however never came. The enemy swarmed over Govans works on our left & swung around in our rear. The troops we heard coming in our rear were not our reenforcements so longingly hoped for but blue coats who came up behind us, poured one volley into us from the rear & called again to us to surrender. The right of our regiment was not completely surrounded so they escaped but for the left of our regiment there was no escape so we were captured. Many of our other troops were also captured but the rest of Our brigade fell back about one half of a mile & reformed. Capt Fayette Hewett hurried a battery into position & opened on the advancing enemy so fiercely that they thought it was only our first line they had captured & persued no further.

This Battle of Jonesboro was the fall of Atlanta. It was

16 Henry C. Boyd of Cloverport, Kentucky. Thompson, 835.
17 Stephen W. Rowan of Livermore, Kentucky. Thompson, 825.

a matter of life & death to keep this horde of yanks from
advancing further because Genl Hood had not yet gotten
his army safely out of A[t]lanta & this was our only road for
retreat. General Hardee made a determined stand at this
place, notwithstanding the disaster to part of his line. He
massed several batteries & concentrated their fire upon that
part of the enemies line that had captured us. If the assistance of these batteries had come to us fifteen minutes
earlier our line would never have been broken, but they
were the first of the troops falling back from Atlanta &
after straining every nerve to get to us sooner were only able
to get to our hard pressed troops in time to save us from
utter disaster.

The furious fire from our Batteries & our insignificant
earthworks with only a hand full of men to defend them
convinced the enemy that our main line was yet behind for
them to meet before they could advance further & they were
therefore content to hold the ground already gained & wait
for the morrow to renew the attack.

Those of our command who were captured were hurried
under guard to the rear. Our batteries which were directed
against the enemy were now bursting shells in the midst of
our men who were prisoners as well as amidst our captors.
One shell which burst right amongst us almost tore Ed
Hagans[18] arm off. He cried out, "They got me that time
instead of getting a yank."

The blood spirted over all of us showing that an artery
was ruptured. Booker Reed & I took a handkerchief which
I was fortunate enough to have, tied it around the arm above
the wound, took a little stick & put through the handkerchief
& twisted the handkerchief tight until we stopped the flow of
blood & Booker helped Ed back to the Yankee hospital while
I helped John Webb[19] back. John was second Lieut in Co D

18 Ed Hagan was from Marion County. Thompson, 819.
19 Lieutenant John H. Webb of Cynthiana had fought in every engagement of the Brigade from Shiloh to Jonesboro. Thompson, 831.

of our regiment & had a terrible wound in the head of which he died in a few weeks time.

It was dusk by the time we got back to the field hospital & I could not help feeling sorrow as well as satisfaction when I beheld the work we had made for their surgeons. The dead & wounded in great numbers were here. I saw that their surgeon would be working all night with their wounded & many of our men who were captured were suffering much from their wounds & I had a flesh would [wound] which bathing & simple serit[?] & a bandage would make more comfortable so I went to the Surgeon & said to him that many of our men there were very uncomfortable from their wounds, that I saw he would be busy all night with his own men, so if he would give me a basin & bandages & salve that I could do a good deal to add to the comfort of our boys.

He said, "Bully for you, my man. I will attend to your boys as soon as possible but I must look after my own boys first," to which I assested [assented] as being all right.

He gave me all the pariphernalia & told me to come to him if I wanted any thing else or any instruction. I washed all our boys wounds & bound them up & did what I could for them & washed my own wound & bandaged it as best I could. Poor John Webb suffered a great deal & so did Ed Hagan. John's wound seemed to me to be a scalp wound for I washed it & felt the scull all along the course the ball had traveled & it did not seem to me that the skull was fractured, but he was taken to the yankee hospital at Atlanta & died in about two weeks.

I had lost my cap & also my blanket in the fight so I helped myself to a hat which was lying over the face of a dead yank & I knew he would never again need the blanket which was spread over him so I took that also & his over coat cape. The Ambulances were hauling the wounded all night coming & going to the permanent hospital so I thought this should be my night to make my escape. I thought with a yankee hat on & a yankee blanket over my shoulders I could walk away & no body notice. I first tried it on at the back gate for this field hospital had taken possession of the house & yard of a citizen. I was turned back from the back gate by the guard & none of my pleas for permission to step just outside the guard line would do.

I tore a paling off the side fence a little later hoping to slip through the guard line but the guard turned & saw me just as I thought I could carry out my purpose [and] he ordered me back. I then thought I would help load an ambulance & walk off following the ambulance but they were too watchful for me. So the morning came & my night of wakefulness brought not the opportunity for me to escape.

The next morning all those who were able to march were marched over to the head Quarters of the Union Genl Jefferson C. Davis.[20] He ordered a tent fly pitched for us, directed that rations be issued to us and that wood & water & cooking utensils be brought to us. We had the best breakfast that morning we had eaten for many a day, good genuine coffee, hard tack & bacon. Before he sent us to our quarters he said to me, "My good fellow you seem to have been wounded. Has your wound received our Surgeons attention?"

I told him I had dressed it the best I could.

He replied, "That wont do. Here orderly take this man to the surgeon & have his wounds dressed," & I was carefully & skilfully ministered to by their surgeon.

Our Army had fallen back to Lovejoy Station thus leaving the enemy in full possession of Atlanta & Jonesboro. They burned the R. R. depot & tore up even the rails leading Southward; they piled the rails together & then took the crossties & built great fires over the rails & when red hot they had great big iron hooks for handling the red hot rails which they would take & wind them around a telegraph pole.

[20] Major General Jefferson C. Davis commanded the Fourteenth Union Army Corps, which had formed the spearhead of the Union movement from the left or north.

We remained here for three days. The next day they marched us up to Atlanta & put us in a prison pen which we had used to put Federal prisoners in. It had a large frame building in the centre but not large enough to shelter all of us from the rain or from the sun, both of which we had an abundance of. The rations of hard tack, bacon & coffee were so good that we felt we would soon be growing fat. Every day they sent emissaries in to ask if some did not want to take the oath of allegiance to the United States. They would stick hand bills all around offering amnesty & transportation home to any who would take the oath not to fight again in the confederate army but I rejoyce to say not a Kentuckian would listen to them.

Soon we were sent to Chattanooga & put in a pen with not a bit of shelter. It was a block right in the business part of the city with every house burned down and the chared ruins tumbled in upon themselves. To get a level spot to lie down we had to pile the bricks to one side out of the way.

They seem to think they have been treating us too good, [for] the rations now are cold corn bread & cold beef & no coffe & scarcely any water. They put their posters offering amnesty & transportation all around & send in their emissaries urging the men to go home & stop fighting, saying "Dont you see the Confederacy is whipped?" But thank God not one of our brigade would listen to them.

They kept us in this discomfort for some time, evidently thinking that the thoughts of home & good rations would cause some to weaken, but if any did, it was very few & I know not one that did. Finally we were put on the cars (cattle cars) & sent to Nashville. Here we were put in the penitentiary.

But great was our joy the next day when we learned that Genls Hood & Sherman had agreed to exchange prisoners captured in and around Atlanta. We were sent by rail to Jonesboro & exchanged eighteen days after we were captured.

I walked over the ground in front of the position we defended & there was not a twig which had not been cut down by bullets & there were trees as big as my leg which were actually whittled down by minnie balls. It seemed a miracle that any living soul could have survived that hailstorm of lead.

12 MOUNTED

With the defeat at Jonesboro, Hood, narrowly escaping encirclement, managed to withdraw the remaining troops from
Atlanta and to concentrate the army at Lovejoy's Station,
thirty miles south of Atlanta and only four miles from Jonesboro. Here the two armies faced each other for a week.
Then Sherman withdrew his entire force to the vicinity of
Atlanta.

Hood had still an army of 40,000 veterans and determined to operate on Sherman's line of communications.
By October 1 he had recrossed the Chattahoochee and
busied himself tearing up the railroad at various points
between Atlanta and Chattanooga. Sherman pursued him
for a time until it became evident that Hood's objective was
the recapture of middle Tennessee. Ordering reinforcements
to Thomas and Schofield, whom he had already detached
at Nashville, Sherman turned his back on Hood, leaving him
and his army to the annihilating fate which Thomas was
brewing for him in Tennessee.

With nothing that could be dignified with the name of
army to oppose him, Sherman now determined to sever his

own line of communications and sally forth "to ruin Georgia."[1] Collecting ample provisions for thirty days and sending back to Chattanooga all his sick as well as other impedimenta, he started for Savannah on November 15.

He divided his army of approximately 60,000 into two wings; the right, commanded by Major General O. O. Howard, was composed of the Fifteenth and Seventeenth corps; the left, commanded by Major General H. W. Slocum, was composed of the Fourteenth and Twentieth corps. In addition there was a cavalry division of 5,000 commanded by Brigadier General Judson Kilpatrick.

With Hood in north Alabama preparing for his fatal sally into middle Tennessee, the Confederacy was scraping the bottom of the barrel in an effort to halt Sherman's threatening force. On November 17 General Hardee was assigned command of all forces in Georgia south of the Chattahoochee and was instructed to gather convalescents and local troops to resist Sherman. The bulk of his forces consisted of about 3,500 cavalry under Major General Joseph Wheeler and about 3,000 Georgia militia under Major General Gustavus W. Smith. There was little this feeble force could do but retreat in front of Sherman while harrying his flanks and attacking cavalry units or foragers who straggled too far from the protection of the infantry. Union commanders in this campaign were scornful of their opposition. Their reports are replete with such expressions as, "The enemy kept his troops at a very discreet distance," "the enemy easily repulsed," "the enemy completely routed."

By December 10 Sherman had arrived before Savannah and laid siege to that city. On the night of December 20 Hardee, with no hope of reinforcements, crossed the Savannah River into South Carolina, and next morning Sherman took possession of the "Christmas present" he was to bestow upon Lincoln.

After the fall of Jonesboro the Orphan Brigade had been

[1] Sherman, *Memoirs*, II, 159.

168

ordered to Griffin and then to Forsyth, there to be mounted and henceforth separated from the Army of Tennessee. When Johnny Green returned from prison camp in Nashville he joined the new detail and was thus a part of Wheeler's Cavalry lying on Sherman's flank or retreating sullenly before him.

*S*EPT 19TH 1864. We are back in Dixie at Forsythe Ga. The small remnant of our Brigade, now about 300 men, are gathered together here for the purpose of being mounted, with the hope in mind that the time may come when all that are left of the five thousand young men, good & true, who so gallantly gave themselves at Bowling Green Ky to the Southern cause, may press the enemy back and driving him from our beloved land reach our native Kentucky soil & there recruit our depleted ranks & redeem our state from the oppression of the Despoiler.

We formed line of battle to meet the enemy at Dalton Ga May 7th 64 with Eleven Hundred men in our ranks. In these four months we have had over Seventeen Hundred killed & wounded—a very few have escaped any casualty, but many others have been wounded two or three times—some not leaving the ranks notwithstanding their wounds & others going to the hospital & as soon as possible returning to the ranks only to be killed or again wounded. It was thus possible that we should have 1700 casualties.

From Forsyth we went back, as soon as we secured horses for a reasonable portion of our men, to Griffin & from thence to Newnan Ga where a detail of men were set to work under the direction of Capt Chris Bousche [Bosche] to manufacture saddles for our boys. It was remarkable what good texas saddles he soon turned out. The men would cut the fork from a sapling for the front & the pommel & make the rest of the saddle tree out of plank, then kill a hog, take the hair off in a vat of lime water, stretch the skin over the saddle tree & it was then ready for the leather[er]s.

From Newnan we went to Campbelton on picket duty & from here to Stockbridge on picket duty.

Our boys were so glad to get horses, even poor as these were, that they treated them like they were frail & tender brothers. They would rub them, curry them & wash their feet with the most constant care and solicitude.

One day I volunteered to take charge of a squad to scout on the yankees left & ascertain whether they had any considerable force in Atlanta. Of course I was desirous of bringing back a most accurate report of just where the yankees were, how many & whether they were preparing for a move forward or backward. Some had gone back to Allatoona, but I ascertained they were in great force in Atlanta still. They had been making active preparation for a move but we could not find out which way. I thought I would interview a lady whom I saw standing in the front door of a house near the road & who seemed to be viewing our squad with some anxiety. I rode a little closer to her & asked if there had been any yankee soldiers there that morning & she said yes, fifty or sixty of them, & she said every one of them had these guns that will shoot sixteen times without stopping to load. They were beginning to arm their cavelry with the repeating gun. She said, "Dont you go any nearer for they have better horses than our boys; they have stolen every good horse about here."

But I determined to go still closer to Atlanta notwithstanding I could see their camps very plainly. We rode on up the lane, going up a rather steep hill, I at the head of my squad. Just as I got to the top of the hill I saw the squad the lady had described coming back just towards us. They

171

discovered us just as I discovered them. They were about four hundred yards away. They comma[n]ded gallop; I commanded right about wheel gallop & "boys it's a race for life!"

We wheeled & tore down the hill. For a while we were out of their sight but when they reached the top of the hill our squad of eight men were in full sight. They had fifty men. We whipped & spired [spurred] but they gained on us. They let fly a volley at us & the bullits tore up the dirt all around us. The horse of one of our boys was struck by a bullit but it was a flesh wound. We were in a long lane & they were gaining on us. We pressed our horses to the utmost but the roar of their horses hoofs told plainly they were gaining on us. We were nearing the end of the lane. I caled to my boys, "Take to the woods if we can beat them to the end of the lane." Just then they let fly another volley at us but the balls all passed over our heads.

Thank goodness we got to the end of the lane & dashed out into a path but before we got out of sight, lo & behold, a great big tree was blown down right across our path. All the other boys horses except Robert McCorkle's[2] & mine jumped the log & were soon out of sight. Robert's horse was (a mule) & though no ten rail fence could keep him out of a corn field he would not jump that log. I was behind & yelled at Robt, "Make that mule jump," but he would not jump. & I could not get a chance until he got out of the way.

Just then they shot another volley at us & this put fire enough in Robt's mule to get him over & my little mare flew over like a bird & soon we were out of sight in the woods & the enemy, who were always afraid to follow in the woods for fear of an ambush, abandoned the pursuit & we returned to camp in safety.

We did picket duty around Atlanta until the early part

2 Robert G. McCorkle of Louisville was severely wounded at Shiloh and missed all the fighting from then until the spring of 1864, when he returned and fought throughout the remainder of the war. Thompson, *Orphan Brigade,* 821.

172

of Nov 1864, and at the same time being sometimes drilled in Cavelry drill.

Nov 14th we took position at Stockbridge to oppose a column which Sherman had advanced on that road.

Nov 15th the enemy's cavelry attacked us but when we responded with our long range endfield [Enfield] rifles & gave them such a warm welcome they concluded they had run up on infantry & so withdrew for a while until they could bring up their heavy columns, when we gracefully retired, mounted our horses & rode away.

It was now our duty to hang on the flank of the enemy & annoy him all we could, to attack every marauding party that we could find unsupported by a heavy force & when possible to obstruct Sherman's advance.

From Stockbridge we hurried over to LoveJoy Station & fell upon a force there & drove them back upon their main army. This was a sudden & animated little fight but one in which the enemys chief effort was to get back to their main infantry force. We fell back before Shermans advancing columns, retreating towards Clinton.

Sherman sends parties of marauders throughout the country who burn & destroy every thing that is of the slightest use to civilzed man. He burns the houses, takes every vestage of food or forage, rips open the feather beds, takes the mules & horses & kills the hogs. Indeed, his boast is that if a crow flies over this country after he has been through it, he will have to carry his rations with him.[3]

Just out side of Clinton we charged a party which had burned the planters house. Some of the negroes under the directions of the women had brought the piano & some of the furniture out of the burning house, but the yankee soldiers had torn all the insides out of the piano [to] feed their horses in the body of it, and had broken the furniture into small pieces. We charged them & drove them away,

[3] This boast is generally attributed to General Phillip Sheridan after his devastation of the Shenandoah Valley in Virginia in the autumn of 1864.

killing one of the vandals & wounding others. This was
Nov 20th 1864.

We bivioacked here all night & although the enemy
had left but little to eat for man or beast, the lady whose
house had been burned told us we were welcome to fodder
for our horses & we could get sweet potatoes out of a big
mound in the garden & she thought we could find her hogs
in the woods & we could kill & eat what we needed.

Nov 21st. We followed the enemy cautiously toward
Macon which is about twelve miles from Clinton. We attacked their rear guard & had quite a skirmish with them &
hurried them out of Macon but not before they had applied
the torch, however; while their soldiers were present the
women & the negroes dared not try to extinguish the flames
nor to save any thing from destruction, but after we came
they did. Some of the negroes followed on with the Yankee
army but the large majority stayed with their Mistress & did
what they could to provide the necessaries of life. Great love
& honor is due those negroes who were faithful to the helpless & bereaved women & children of the South. The only
live stock our poor women saved was such as some faithful
negro hid out in the woods or the swamps.

We left the main road here & took a short cut towards
Griswoldville to get between Sherman's army & the Oconee
River. Genl Jos Wheeler who is in command of our forces
wants to delay Sherman as much as he can at this little River.
He wishes also to give by this delay an oportunity to our
people to hide whatever they can as this is the only way to
save anything. Wheelers five or six thousand cavelry can
hope to do nothing with Shermans 50,000[4] men except to
delay them & punish their marauding parties sufficiently
to make them afraid to get far away from their main column
& thus spare some portion of our country from devastation.

We reached Griswoldville before they did & had a brisk

---

[4] According to Sherman's report his forces numbered more than 60,000
men. *O.R.,* Series 1, XLIV, 7.

174

skirmish with them on the afternoon of Nov 21st. They withdrew & waited for their infantry to come up. On the morning of Nov. 22nd 64 they advanced against us again. We drove back their cavelry but soon the infantry was deployed & advanced against us & we were forced back skirmishing with them nearly all day, when we fell back & crossed Oconee River. Here they confronted us early Nov 23d. We disputed the crossing of this river with them, having brisk skirmishes in which both sides used artillery very savagely. We kept them back this day & on the 24th they came at us again but we still had the best of them.

On the Morning of the 25th, however, they had gotten a good ready[?] & they moved upon us in such force they overpowered us & we had to give way & get away in quick order to keep from being captured by a force which had crossed the river higher up. It was an infantry column which had crossed higher up the river & with the hope of cutting off our retreat they were marching rapidly towards Sandersville. They had an hour or two the start of us, but we were mounted & they were not, so we soon overcame the advantage they had of us at the start. But it was a close race to the point where their road came into ours; indeed, they reached it first but stopped a few hundred yards short to deploy in line of Battle & throw out skirmishers & while they were approaching our road in this cautious way we galloped by & looked down from the top of a steep hill & saw their line of infantry advancing upon us, preceded by a line of skirmishers who took a few shots at us but hit no body but a horse on which was mounted two yankee dutch soldiers, prisoners whom our rear guard had to threaten to shoot because when we would trot first one of them & then the other would fall off & swear by "Himmel, Ich can es nicht machen." After seeing the guards gun cocked & pointed at them, however, with a sure determination to leave no prisoner behind us unless he be a dead one, they both clung to that horse. It was really pathetic to see their frantic efforts

175

to cling on after this; the horse was a miserably rough one & they were fat clumsy dutchmen who had never ridden a horse before in their lives.

The road to Sandersville was built through a swamp, being thrown up like a Railroad fill extending nearly a mile with the swamp on each side through which the enemy could not penetrate. We made a stand here to retard them as much as possible. Capt Saml H. Buchannan posted the pickets & was with them when the enemys advanced guard came up. He determined to hold them back until our main force could be formed in line to resist their advance. He had quite a sharp fight with them & drove them back. He then came back to report to our Brigade commander Genl Joseph H Lewis. (Capt Buchanan was our Inspector Genl.) After explaining the position of the troops & the result of the brush he had just had with the enemy he remarked in a casual way, "I have been shot through this leg Genl & I b[e]-lieve I had better go to the rear & have it dressed by the surgeon." This was the first we knew of his being wounded & he treated it as a most casual circumstances notwithstanding he was shot clear through the leg. He went to the rear & we lay down in line of battle to biviouac for the night, first sending details to kill the nearest hogs which could be found & to get sweet potatoes. This was all the rations we could hope to get unless some one should fall over a stray chicken or two. The horse holders were to fall back until they could find some feed for the horses, give them a feed & them [then] come back to us.

Nov 26th. The enemy came at us pretty early. We had the advantage of position having posted our battery so it would sweep that road for nearly a mile. We hid our sharp shooters also in the edge of the swamp & when their battery would reply to ours those keen eyed marksmen would pick off their artillery men, so that our battery had much the best of the fight. This kept up nearly all day when they made a final dash & we fell back but we punished them so severely they did not follow us far that day. The next day we fell back to Davisboro, a place about 12 miles from Sandersville.

Nov 28th we skirmished with them at Davisboro. From there we were gradually pressed back to near Louisville Ga. which is about 12 or 15 miles from Davisboro.

Nov 29th we saw smoke a short distance from Louisville on one road. We mounted our horses & hurried to that point. Here we saw a small cavelry force burning every thing; the out houses & the residence were already in flames. The owner was a widow whose husband had been killed in the Confederate army. She had several small children & one, a daughter about 10 years old, very sick in bed. The enemy, after setting fire to the house & finding there was a sick child inside, did have humanity enough to bring her & her bed out in time to keep her from burning, but so much afraid were they that some money or other treasure was hidden in the feather bed that they took her off the bed, cut the tick open & ran their arms all through it to make sure nothing of any value should escape them.

We charged upon this squad; they fired one voley at us but then skampered away. The poor grief stricken mother was heart broker [broken] for fear her daughter would die from the fright. She moved into one of the negro cabins but whether her grief had yet an other & a more poigniant pang to be added to it in the death of the poor child we never heard.

We fell back to Louisville to take position on the road upon which Sherman's main army was approaching. Our commisary got some meal & molases for us in the town of Louisville, so we ate a good supper & moved to a favorable position to resist a sudden attack, put out our pickets & the rest of us laid down on the ground after feeding & currying our horses & we had a good nights sleep.

The next day, though, Nov 30th 1864, we skirmished with the enemy nearly all around Louisville but that night we withdrew leaving the little town to the enemy. We fell back on the road towards Statesboro, keeping close to the enemy, & had a brush with them every day, Dec 1st, 2nd, 3d & 4th. They left us at Statesboro Dec. 5th. Finding this, our forces were hurried to the Ogeeche[e] River to impede their march. We beat them to this little river & were there on the morning of Dec 6th to oppose their crossing. They tried three different places to cross this day & we drove them back every time. Dec 7th the same experience was had, we having three different skirmishes with them; but that night they crossed at a different point & were making their way towards Ebenezer, a place near the Savannah River where there were some provisions & some stores of amunition. We mounted our horses & rode nearly all night & confronted them at Ebenezer Creek on the morning of Dec 8. We had a sharp little engagement with their cavelry here, when they seemed to abandon the effort to burn the supplies & provisions here & sent marauding parties to burn the homes of the planters. We attacked them & after repeated skirmishes with them this day we drove them towards Eden. This put them between us & Savannah, & at Eden they were to meet another colum of their army, so it made it important for us to get in between them & Savannah. That night we made a detour so as to get betwen them & Savannah. It was a hard ride because we had to go a round-about way & our horses were suffering for feed.

On the morning of Dec 9th, however, we were ready for them & they found us confronting them on exactly the opposite side from our position the day before. Their reenforcements, however, came up & attacked us, [and] after a brisk skirmish we fell back a few miles & formed at a favorable position across their road. When their advanced guard came up we opend fire on them. They attempted to drive us off but could do nothing with us until their artillery came up & opened on us. The defenses & obstructions which we had thrown up with rails could not withstand artillery, so we had to retreat, but we kep this up during the whole day, having frequent brushes with them until near Pooler['s] station. Here we mined the road, placing some bomb shells in the road which just at this point was a plank road; a few planks were lifted, some percussion shells were placed under these planks & about one quarter of a mile away just at the other edge of the swamp we had our artillery ready & when the first bomb exploded our artillery, which until then was out of sight, wheeled into line & opened on their Cavelry column which was in advance. They were thrown into great confusion & rout but only one of their horses was killed & but one dead man was left on the road.[5] It was some time before they advanced again & then only after shelling us for nearly one hour; we, however, held them back until night. But neither our men nor horses had any thing to eat, so we left only a squad to picket this place while the rest of the command fell back to the outskirts of Savannah. Here we got provisions for the men & also for our horses & sent some to the picket force left near Poolers station. It was at this last fight that poor Lt Fielding Forman[6] received a wound from which he died a fews days later.

Dec 10th. The enemy were on us early this morning, but we had sent our horses to the rear & taken position in the trenches around Savannah. So when the yankees came up & got a volley from our enfields & found we had reached the defences around the town they withdrew for a time to let Sherman's whole army come up.

Genl W. J. Hardee is here in command. We have seen a great deal of service with him & the men all admire him. He has gotten together here about Six or Seven Thousand militia. Old men from 50 to 60 years old & boys of 14 to 16

[5] As a result of this mine explosion Sherman ordered some prisoners to march in front with picks and spades to dig up the torpedoes or else to explode them themselves. By some coincidence no more explosions took place. Sherman, *Memoirs*, II, 194. Sherman does not mention the Confederate battery opening on him at this point.

[6] Fielding Forman was from Hartford, Kentucky. Thompson, *Orphan Brigade*, 825.

have rallied to the defense of our South Land. The odds, however, are greatly against us but our men have not lost heart. Genl Hardee has man[n]ed the defenses, & Sherman with his 50,000 [60,000] men gives us work to do every day. There is not a day we do not have heavy cannonading & sharp fighting, Somtimes only brisk skirmish fire & sometimes an assault, but we drive them back & repulse his every effort to break our lines. One day, however, Dec 13, his fleet steamed up the mouth of the Ogeeche[e] River & to-gether with the land forces made a most fierce & determined assault & captured Fort McAlester [McAllister]. This constituted our extreme left.

We readjusted our lines & took position in the inner line of works & kept up our daily fighting. But the land & Naval forces of the enemy had now formed a junction & they could take their time. Daily skirmishing kept up until Dec. 22 [20]. Our horses had been sent across the Savannah river into South Carrolina & we had laid aside our spurs, taken our Enfield Rifles into the trenches & caused many a yankee to bite the dust.

But Hood had fought the battles of Allatoona, Franklin & Nashville & had his army almost annihilated & was in rapid retreat towards Decatur Ala with the main part of his force; [and] Cheatham was coming towards Augusta.

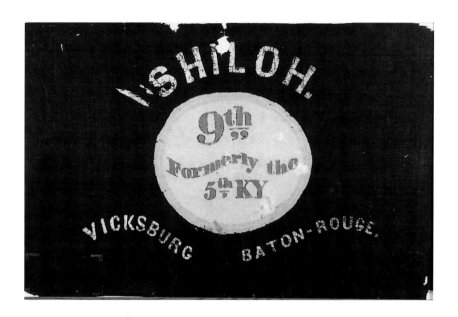

Hardee pattern battleflag of the Ninth, formerly the Fifth, Kentucky Infantry bearing the battle honors "Shiloh," "Vicksburg," and "Baton Rouge." The flag, proudly used by the Ninth Kentucky Infantry at Stone's River, Chickamauga, Chattanooga, Atlanta, and the Carolina campaigns, is the banner that Johnny Green would have remembered most in his years of service in the Ninth Kentucky.
Courtesy of I. Beverly Lake, Wake Forest, North Carolina, and the Museum of the Confederacy

Gen. Benjamin Hardin Helm. Two-time commander of the
Orphan Brigade, Helm hailed from Elizabethtown,
Kentucky. He was married to Emily Todd, half-sister of
Mary Todd Lincoln. Commanding the First Kentucky
Cavalry at Shiloh, the "Beloved and Gallant" Helm was
elevated to command of the Orphan Brigade and led it at
Baton Rouge, where he was wounded, and Chickamauga,
where he was killed. Johnny Green referred to Helm as the
"Idol of his men." Helm is buried in the family cemetery in
Elizabethtown.
Library of Congress

Desperate fighting in the dense thickets at Chickamauga. There General Helm was mortally wounded leading the Orphans to "within a few yards of the enemy's works."
Library of Congress

Col. John W. Caldwell. Born in Russellville, Kentucky, Caldwell practiced law in his hometown before the war. There he raised what became Company A, Ninth Kentucky Infantry. He assumed command of the Ninth Kentucky upon Colonel Hunt's resignation after Stone's River. Caldwell "had fast hold upon the hearts of all the men and officers," remembered Johnny Green.
Ed Porter Thompson, *History of the Orphan Brigade,* 434

Lt. Col. John Cripps Wickliffe. Born in Bardstown to a distinguished Kentucky family, Wickliffe practiced law there before the war. He raised what became Company B, Ninth Kentucky Infantry in Nelson County and rose to command the Ninth Kentucky at Chickamauga when Colonel Caldwell was wounded. He was Lt. Henry Curd's brother-in-law and the cousin to Margaret Wickliffe, Gen. William Preston's wife. He is buried in the Lexington Cemetery.
Ed Porter Thompson, *History of the Orphan Brigade*, 447

Maj. Benjamin Desha. Born in Harrison County, Kentucky, Desha raised what became Company D, Ninth Kentucky Infantry. He was so severely wounded at Shiloh that he was compelled to leave the service. He returned in the spring of 1863 and rejoined the Ninth Kentucky. Johnny Green recalled Major Desha being severely wounded in the arm at the battle of Jonesboro, Georgia, on August 31, 1864. He was Capt. Joseph Desha's brother.
Confederate Veterans Ass'n of Kentucky, *Constitution and Bylaws*, 48

Gen. Joseph H. Lewis. Born in Barren County,
Kentucky, and a Glasgow lawyer before the war,
Lewis raised and commanded the Sixth Kentucky
Infantry until the death of General Helm at
Chickamauga, when he assumed command of the
Orphan Brigade. Lewis led the brigade until the
end of the war. "He is a brave, kind man,"
recalled Johnny Green, "but we feel that no man
can fill our Ben Hardin Helm's place."
Ed Porter Thompson, *History of the Orphan
Brigade*, 387

Gen. Joseph Eggleston Johnston. Commander of the Army of Tennessee from Dalton, Georgia, to the gates of Atlanta, Johnston restored enormous confidence in the troops even though he engineered a campaign of retreats. Johnny Green deeply admired Johnston. "I believe Mars Joe will do what is right but if he has to surrender," Green recalled a fellow Orphan saying in the days before the end of the war, "I just wish I had a barrel of whiskey."
Library of Congress

 The defenses of Atlanta, east of the city near the Georgia Central Railroad tracks and just north of the position of the Orphan Brigade. Library of Congress

Gen. John Bell Hood. Named to command the Army of Tennessee on July 18, 1864, at Atlanta, Hood ordered repeated attacks against Gen. William T. Sherman's Union armies, which were virtually surrounding the city. "The boys have no objection to [General Hood]," wrote Johnny Green, "but they dont think there is another Genl in the world equal to Genl Joseph E. [Johnston]— except Genl R.E. Lee." Library of Congress

Gen. Leonidas Polk. Wing commander in the Army of Tennessee, Polk had been the Episcopal Bishop of Louisiana before the war. At Chickamauga, Gen. Benjamin Cheatham yelled for the men to "give em Hell." Polk then said to the Orphans, "Boys! You are going at them again . . . go at them and give [them] what Cheatham said." Polk was killed at Pine Mountain, Georgia, on June 14, 1864, near Johnny Green. Green recalled that an artillery shell "passed clear through the General, killing him instantly." Library of Congress

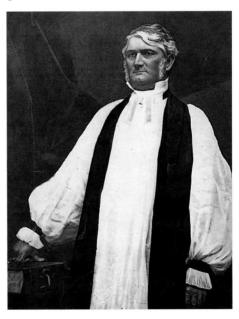

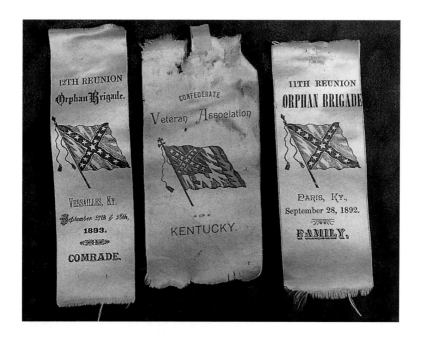

Orphan Brigade ribbons for the 1892 reunion in Paris, Kentucky, and the
1893 reunion in Versailles, Kentucky.
Collection of Kent Masterson Brown

13 SURRENDER

After the fall of Savannah, Sherman spent more than a month in preparing for the final phase of his grand campaign—the march through the Carolinas in contemplation of a junction with Grant for the knockout blow against Lee. Meanwhile, the Confederacy was making desperate extemporizations in an effort to gather sufficient force to prevent the junction. Lafayette McLaws and Wade Hampton were sent from Lee's army to help sustain morale in South Carolina and to stimulate recruiting; Hardee was summoned from Charleston, where he had gone after the fall of Savannah; the remnants of Hood's Army of Tennessee, without Hood, were regrouped under Cheatham, Stewart, and S. D. Lee and rushed to Carolina; and Daniel Harvey Hill was recalled from retirement in North Carolina. Later, Joseph E. Johnston, unassigned since his removal from command of the Army of Tennessee the preceding summer, was named commander of all, with Beauregard his second in command. Johnston's total effectives were about 18,000.

Sherman left Savannah with an army of 60,000 on February 1, 1865. The roads north were held by Wheeler's Cav-

alry, who had felled trees and burned bridges to obstruct the march, but Sherman's veterans brushed the roadblocks aside, bridged the swollen streams, and marched on with great rapidity. On February 17 his right wing entered Columbia, and that evening a large part of the city went up in flames. Sherman denied responsibility for this vandalism, but there seems little doubt that he and his soldiers were eager to make South Carolina "feel the utmost severities of war."

From Columbia, Sherman moved on to Fayetteville, North Carolina, with Hardee retreating before him and delaying him as much as he could. From Fayetteville he determined to move on Goldsborough and was proceeding there when Johnston united his force before the left wing at Bentonville on March 19. Johnston's plans were well formed to annihilate this wing while it was beyond support of the right wing, then fall on the right wing to defeat it. The plan might have succeeded had not a Confederate deserter warned General Slocum of the trap he was approaching. Slocum sent at once to Sherman for aid, and although Johnston won some temporary success, Slocum was strengthened and Johnston had to retreat. On March 23 Sherman rode into Goldsborough, where his army was joined by those of General Schofield and General A. H. Terry, marching inland from the coast.

This concluded one of the most remarkable marches of any army in the war, or perhaps in any war. The army had come 425 miles from Savannah, crossing enroute five large, navigable rivers, at any one of which a small, well-handled force might have made a crossing difficult. The country traversed was generally a wilderness, frequently a swamp where roads had to be corduroyed to move guns and wagons. This journey had been accomplished in midwinter in fifty days' time, the army averaging ten miles per day. It reached Goldsborough in superb condition.

With the concentration of the three Union armies at Goldsborough there was no possibility that Johnston's small force might offer effective resistance to Sherman's advance on Lee's rear near Richmond. Then on April 9 Lee surrendered to Grant, and five days later Johnston made overtures for his own capitulation, which was concluded on April 26.

*T*HE NIGHT OF Dec 22nd[1] 64 we evacuated Savannah, marched across the very long pontoon bridge over into South Carolina & then burned the bridge & left Sherman & his gun boats in possession of Savannah.

It is sad indeed to realize that the yankee army has so devastated our dear Southland [and] That our armies have not yet been able to hurl them back & teach them that coercion is a sin which a wicked tyranical majority can never fasten upon a liberty loving people. Our cause is just & surely God will not let us fail. The Lord loveth whom he chasteneth & we must renew our faith in him, meekly, faithfully serve him, never faltering, never wavering in courage and devotion. We must do our duty to God & our Country & notwithstanding it all looks very dark now, he will yet lead us to victory. We must cheer up [for] it is darkest just before day. Day must be near at hand for us, for it certainly is dark.

Dec 25th 1864 *Christmas.* Peace on Earth, Good will to men should prevail. We certainly would preserve the peace if they would go home & let us alone. Before hostilities began, our government sent commissioners to Washington proposing that commissioners be appointed by both the US.

1 The Confederates evacuated Savannah on the night of December 20. *O.R.,* Series 1, XLIV, 776.

Governm't & the Confederate States to adjust all matter of
Equity, & that for the forts & other Government property
taken we would pay justly & pay our just proportion of the
Government debt,[2] but Lincoln would hear to none of it.

We have gotten our horses & are biviuacked near the
Savannah River. We have some glad titings any how. Our
commisary sends word for each Orderly Sergeant to come to
his wagon & he will issue one piece of soap to each man.
This is indeed good news. Since the Skirmish began at Stockbridge Nov 15th we have not had a chance to wash any more
than our faces occasionall & never our feet or bodies until
now. We have never had our clothes off & no clean clothes
until now. The quartermaster brought clothes out from
Savannah to issue to us; they would otherwise have been
burned up in Savannah.

I got my piece of Soap & took a bath in the Savannah
River. Lathered well & then soused in good & took a swim.
It was pretty cold too. I donned my new clothes, cotton
under clothes & grey Jeanes Jacket & trousers, & washed as
best I could my old clothes, dried them & put them in my
feed sack. As there was no cooking utensil in the regiment
except a coffee pot or two I had to do my laundry work in
cold water & you can gess it was poor.

Jan 1st 1865 Sunday. It is growing cold. The regiment
was assembled for divine service & The Rev H H. Kavanaugh
preached for us. His text was, "Let not your hearts be
troubled, ye believe in God believe also in me." He made it
very plain that all we had to do was to have faith, keep our
powder dry & take good aim & that finally the victory would
be ours. He said the ways of God are past finding out, but
"He doeth all things well." The Israelites were doomed to
wander in the wilderness forty years but finally they gained
the promised land.

2 President Davis appointed as commissioners to the United States government M. J. Crawford, John Forsyth, and A. B. Roman. They were empowered
"to agree, treat, consult, and negotiate of and concerning all matters and
subjects interesting to both nations and to conclude and sign a treaty." *O.R.*,
LI, pt. 2, p. 8.

The Service had to be brought to a hurried close & boots & saddle[s] was sounded & we hurried off to Sisters Ferry where it was rumored the enemy were about to cross from Georg[i]a over into South Carolina. We rode down there & took position [where we] could see yanks across the river but they were not crossing; a few harmless shots were exchanged. After a while a gun boat came steaming along.[3] We fired at the pilot & others visible, [but] he soon dodged behind his armor plate & we could do him no harm. They let loose several shells at us & we poured so many minnie balls in their port holes that they almost ceased fireing but steamed right along & got behind a turn in the river, where they shelled us furiously & killed one or two of our horses & we could do them no harm. They steamed on up the river & we withdrew. We rode towards Hardeeville.

The wind is very pierceing. It has grown very cold & the snow is coming down like a northern Snow Storm. We ride until about 2 oclock at night & halt, feed our horses out of our feed sacks & lay dow[n] & rest. The ground is covered with two or three inches of snow, & it is very cold; it must be about freezing; we halt in a pine woods but green pine wont burn any better than wet shucks. But by feeling in the snow with our feet we find a good many pine knots, called down here light wood knots. We gather a number of these, start a fire against a fallen pine log, scrape the snow off the ground in front of the fire & lie down, wrap up in our blankets & sleep the sleep of the just.

Jan 2nd we hurry to Purysburg where we have a slight skirmish with the enemy but they do not press us much but pass on towards Hardeeville where we meet them again on Jan 3d & have a brush with them & fall back. We hover around their flank trying to annoy them as much as possible, find out what their plans are & keep Genl Joseph Wheeler posted about them.

[3] This was probably the gunboat *Pontiac* of Admiral Dahlgreen's fleet. *O.R.*, XLVII, pt. 1, p. 18.

Jan 20th. We have been dodging first in front of them, then behind them & sometimes at night riding so close to them that the sound of their horses foot tread warned us to take to the wood & let them pass, as we knew their force greatly outnumbered ours & [besides] we had received orders to hurry on to Salkahatchie River, to be sure to be there by day light & in position to resist a force expected to attempt to cross there.

We were there after a long ride, many miles of it through swamps where, by the way, The colum came to a sudden halt. A light shone which seemed very much like the glow of campfires. This was a dilemma, [for] we must be at Salkahatchie River by day light. We had taken this swamp road because the yanks held the other with a large force. If the enemy was in our front we must attack them & cut our way through. We got ready for attacking them & sent forward scouts to ascertain their position & as much as we could about their force. The scouts went forward cautiously but they never could catch up with the light & finally it was discovered that the luminosity was the will o the wisp which had kept us in momentary expectation of charging upon the enemies camp. We reached the Salkahatchie River none too soon for The enemy were upon us early on the morning of the 20th.

We keep them back throughout the 21st, 22nd, 23 & 24th but late on [the] 25th, after keeping us busy in front, they crossed higher up & we had to retreat towards Ennis' Cross Roads, where we had a brush with them on Jan 27th. We were then ordered in the direction of Combahee River, where we had to make a 35 mile ride & had a skirmish with the enemy on Jan 28th. That night about midnight we hurried off to Robertsville, about 25 miles, & met the enemy Jan 29th. After that we moved to Lawtonville & had quite a brush with a cavelry force of the enemy on Jan 30th and drove them off. We camped here the next day.

Feb 1st 1865 we were ordered to a point on the Salke-hatchie River to hunt for the enemy & hang onto his flank.

Feb 2nd we found & attacked him. The day was consumed in advancing & at times retreating, the enemy trying to cross first at one point & then at another on Salkahatchie River, but we skirmished with him at one place & then at an other within a radius of about 5 miles on both the 2nd & the 3d of Feb 1865. The night of the 3d the enemy crossed at another ford on this river & went on & left us.

Hearing of a party of mauraders about Buford's Bridge we hurried over there & made a charge upon them & drove them off in the direction of Lawtonville, where we followed them, caught up with them & had several men & two horses wounded. This time we fought them on the opposite side of the town from our fight with them on Jan 30th. We hung to them; they made a stand at Salkehatchie Swamp & we fought them there on Feb 5th. They fell Back towards Barnwell & here again we caught up with them & fought them on Feb 6th. They were next encountered at Little Salkehatchie River, a distance of about 20 miles off. Both our men & horses were greatly exhausted. After riding nearly all night we came to a plantation where they had some corn & fodder, so we stopped to feed horses & men.

We found the sweet potato bank & also some hogs. A detail was made to kill as many hogs as were needed & give a receipt to the owner for hogs, potatoes, corn & fodder consumed. The hogs were skinned & cut up, each man getting his portion of hog & potatoes. Each mess would scoup a hole in the sand, put the potatoes in that hole, cover them over with sand, then build a fire right over them, get a stick, put the piece of pork on the end of the stick & prop it in front of the fire to cook, then lie down to catch a nap while our food was cooking & the horses eating.

In about 3 hours the bugle called us to boots & saddle[s]. We then had to saddle, scratch our potatoes out of the fire, take our meat in our hands, mount & eat as we hurried along.

If we had been fortunate enough to have any salt for our pork it would have been all right, but such as it was, in our half starved condition we ate with an appetite & were thankful to get it.

Feb 7. We came up with a party of the enemy & attacked them at Blackville. They fell back towards Edisto River where we followed them & had a skirmish again with them as they crossed the Edisto Railroad bridge.

The country is so full of yankee cavelry we find them on all sides of us.[4] It is first a hard ride to catch up with them & have a fight & the next thing is fight them & finding them too strong for us, run as hard as we can to get away from them. We rode all night Feb 7th to catch a party at White Pond, attacked them & were soon sorry that we had, for they were so much stronger than we were that we had to use both skill & bluster to get away from them before they got a chance to eat us up. They pressed us so close that we had to turn & give them another fight about noon at Williston; here we divided our small force into three columns, each being very small, but we succeeded in fooling them into the belief that we had fallen back upon heavy reenforcements & were only trying to lead them into a trap. Our left detachment first attacked them, then the right & a few minutes later our centre colum made a fierce charge upon them. So bold were we that they fell back believeing that they had just escaped falling into a trap which they credited us with having laid for them.[5] It is true we had laid a trap but it was one intended to scare them sufficiently to make them go slow so as to give us a good chance to run & we did begin running as soon as they fell back & we were rejoiced to have the op-

---

[4] Actually Sherman had only 4,200 cavalry at this time. He did have an undisclosed number of mounted infantry which Green may have taken to be cavalry (O.R., XLVII, pt. 1, p. 43). The Confederate cavalry under Wheeler and Butler numbered 4,900. *Ibid.*, 1060.

[5] Union accounts of this engagement give quite a different picture. They portray a complete rout of the Confederate forces, who retreated in wild flight a distance of five miles or more until the pursuit was called off. *Ibid.*, 891, 896, 898-99, 901.

portunity, for these two fights in this one day were more than we hungered for; this was Feb 8th.

The Yanks seem to be moving on Aiken & Wheeler has a considerable force of Cavelry in this vicinity. He stationed us at a point on the South Edisto River where we had a fight with the enemy on Feb 9th & afterwards fell back upon Aiken & there skirmished with the enemy; he [the enemy] brought up a large force & pressed us back but Genl Wheeler brought a considerable force into action & drove him back. But he [the enemy] seemed determined to hold this point & took up a strong position & fortified. That afternoon Genl Wheeler sent us after a raiding party moving towards Augusta Ga. We encountered them at Johnson's Station & drove them back.

By Feb 12th we were engaged with the enemy at North Edisto River where we confronted him, skirmishing with him also on the 13th & the 14th. On the 15th we fought him at Congaree Creek but all we could do was to delay him temporarily, for he sent another party to a ford a little higher up & crossed over & went on to Columbia leaving us behind. We followed him on the 17th & skirmished with his rear guard & picked up a few stragglers.

The devastation which Sherman committed in Columbia was barbarous. The Court house, depot, hotels & many residences besides all the business parts of the town he burned; the gas lamps were knocked down & because the Roman Catholic Nuns had taken many Confederate wounded Soldiers into their building to nurse them, the Vandals burned the Nunnery to the ground.[6]

6 Responsibility for the burning of Columbia, South Carolina, is a most controversial question. General William B. Woods in his official report said he was assured by responsible citizens of the city that the fire had been started by drunken Negroes (*O.R.*, XLVII, pt. 1, p. 252). Another Union general stated that it was started by criminals released from the prison when the Confederates evacuated (*Ibid.*, 242). Sherman stated that the fire was started by Confederate General Wade Hampton, who ordered all cotton to be fired when he evacuated (*Ibid.*, 21). In his *Memoirs*, however, Sherman admitted (II, 287) that he made this charge against Hampton purposely to "shake the faith of his people in him, for he was in my opinion a braggart,

Sherman & his army passed on towards Goldsboro N C but we were ordered to the Vicinity of Camden S. C. where a severe engagement was fought during the revolutionary war.

We drove a small force of the enemy out of Camden on Feb 22 & drove them to the Wateree River where they met reenforcements & skirmished with us the 23d, 24th & 25th, when they retired & we followed them & again engaged them on the evening of the 25th at Westville.[7]

On the 26th they made a stand at Lynch's Creek where we overtook & drove them off[8] after several hours skirmishing.

Since we left Aiken we have been in a section in which, in accordance with Genl Shermans orders, nothing was left undestroyed which could be used by man or beast. The inhabitans left here would starve to death if they had not been able to hide in the swamps or bury where it could not be found a scant supply of food. For days at a time we have had nothing to eat except the corn from our feed sacks intended for our horses & so constantly have we been riding & fighting that sometimes we could not find time to stop long enough to build a fire & parch the corn. Indeed I have sometimes longed for an other opportunity to get such a breakfast after an all night ride as we had last November in our campaign through Georgia, when we had chased & fought all day & ridden all night without one bite to eat & still the next morning we were pressing hurriedly on to forestall the enemy, with no sign of rations in sight. The Colonel while riding along noticed two trees filled with black Hawes [haws]. Some one said, "They are good to eat & they are the largest & best looking I ever saw."

The Colonel said, "Well then we will all get our break-

---

and professed to be the special champion of South Carolina." All accounts agree that a tempest was blowing at the time, so that the fire, whether started by accident or design, was aided by the elements.

[7] West's Corners, South Carolina. This was such a minor affair that it can hardly be dignified as an "engagement." *O.R.*, Series 1, XLVII, pt. 1, p. 322.

[8] Union reports all agree that the Confederates were driven off in this minor engagement. *Ibid.*, 342, 349.

fast off these trees," and the regiment was halter [halted] there & the boys were told the only breakfast in sight for them was what could be gotten off those Hawe trees & we all ate thereof heartily & were glad to get something to fill that aching void within.

We are still kept busy chasing & being chased by the enemy, Now & then having some men & horses wounded. But as our business is to whip such yankee forces as we find which we can whip & to be sure not to get whipped, our casualties are not large, for when we attack an inferior force they get away as fast as they can & when the force proves to be too strong for us we get away as fast as we can. As ours is now a detached force, however, we are pretty careful to pick out a force not too large.

In this kind of campaigning we met the enemy & had fights with them more or less severe at Wilson's store on March 1st, at Wadesboro on March 2nd and later this same day at Thompson's Creek, & renewed it again at the same place March 3d & at White's store on March the 4th and at Wadesboro & Bethel Chu[r]ch on March 5th. This was a nice little country church where we supprised the yanks tearing the carpet off the floor to make saddle blankets. We captured two yanks here & the others scampered off as fast as they could. At Green Springs we again met them on Mar 10th & chased them for 15 miles to Monroe's Cross Roads, where they made a stand again & we again drove them.

We now were comparatively inactive until April 5th when we engaged a party on the Santee River.

On April 8th a marauding party under a Federal General Potter[9] we confronted at Sumpter.[10] We found two old pieces of cannon here which had been used by the militia. We took these & pressed them into use & got some of our men

9 Brigadier General Edward E. Potter was sent from Georgetown, South Carolina, on April 5 for the purpose of destroying railway rolling stock between Camden and Florence. The expedition was highly successful. *O.R.*, Series 1, XLVII, pt. 1, pp. 1025-27.
10 Sumterville, South Carolina.

to work them. [We] took up our position in the edge of the town & waited for the enemy. Our line ran through a church yard which was used for a grave yard belonging to a very pretty episcopal church.

The enemy approached very carefully on the 8th. We opened on them & the fighting was very brisk but we made it so hot for them that they withdrew. The next day they received quite heavy reenforcements & came at us again & we repulsed them. They withdrew a short distance & entrenched & brought artillery which was too much for our old guns. They dismounted them [the Confederate guns] & about this time our Commander discovered signs that they were preparing to flank us & we fell back a few miles to Dingles Mill.[11] Here we prepared an ambu[s]cade for them. The road crossed a stream which had become swollen until it was nearly belly deep to the horses. It was about one hundred feet wide & the cavelry must necessarily come through there slowly. We placed our regiment in a woods within rifle shot of this spot & fell back. The enemy approached carefully & when the head of their column was about the middle of this stream some of our boys opened on them & killed a good many but it allarmed them & sent them scurrying back. The plan would have been more disasterous to the enemy if the few of our men who opened on them had held their fire until the stream was full of their men, for every one of them would have been shot before they could have ridden back through that water.

They retreated & let us alone after that, but another colum of Potter's troops was marching upon Statesburg & we hurried there to head them off from Camden where we had many supplies & some RR. cars & locomotives. We fought them around Statesburg on the 15th & 16th [and] on the 17th of April. They then gathered so much force that they pressed

11 General Potter reported that he turned the enemy's position "routing him completely, capturing a battle flag and three guns." (*O.R.*, Series 1, XLVII, pt. 1, p. 1026). His report does not indicate that he considered the resistance serious.

193

us back to Camden where we resisted them quite obstinately. But they sent a cavelry force around to the rear of the town & destroyed some of the Railroad property but the most of the rolling stock had been sent to the neighborhood of Boykins Mill. Here we had quite a fight with them, driving them back repeatedly. Our flanks were proctected by an almost impassable swamp & not withstanding they would constantly bring fresh troops against us in overwhelming numbers, we would drive them back with great loss to them & but small loss to ourselves. They could come at us only along a straight road about 50 feet wide running through this swamp for a half mile & as Straight as an arrow. When the road would get full we would just mow them down & then those who could would get out of the way as fast as they could. But they had such great numbers that they sent a heavy force some distance off on our right flank to cross the swamp & flank us out of our position.

We engaged them at Bradfords Springs this same day but they were too many for us & we fell back, they pressing us pretty closely. On Apr 19th we fought them at Beech Creek & at Denkins' Mill & again skirmished with a detachment near Camden, driving them through Statesburg where they got reenforcements & turned upon us & we in turn fell back.

April 20th we tried to drive them back but they were too strong for us & after a sharp skirmish at Middleton they burned a lot of RR. cars laden with supplies & a number of Locomotives were destroyed.

Apr 21st we had gotten together some reenforcements & determined to attack the enemy in an entrenched position he had taken near Middleton. We were drawn up in line of battle, Skirmishers wer deployed & the fighting had begun; but suddenly the retreat was sounded. We fell back & the question passed from mouth to mouth—"What is the matter?"

Our boys generally were very confident that we were about to run over & capture the force in front of us. The

194

boys of Company A of our regiment were very anxious for another chance at the yankees, for Geo Doyle,[12] a great favorite in their Company, had been killed by them two days before in our skirmish near Statesburg.

Finally we were marched about three miles to the rear. The rumor now came floating to us that Genl Robt E. Lee had surrendered & that Genl Joseph E Johns[t]on had entered into an agreement for an armistice.[13] This news came as a great shock to us. We none of us ever dreamed of such a thing as Genl Lee ever being forced to surrender & we thought the army left to us would be carried to the Trans-missippi department & the war continued until our independence was granted.

As we were marching to the rear Billy Fox[14] & I were side by side & I said, "Billy what do you think? Do you believe Mars Joe will surrender?"

Billy replied, "I dont know; I believe Mars Joe will do what is right but if he has to surrender I just wish I had a barrel of whiskey. I never was drunk in my life but if that is true I would like to go out in the woods & die drunk & bury all my sorrows."

We reached our horses & fed & biviouacked & the next morning our worst fears were confirmed. Soon after this we learned that we had all been surrendered & that we were to ride over to Washington Georgia & be paroled. This was the blackest day of our lives. A great gloom settled over the command; all was lost & there seemed to be no hope for the future.

---

12 It was alleged by the official historian of the Orphan Brigade that Doyle was killed by Negro troops after his capture. Thompson, *Orphan Brigade*, 810.

13 Lee had surrendered on April 9. Johnston had opened negotiations with Sherman five days later, but it was not until the eighteenth that they signed an armistice to last while the terms of surrender were forwarded to Washington for approval. On the twenty-fourth Grant arrived at Sherman's headquarters with word that the terms were disapproved. The truce was to expire on the twenty-sixth, but by that time a new arrangement was reached and the surrender was effected (*O.R.*, Series 1, XLVII, pt. 1, pp. 31-34). News of the truce did not reach some units until April 21. *Ibid.*, 1026.

14 William Fox was from Louisville. He fought with the Brigade throughout the war. Thompson, *Orphan Brigade*, 818.

We went back through Camden. The bridges over the Wateree & over the Congoree [Congaree] had been destroyed, so we swam our horses across & proceeded to Augusta to cross the Savannah & finally On May the 5th we reached Washington Ga. Here we biviouacked & prepared muster rools to give to the paroling officer "Lot Abraham" [?] who was provost marshall for Genl Wilson[15] of the Uion army.

The night of the 5th of May Genl Breckinridge, Genl Duke[16] & President Davis & some of the officers of his cabinet besides Genl Breckinridge came to this little town. We took heart for a few minutes, for we thought possibly he has determined to take us across the Mississippi & continue the fight, but we learned, no, we were to surrender & be paroled the next day, but our President & our Genl Breckinridge would try to escape to some foreign country. We had been granted parole but a price had been set upon their heads [and] We were all anxious for their safety.

The Confederacy had not paid us even in our depreciated currency, but now a large goods box of Confederate money [was] set open in our camp & we were told to help ourselves if we wanted any. Some specie belonging to our poor country had also been sent here to be distributed to us. I got, I think, $2.50 in silver & I believe each officer got $5 in gold.

May 6th 1865 we were paroled.

[15] Major General James Harrison Wilson, who had distinguished himself as a brilliant leader of cavalry.

[16] Basil W. Duke was born in Scott County, Kentucky, and was educated there and at Centre College and in law at Transylvania. He practiced law in St. Louis before the war, where he was a leader in secessionist activities. He married a sister of John Hunt Morgan and, joining Morgan's "Lexington Rifles," was chosen a first lieutenant. When this unit was organized as the Second Kentucky Cavalry he was appointed lieutenant colonel and later colonel. He took a conspicuous part in Morgan's raids. He was wounded at Shiloh and was captured with Morgan in his Ohio raid in 1863. He was appointed brigadier general in September, 1864, and served in eastern Kentucky and western Virginia. When Lee surrendered, Duke endeavored to join Johnston in North Carolina. He was assigned as an escort to Jefferson Davis in his flight into Georgia. After the war he settled in Louisville, where he was a prominent lawyer and was active in politics.

14 HOMEWARD

We were permitted to keep our horses & side arms. I am sorry to say that I did not keep my Sergeant Majors sword. I was foolish enough to be a little ashamed that the war should close before I was entitled to carry a commissioned officers sword.

What to do was now a problem. $2.50 in silver, a pocket-full of confederate money, a horse & one days ration, but no home & no one on whom I had any claim.

Jim Bemis & Dr Hester & I determined to start in the direction of Talledega Ala where Dr Hester had an aunt living. We started early on the morning of the 7th [of May]. We rode without breakfast but about noon we stopped at a farm house of good appearance & asked if we could buy our dinners. The owner was a widow. "Come in gentlemen," she said [as] the tears came to her eyes. "You certainly can get your dinners but you can not pay for it. My husband was killed in the confederate army & I pray God to bless every one of you boys."

After dinner we rode on & about sun down we began to watch for a good looking farm house & when we asked if we could buy food for our horses & ourselves we were told by the old gentlman, about seventy five years old, that such as he had we were welcome to without money & without price. He had one son killed in the army of Va & one killed battling for the south at Chic[k]amauga. His gin house & barns had been burned by Shermans men & his house had been set afire by them but Wheelers men came up just in time to extinguish the flames. When we told him we were some of Wheelers men but not the ones who had saved his house he was rejoiced to grasp the hand of any man that rode with Joseph Wheeler.

We were caught in a very heavy rain one afternoon & as we were no longer soldiering we concluded to stop at the first house in sight. It was a rather poor looking house but two dessolate chimneys standing close by told of the destruction of the main house. We asked if we might buy food for our selves & horses & the owner, a widow, said we were welcom to such as she had but she could not take any pay. She had given her husband & her son to the Confederacy & she could take no money from a Confederate soldier. Her son was killed, her husband wounded, & she did not know whether he was ded or alive now. She longed for news of him.

When we reached [the] Chattahooche[e] River we had to make our horses swim the river but we found an old negro man who was still sticking to his master, a one legged Confederate soldier about twenty years old. This good darkey ferried us across in his dug out & when we rather pressed a silver half dollar on him for ferrying three of us over he said, "No sir ree. I cant take no money from a confederate soldier for a little thing like dis; You know I was a soldier myself till Old marster the Colnel got killed in the seven days battle at Richmond. Den I brung him home and had to stay & take keer of old Miss while Mars Jemes he went to de war, & den when he lost his leg at Ric[h]mond I had to go on & fetch him home."

We went to the home of Dr Hester's aunt, a young

widow whose husband had been killed at the battle at Nashville just a few months before. She had a large plantation & had possessed a grist mill run by water power until [General James H.] Wilson in his raid had burned it down. She had one faithful old mam[m]y & one negro man still loyal to her & they were trying to make a living for her & her little four year old boy. Here we were entertained for a week & not one cent would she let us pay.

I then left Dr Hester & Jim Bemis & started on by myself to Florence Alabama where I had clerked before the war for three months with McAlester, Simpson & Co. Mr McAlester, an old man, still lived there & I went to his home. I crossed the Tennessee river at Whitesburg Ala May 29th 1865. An old Negro man with a skiff took me & my saddle & bridle across in his skiff. I seated myself in the stern & held my horse by the halter to have her swim across at the stern of our boat. We started all right but my horse was not following just right & I jerked the halter. This ducked her & caused her to struggle a little which in turn upset me & I went headlong into the river. The old man caught my horse's halter & held out an oar to me & said, "Marster you better come in de boat. You get drowned out dere ef you dont mind."

With his assistance I scrambled into the boat & he ferried me safe across & when I asked him what he charged he said, "Oh nothing at all." He said he "knowed the Confederate soldiers could not get home ef *they* own people did not help them along."

Whitesburg is about ten miles from Huntsville, about 80 miles from Florence & about the same distance from Talladega. I have been three days riding from the latter place, taking it very leisurely & stopping about sundown at whatever house was in sight, & never have I found any one willing to charge me any thing for accommodation & feed for myself & horse.

I am told the country from Huntsville to Florence along

199

the line of my road is dessolate & infested with gorillas [guerillas], & for my two days ride from Huntsville to Florence I had better provide myself with rations. This I bought in Huntsville, two loaves of bread & two lbs of middling for a cost of 50 cts in silver. This seems cheap compared with $500 which Dr Hester told me he paid in confederate money last December for a pair of boots.

I rode about five miles out on the road towards Florence. All the barns & gin houses & fences have been burned by the yankees & the negroes have almost every one of them deserted their homes & flocked to the yankee camps or near them.

At Huntsville I stopped at a house where there was an old man about 70 years old chopping wood to cook the supper. I asked if I could stay all night & get something to eat for myself & horse & he said I was welcome to such as he had, but he would have to ask me to get corn out of his crib to feed my horse for there was not a negro on the place. They had every one left & stolen all the chickens on the place the night they left. The yankee soldiers had money to buy any such things brought to their camp & the entire community had been robbed of every thing of the kind.

The old gentlemen's wife cooked the supper & the breakfast; the coffee was made of sweet potatoes cut into little cubes about the size of the end of your little finger & parched; for sweetening we had sorgum molases, called Long Sweetening. The old gentlemans son owned a plantation about five miles away. He was a Col & fought with Johns[t]on's army at Goldsboro N. C, where he was wounded. They heard from him through a friend after the battle saying some kind people in N' Carolina were nursing him & sent word that he would get well & be all right but since then the whole country had been in such chaos with no mails & no communication they had heard no further news from him & of course were in dreadful suspense. The old man had lost two grandsons in our army.

When I offered to pay, the reply was the same as always

on our journey home; he could not charge a confederate soldier any thing; "This is all we can do for them & they certai[n]ly are welcome to it."

The next day's ride was through a very wild & dessolate country; I rode about 40 miles & at night fall hitched my horse to a sapling & made my bed in the woods very near my horse. Way in the small hours of the night a snort from my horse wakened me. I sat up on my blanket & there at my horse's head I saw a great big negro trying to untie the halter to steal my horse. I siezed & cocked my pistol & leveled it at him & called out to him to get away from there or I would blow a hole in him. He did not wait upon the order of going but as our colored brother would say, "He farly flew." I slept with one ear open the balance of that night for my horse was my entire capital & I did not want to walk that 40 miles to Florence either.

I took an early start the next morning & just at dusk I rode up to Mr McAlesters house. He was away but Mrs McAlester & her son John, about 10 years old, & Robt, about 8, & Bessie, a dear little girl nearly 7, rushed out to see me & were as glad to see me as if I was the son of the family. Aunt Polly, the black cook, hugged me & said, "Fore de Lord you aint as big as you was when you went away. Dey sholey aint give you enough to eat. Never min honey, we'll find something fur you to eat."

Uncle Simon, who had also remained faithful, said, "He may be little but I bet you he could shoot yankies all right." He took my horse & both man & beast had found a haven of rest & a hearty welcome.

Florence had experienced a scourge of bushwhackers, outlaws who pretended to be union when the Union soldiers were in possession & pretended to be Southern when Southern soldiers were in control, but robbed & even murdered when neither army was present. Just before the surrender they made a raid into Florence just at night, caught old man Forcht, a wealthy jew, & threatened to burn his store if he made any protest against their taking every thing they wanted out of his store, & then put a rope around his neck & threatened to hang him if he did not get them $1000 in specie. He took them to a spot in his cellar & dug up $200 in gold & gave them, but they swore they knew he had more & they would certainly hang him if he did not get the $1000. He protested that was all he had in the world & they dragged him with the rope around his neck to a tree in the yard, threw the end of the rope over a limb & pulled him up until his toes could barely touch the ground. [When] he beckoned that he would give them the money, they then let him down & he led them to a spot in his garden where he directed them to dig. Here they dug up $1500 & took it.

They went to every rich man in Florence & if he was at home they robbed him & if not at home they stole all the silver they co[u]ld find & upon finding Dr Hargraves away from home they burned his house.

They came to Mr McAlester's house after robbing his store. Simon, however, had brought the allarm & Mrs Mc-Alester had wrapped up some bread & meat in a bundle & made Mr McAlester put what money he had at home in his pocket & rush off to Cypres swamp. From there he was to make his way to Decatur, where there was a yankee force, & appeal to them for protection for Florence.

The bushwhackers came to Mr McAlesters home & demanded him. When told he was not any where near but had gone to Decatur to get soldiers to come down & protect the people they would not believe it but broke right into the house, ransacked every nook & corner & ran their bayonets through all the feather beds, hoping to discover silver ware hidden there. Aunt Polly had already taken it, put it in a coffee sack & put it in her trunk & put her clothes on top of the sack. They came even into her room & searched, she all the time abusing them for *poo* white trash; they would not even let a *poo* nigger alone. "Come on in here [and] look for you selves. Steal my petticoats ef you wants them," &

with this [she] lifted the top of her trunk open. They felt sure there was nothing in there or she wo[u]ld not have been so quick to open the trunk, so they searched every thing else but simply glanced into the trunk & never discovered the family silver plate hidden in the bottom of that trunk.

At an other time a similar band went to the country home of Mrs McAlesters Uncle Mr John Wilson, an old man 75 years old. [When] they demanded money, the old man ordered them off his place, [but] they siezed him, stripped him & said if he did not produce $1000 they would burn him to death. He still defied them, saying he had no money about the place & it would do them no good to burn him, that what money he had was in a bank in Louisville Ky. They built a fire on his hearth. Two of the villains taking hold of his arms & head & two of them taking hold of his feet, they placed his bear back on the fire & again demanded money. He said, "Kill me at once, for you will never get money here."

They built up the fire more fiercely & the old mans sufferings were intense. Cooney Foster, a Grand son 12 years of age, got an old shot gun that had been hidden away, loaded it & rushed into the room & fired upon them & wounded one. They fired upon him & wounded, but did not kill him. They, however, began to fear that others might come & attack them & they set the house afire & left. When they had left one of the negro women extinguished the flames & helped the old man & Cooney into bed & got word to some of the neighbors. The old man died in a few days but Cooney got well.

Mr McAlester could get no force sent from Decatur, for notwithstanding Richmond had fallen the Federals were rushing all their spare men to attack Lee & Jos. E Johns[t]on. When he reached Louisville, however, and explained the situation to the commanding general, he sent Lieut' Col Wm L Buck, commanding the 8th Michigan Cavlry, to establish a post here. This put a stop to such brutal outrages but petty thieveing was continuous.

I was notified that I would not be permitted to wear my uniform so I had to get citizens clothes.

I soon found I could make myself & my horse useful plowing & cultivating the garden & chopping & hauling fire wood. Just as the garden began to produce pease & potatoes large enough to eat, some marauders came each night & stole all that were fit for use.

I told Mrs McAlester if she had a gun around the place I would put a stop to it. We dug up a double barreled shotgun & a box of amunition. I cleaned up the gun & got it ready for use, but concluded I had better first go & see the Lt Col commanding the soldiers. This I did. I told him our living was dependent on our garden & that some one was robbing it every night. He said he could not guard every potatoe patch in the county. I said, "If you will just say the word I will guard ours."

He replied, "All right."

With that I loaded my arsenal, took my blanket & undertook to sleep with one eye open in our garden; this was the latter part of June. No thieves came for seve[r]al nights & Mrs McAlester tried to persuade me to give up the guard. She said, "Those marauders always take their guns with them & they might kill you."

But I continued to do guard duty.

After a few nights the sound of voices wakened me about 12 oclock at night. I was under the shadow of a tree [and] I sat up on my blanket. Two men were in the garden walking to the potatoes [and] one had his carbine. I waited to make sure that theft was their purpose. They squatted down in the potatoe rows & began rooting for potatoes, each with a knife. I watched for a while [so] that they might begin to fill their sacks, for each seemed to have a sack thrown over his shoulders. Having grabbled a considerable number of potatoes each drew his sack from his shoulders & began to fill. At this moment I called out, "Surrender there!"

They each jumped to their feet & the one with the

carbine reached for his gun. With this I blaized away with one barrel of my gun & again called out, "Surrender there!"

With this they both took to their heels, ran & jumped over the fence. I wanted them to keep on runni[n]g for they had an army gun with them of long range & deadly load while my gun was loaded only with bird shot. So to encourage them to keep on running I shot the second barrel at them just as they jumped over the fence. I then got behind my tree & reloaded for fear they would stop behind the cover of the fence & open on me with the carbine. But they kept running, much to my delight.

I gathered up their sacks with potatoes in them & went home. The shots had wakened Mrs McAlester who was now much alarmed for fear they would send & arrest me. We put out all the lights & kept quiet. Soon a squad of soldiers came, tramp, tramp, right up to the house. But the garden being across the street or road they could not hold the house responsible for what happened in the garden. They, however, marched all around the garden & then came back & marched all around the house but seeing no sign of life went back to camp.

The next morning I gathered up the two sacks with the potatoes in them & went up to Lieut Col Buck's quarters & said, "Col you know you told me I might guard our potatoe patch & last night I shot at two men who were robbing our garden. I dont know whether I hit them or not, but they ran off & left these sacks with these potatoes in them that they had grabbled out of our patch; & these are feed sacks with the name of your regiment on them."

He replied, "Young man you need be in no doubt about your marksmanship, for the Surgeon has been busy ever since you shot them, picking shot out of their backs. Now what have you got to tell about the shooting, for they say they had been to the river fishing & were coming along the road home when a regular volley was fired at them from ambush."

I told the facts just as they occurred & S[ai]d, "Their tracks are in the garden & some of the shot did not hit them, for a lot are in the top plank of the fence."

He said, "This bushwhacking charge is a very serious charge, sir."

I asked him to make the men describe accurately the place in the road they claimed to have been bushwhacked & then to send an officer with me & see if every thing did not prove the truth of my account. He did this & then said, "Young man, many a man has been tried by a court marshall & shot for a case that at first looked no worse than this. But I believe you have told the truth & I will let you go, but dont you shoot any more soldiers."

Some of the soldiers after this threatened to get the damned rebel that shot those two Union Soldiers, but I paid no attention to them & went in & out as I had occasion to. A short time after this as I was going to church with Mrs McAlester & passed by their camp, some of them yelled out, "O, Reb—what will you take for that shot gun?"

I have no doubt that Lt Col Wm L Buck of the 8th Michigan Cav'lry saved my life by not having me court marshalled, for a court of that kind would have believed their own men instead of a rebel & to fire on a Union Soldier from ambush at that time was death.

Mr McAlester came home pretty soon after this. I owed a little bill at his store [and] I told him I wanted to sell my horse & settle up. He bought my horse for $150—took out what I owed him & left me about money enough to pay my way home to Ky.

When I got to Nashv'l I learned I could get free transportation to Louisville on the Railroad if I would take the oath of Allegiance to the United States & if I did not take the oath I could not travel on the railroad at all. Capt Dan Parr's Steam boat The Tempest was at the wharf about to leave for Louisville. He said, "Pay your passage & keep your mouth shut & you can travel on my boat without taking the oath." So I paid & took passage & landed at Henderson Ky all safe.

Here I found my father who, having been twice arrested during the war as a Southern sympathizer, was barely able to make his own living. Of course it was a great joy to both of us to be to-gether again, but being out of money I had to get to work at once. A friend of my father's, Mr Barret, owned some woodland about 4 miles from Henderson. He said if I would chop wood from his land & haul it to town & sell it I might have half, he furnishing the woodland & an ox team, I to do the chopping & hauling. I formed this partnership immediately & the next day was hard at work chopping. This work continued until a carbuncle on my hand forced me to discontinue. I then came to Louisville & Mr A. D Hunt secured a situation for me.

JOHN W GREEN *Serg'nt Major*
9th Ky Regt Inftry C S. A.
Orphan Brigade

INDEX

209

214

See also McAllister, Simpson, and Compan

McAllister, Mrs.: 201–205 *passim*

McAllister, Bessie: 201

McAllister, John: 201

McAllister, Robert: 201

McAllister, Simpson and Company: xxviii, 7. *See also* McAllister

McClarey, Mike: 65–66

McClarty, Capt. Clint: 13

McCook, Maj. Gen. A. M.: 63, 89

McCook, Brig. Gen. Daniel: 145

McCorkle, Robert G.: 172 and n

McKay, Lieut. Henry Clay: 139 and n

McLaws, Maj. Gen. Lafayette: 181

McLean, Lt. Thomas A.: xv, 129 and n

McLemore's Cove, Ga.: 86

McMinnville, Tenn.: 73, 74

McPherson, Maj. Gen. James B.: 125, 143, 144, 145

Marietta, Ga., battle of: xxi, 126, 135

Marietta and Canton Road, Ga., skirmish on: 137

Merry Oaks, Ky.: 14

Michigan troops, Eighth Cavalry: 203

Middleton, S.C.: 194

Mill Creek Gap, Ga.: mentioned, 117; battle of, 127

Mill Springs, Ky.: 21

Miller, Len S.: 10 and n

Mines, land: 179 and n

Missionary Ridge, Tenn.: battle of, xxi, 102–103; mentioned, 86

Mississippi Railroad: 42

Mississippi troops: xvii

Mitchell, William: 11

Monroe's Cross Roads, S.C.: 192

Monterey, Miss.: 19

Moore, Col. A. B.: 57 and n

Moore, A. J. (Gus): xv, 70 and n, 71, 72, 142

Moreman, S. M.: 51

Morgan, Maj. Gen. John H.: xvii, xix, 30, 53, 54, 196n

Mortar boats, *see* Gunboats

Mortar shells: 43–44

Morton, Miss.: xx

Mud River, Ky.: 11

Murfreesboro, Tenn., camp life at: 17–18

Nash, Walker: 158 and n

Negley, Maj. Gen. Jas. S.: 88

Negroes: 4, 5, 174, 200, 201, 202–203

Nelson, Maj. Gen. William: 22

New Hope Church, Ga., battle of: 125, 131

Newman, Capt. Price: 11 and n, 31, 32, 140

Newnan, Ga.: 170

New Orleans, La.: 38

North Edisto River, S.C.: 190

Oakland, Ky.: 13n, 14

Oconee River: 174–75

Ogeechee River: 178, 180

Oostanaula River: 129

Orphan Brigade: origin of name, xvi; summary of organization and service, xvi -xxii; retreats from Ky., xvi, 16; at Shiloh, xvii, 24–37 *passim*; retreats to Corinth, xvii, 34; at Tupelo, Miss., xviii, 42; at Vicksburg, Miss., xviii, 38, 42; malaria epidemic, xix, 47–48; at Baton Rouge, xix, 45–47; and Bragg's Ky. campaign, xix, 39, 48–49; at Murfreesboro, xix, 50–69 *passim*; at Hartsville, Tenn., xix, 56; at Stone's River, xx, 62–63, 64, 68 and n; at Manchester, Tenn., xx, 72, 74; in Mississippi (1863), xx, 75, 78–79, 82; at Chickamauga, xx, 88, 96; at Missionary Ridge, xxi, 104–105, 107; reorganization (1863), xxi; at Dalton, Ga., xxi, 117, 120–23; retreat to Atlanta, xxii, 133; at Atlanta, xxii, 144, 146; mounted, xxii, 168–69; extraordinary quality of, xxiii-xxvii *passim*; mentioned, 10, 49–50, 85, 120 and n, 170, 171, 172–73

Orphan Brigade, Second Regt.: xvii, xix

Orphan Brigade, Fourth Regt.: xix

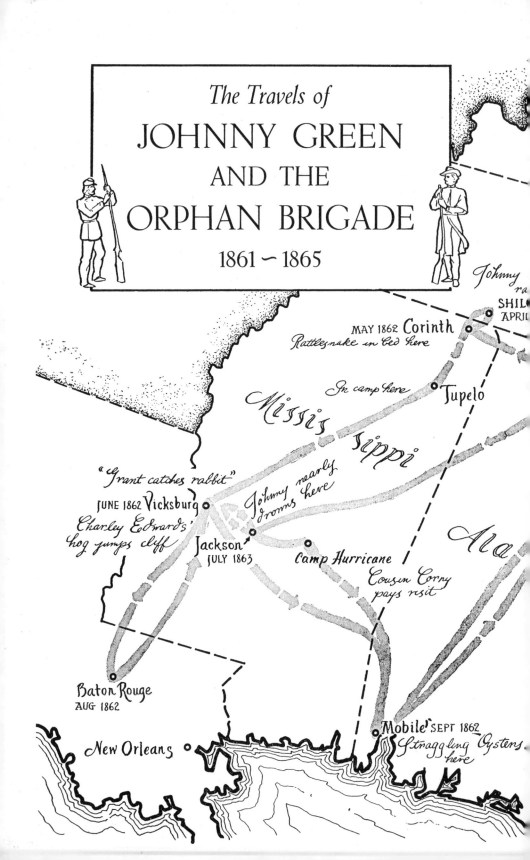

The Travels of
JOHNNY GREEN
AND THE
ORPHAN BRIGADE
1861 – 1865

Johnny
ra
SHIL
APRIL

MAY 1862 Corinth
Rattlesnake in bed here

In camp here Tupelo

Missis sippi

Johnny nearly drowns here

"Grant catches rabbit"
JUNE 1862 Vicksburg

Charley Edward's
hog jumps cliff

Jackson
JULY 1863

Camp Hurricane

Cousin Corny
pays visit

Ala

Baton Rouge
AUG 1862

Mobile SEPT 1862
Straggling Oysters here

New Orleans